COMHAIRLE CHONTAE ROSCOMÁIN
LEABHARLANNA CHONTAE ROSCOMÁIN

1. This book may be retained for three weeks.
2. This book may be renewed if not requested by another borrower.
3. Fines on overdue books will be charged by overdue notices.

D1356136

Raw emotion:
A tearful John Hayes
takes in the joyous scenes
after Munster's Heineken
Cup final victory

BEYOND OUR WILDEST DREAMS

1995–2006
THE STORY OF MUNSTER'S HEINEKEN CUP ODYSSEY

CIARAN CRONIN

Editors
Declan O'Brien and Joe Coyle

Photographic Editor
Joe Coyle

Production Editor
Mark O'Neill

*All photographs courtesy of Sportsfile
unless otherwise stated*

Published by:

Tuatha na Mumhan Books,

54 Pococke Lower,

Johnswell Road,

Kilkenny,

Ireland

Tel: +353 56 7752968

Email: tuathamumhan@eircom.net

ISBN-10: 0-9553630-0-4

ISBN-13: 978-0-9553630-0-9

A CIP catalogue record for this book is available from the British Library

All photographs courtesy of Sportsfile unless otherwise stated

Designed by:

Design at DBA,

56 Carysfort Avenue,

Blackrock,

Co Dublin

Printed and bound by Bath Press

CONTENTS

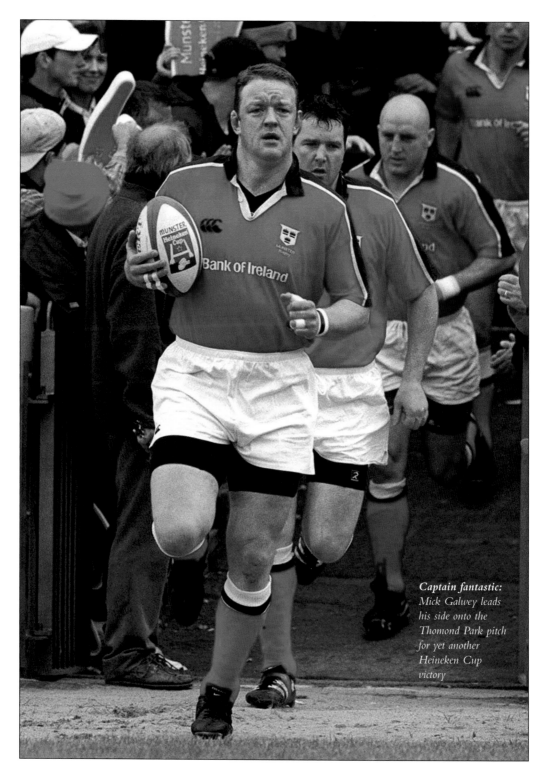

Captain fantastic:
*Mick Galwey leads
his side onto the
Thomond Park pitch
for yet another
Heineken Cup
victory*

FOREWORD

Who would have thought when we took to the field in Thomond Park against Swansea back in November 1995 that the Heineken Cup would go on to play such a big role in all our lives? Not the 15 players who ran down the tunnel that day anyway. Rugby was changing rapidly since the game turned professional and we weren't quite sure how the competition would evolve. As it was, a decent crowd turned out in Limerick that afternoon but I often wonder what would have happened had Pat Murray not crossed for that late try to snatch victory in the dying minutes. Our proud Heineken Cup record at Thomond Park has been a huge motivational factor for Munster down the years but had we lost our first game in the competition, that glorious run would have been over before it even started.

People always ask about a turning point and aside from that first victory, the day we went to Vicarage Road and beat Saracens certainly stands out. There were only a couple of hundred fans with us in London that day – family members, close friends and a few hardcore rugby men and women – but after our stunning comeback in London, the numbers following us on away trips grew steadily. Our fanatical supporters have played a huge part in our Heineken Cup adventures across the continent but it always pleases me when I see the old crew at games.

When I did hang up the boots after 48 appearances in the competition, the thing I missed most was the comradeship within the squad. The Munster team spirit is one of the most unique I've experienced in sport, with everybody involved in the set-up always being made to feel equally important.

It was that factor, more than anything else, that got us out of so many tight situations over the years and that's why when Anthony Foley finally lifted the Heineken Cup, everyone involved in the 11-year odyssey felt as though a weight had been lifted from their shoulders. The win felt every bit as good as we hoped it would.

Mick Galwey

For my parents, Mary and Mike, and for Andrea,
thanks for all your love, patience and support

INTRODUCTION

The owners of the B&B in Carmarthen were going out of their minds. They had three double rooms which brought them a few extra quid every now and then. It wasn't exactly what you'd call a thriving business but the money was handy and the company welcome. The town wasn't the most popular spot in Wales and aside from the few tourists who came to visit the nearby boathouse where Dylan Thomas composed much of his poetry, the B&B didn't take up much of their time. Then came the deluge of May 2006.

For the fortieth time on one particular day, the phone rang with another Irish voice asking if there was any room at the inn. "We'd take anything going at all," each voice would invariably say. "Anything you have free." But the rooms had been fully booked for weeks and the owners asked once again, not quite believing the answer each time they heard it: "Why on earth do so many Irish people want accommodation this weekend?" "The match," each voice answered. But the match was in the Millennium Stadium, more than 55 miles away. Could they not stay any closer to the Welsh capital?

Had the B&B owners taken a walk down Cardiff's Mary Street on the morning of Saturday, 20 May, they would have copped on pretty sprightly. A sea of red had engulfed the city, as tens of thousands of Munster supporters flocked to the Welsh capital for their side's Heineken Cup final meeting with Biarritz. There was barely room to walk down Cardiff's main thoroughfares, and while the initial plan of the South Wales Police was to shut the streets around the ground to traffic at 1pm, the sheer volume of fans searching for a coffee, a bite to eat, or a pint or two to steady their nerves, forced the constabulary to put their plan into operation much earlier.

Once again, Munster's support was defying all conventional wisdom. They'd come from every parish in the province and a fair few corners of the rest of Ireland, while more than a few hardy souls had even traversed the globe. They were determined that trivial considerations such as transport, accommodation or match tickets were not going to stand in the way of their progress to Cardiff. For some, the travel plans bordered on insane. Flights to Cardiff, Swansea and Bristol had been booked out months in advance and places on ferries were as scarce as hens' teeth. As a consequence, regional airports the length and breadth of southern England became staging posts for the advance on south Wales. Backwaters of Britain's aviation infrastructure such as Exeter and Bournemouth experienced passenger numbers they

Standing on the shoulders of giants: *Munster's Paul O'Connell tries to get away from Serge Betsen of Biarritz in the Heineken Cup final as Dimitri Yachvili and Anthony Foley watch on*

could barely have dreamed of, as red-clad hordes poured through their small arrivals halls from late on Thursday to early Saturday morning.

Supporters were equally inventive in how they sourced tickets and accommodation. Ireland's recent love affair with foreign holiday home ownership was put to good use by those who had invested in the south of France. A few days' sun in early May tied in nicely with day trips to Biarritz and the purchase of tickets that couldn't be got for love nor money back home. The needs of hundreds were answered in this way.

Meanwhile, on the accommodation front the couple from Carmarthen weren't the only poor souls in the tourism sector to be plagued in the run-up to the game. It wasn't unusual for unsuspecting landlords to let rooms to one or two lads, only to find a small platoon arriving on their doorstep the evening before the game. To their credit, most hotel and B&B owners did their best to accommodate the overflow. Few were left stranded and those who were did the only logical thing in the circumstances and partied through the night.

That weekend was carnival time in Cardiff. The men and women from Ireland's south-west had journeyed in the belief that Munster were about to complete an amazing sporting odyssey. An epic trial of patience and pain which had lasted 11 gruelling seasons and taken the country's most popular provincial side, and their fanatical supporters, to every rugby stronghold in Europe was about to end – or so they prayed. They had beaten the best England, France, Wales, Scotland and Italy had to throw at them but, somehow, they never managed to seal the deal. Always close, but no cigars.

But May 2006 was going to be different, they could feel it in their marrow. It was going to be Bordeaux 2000 all over again, when Mick Galwey led Munster to victory over the kingpins of French rugby, Toulouse. It was going to be like those great days in Thomond Park when Gloucester and Sale were humbled in the final matches of the pool stages. There would be no talk of Northampton at Twickenham in 2000, or Neil Back's intervention in 2002. The touch judge's poor call which denied John O'Neill in Lille in 2001 would be put right, while the lack of self-belief which had cowed the men in red into believing that they couldn't beat Biarritz in San Sebastian the previous year would not be repeated. This was Redemption Day.

And so, as the clock ticked towards 3pm on that fateful Saturday, and the Carmarthen couple dealt with the lodging queries of the final wave of Cardiff-bound supporters, the stage was set for Munster's finest hour.

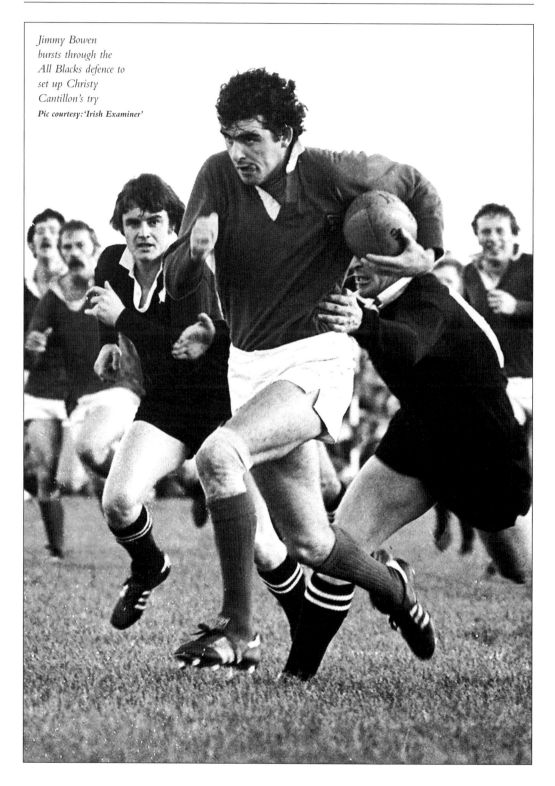

Jimmy Bowen bursts through the All Blacks defence to set up Christy Cantillon's try
Pic courtesy: 'Irish Examiner'

CHAPTER 1

OLD SCHOOL

The 31st of October, 1978. Munster 12, All Blacks 0. A date and score line that most Munster people can rattle off the tongue just as easily as their five times tables. The team? An easier line-up for some to recall than the dozen who hung around with Jesus. Larry Moloney at full-back, Moss Finn and Jimmy Bowen on the wings, Greg Barrett and Seamus Dennison in the centre, Tony Ward and Donal Canniffe, the half-backs. And the forwards. Gerry McLoughlin, Pat Whelan and Les White in the front row, Moss Keane and Brendan Foley right behind them, Christy Cantillon, Colm Tucker and Donal Spring in the back row.

But while 1978 has become a milestone in Munster rugby lore, there had been other great days. In January 1958, there was a 3-3 draw against Australia at Thomond Park, while nine years later they took that next step by beating the Wallabies 11-8 at Musgrave Park. More dates, more history. A draw against the All Blacks in Cork in 1973, a narrow 13-15 defeat to Australia in the same city three years later. Special days one and all, special afternoons that had helped to mould the Munster identity, the honest and noble struggle to knock the big guy from his perch.

If honest and noble were the characteristics of Munster's efforts against the international sides who came knocking every couple of years, then Tom Kiernan was the very embodiment of it all. A full-back by trade, the Corkman was a born leader of the teams he played in and those he later coached. If you thumb through those famous victories and close calls, you'll spot a common link. Full-back in the team that lost 6-3 to the All Blacks in 1963? Tom Kiernan. Full-back and scorer of eight points in the victory over Australia back in 1967? Tom Kiernan. Full-back on the team that drew with the All Blacks in 1973? Tom Kiernan. Coach to the team that will be forever remembered for their deeds back in 1978? Join the dots.

His foresight in preparing for the All Blacks victory is what stands out. It started back in September when the squad went on tour to London for four days towards the end of the month. They played two fixtures and both were disasters, losing 33-7 to Middlesex and drawing 15-15 with a scratch Exiles selection. But the games showed exactly what Kiernan needed to work on and the intensive training sessions began.

For some reason, the old army barracks in Fermoy and a pitch by the banks of the River Blackwater was the squad's training base for the weeks leading up to the game. The training was gruelling, as Kiernan pushed his panel to the limit each evening. Once the wily old campaigner had called a halt, it was back to the Grand Hotel in the town to get changed, eat a sandwich, drink a cup of tea, and disperse to Cork, Limerick, Dublin or wherever. This was repeated twice a week for seven weeks. But the thorough preparation paid off on the final day of October '78 when Kiernan's side reaped a glorious reward.

It was a massive result for Kiernan. He had established his credentials as a top-class coach, a reputation that was enhanced when he led Ireland to their first Triple Crown in more than three decades in 1982. But if Tom Kiernan's legacy as a player and coach ranks among the best, then his influence as a rugby administrator was just as profound.

His finest hour among the blazers was arguably the 1995 initiative which led to the establishment of the European Cup. Following the success of that year's Rugby World Cup in South Africa, the International Rugby Board (IRB) bowed to the inevitable and abandoned rugby union's amateur ethos. As the rugby fraternity slowly began to catch on to the complexities of the all-new professional world, Kiernan and Vernon Pugh of the Welsh Rugby Union decided to act. The pair realised that brave decisions were needed if the rugby nations of the northern hemisphere, particularly Ireland, Scotland and Wales, were to keep pace with their counterparts south of the equator. The southern hemisphere's Super 10 series started in 1993 and it was a resounding success. In the summer of 1995 the competition admitted a further two teams to the fold and signed a 10-year, multi-million dollar deal with Sky Television. It was against this background, and while most countries were still in South Africa towards the end of the World Cup, that Pugh, with the help of the IRFU's IRB representative Kiernan, called a meeting of the Five Nations in Johannesburg to discuss the creation of a European equivalent to the Super 12. Their idea was met positively by most unions and it was agreed that the first European Rugby Cup would be run during the upcoming 1995/96 season.

The European Cup initiative by Kiernan and Pugh was a brave one, but both men knew that radical changes were necessary if professional rugby was to survive along the continent's Celtic fringe. In retrospect, provincial rugby was the perfect professional model for Ireland. The provinces had history and tradition aplenty, and none more so than Munster.

Legend in the making: *Munster coach Tom Kiernan follows the drama unfolding at Thomond Park as the province overcome the mighty All Blacks*

The game in the province evolved differently in the two main centres of Cork and Limerick. Cork followed the more traditional route, the game taking hold following the formation of the rugby club at Queen's College, Cork – an institution that would later become UCC. Cork County and Cork Bankers were a couple of early outfits by the Lee but the clubs which were to dominate the Cork rugby scene for the next century were established soon after. Cork Constitution came into being in 1892, with Dolphin RFC following 10 years later.

Things were a little different in Limerick. There was no university in the city to kickstart the process but William Barrington, a former pupil of the famous Rugby School in England, and Trinity graduate William Stokes were credited with forming the first club in the province, Limerick County, in 1876. That particular club, based at the Market's Field in the city, existed for 29 years before its star faded. But by 1884, both Garryowen and Shannon had been founded and the life-long love affair between Limerick and rugby was well under way.

What has intrigued most about Limerick rugby is how the game was played by the masses, not just the upper and middle classes. After the foundation of Garryowen and Shannon, clubs began to sprout up all over Limerick city and county. These clubs certainly helped enhance the sport's popularity but the British army also played a leading role in spreading the rugby gospel. Like most Irish cities in the late 19th century, Limerick was plagued by poverty. For many young men consigned to the drudgery of life in the city's slums, there were just two escape routes, emigration or the army. "Join the army, see the world" was the catch-cry of the British army recruiters and many did just that, even if the seeing the world part didn't work out for everybody who signed on the dotted line. But while they were stationed in the city, the young recruits learned to play rugby. It fast became their pastime of choice, the physicality of the game attracting many to the sport.

But to talk exclusively about rugby in Cork and Limerick would be to ignore the development of the game in the rest of the province. Rugby's growing popularity in Tipperary, Kerry and west Cork, and the widespread support which the provincial side enjoys across each of the six counties, has been the source of widespread discussion. However, it could be argued that rugby has always been strong in these areas. For example, Nenagh Ormond, Clanwilliam from outside Tipperary town, Bandon and Tralee were among the eight participants in the first ever Munster Senior Cup in 1886. Indeed, the lads from Tipp could claim to have an even older association with the game of rugby than either Limerick or Cork. For it could just be that the schoolboy credited with creating the game, William Webb Ellis, may well have been born in the Premier County.

The origins of rugby football are well known to most followers of the game – the official version of the story, that is. William Webb Ellis, a pupil at the famous public school at Rugby, was playing a game of association football with his friends after school when he picked up the ball and ran past the opposition with the pig's bladder tucked under his forearm. Everybody on the field, and there would have been quite a few of them back then as the rules of football were quite loose, stared in amazement as their fellow student broke their game's one and only law – you couldn't handle the ball. The legend goes that Webb Ellis snapped up the ball and ran on a whim. But if some rugby historians are to be believed, then there may have been another reason for the young schoolboy's actions.

Although Webb Ellis is believed to have been born in Manchester in 1806, it is also possible that he was a native of Clonmel, Co Tipperary. Webb Ellis's father, James Ellis, was an officer in the Dragoon Guards regiment of the British army and the very nature of his job meant that his family were constantly on the move. In the year of William's birth, 1806, army records show that his father's regiment was stationed in

Dundalk, Dublin and Clonmel. But whatever the doubt surrounding William's birthplace, there's no disputing that he had many Irish cousins, in Co Tipperary in particular, and that he was a regular visitor to Ireland during the summers of his childhood.

William Webb Ellis

It was during these visits, some suggest, that the young Webb Ellis discovered the game of caid, an early form of Gaelic football. Caid was a ball-carrying game which took two forms. The first was called cross-country caid, where two parishes played each other in an often brutal fashion in an attempt to work the ball past a certain mark in the other team's parish. The second was field caid, where the game was played with equal fervour within a defined space and with a definite number of players. There's little doubt that the young Webb Ellis would have seen this game played and possibly even joined in. And whether he decided out of devilment to pick up the ball that afternoon on the Rugby playing fields back in 1823, or was merely showing his schoolmates what his cousins played back in Tipperary, no one will ever know. However, the thought that rugby football was created by a Munster man or inspired by Munster people is a tempting one, and one that captures the imagination.

***

It was a full 52 years after Webb Ellis's intervention that Ireland played their first rugby international. They travelled to the Oval in London to play England, but it wasn't until later that year that the first interprovincial game was played. Ulster and Leinster met on 27 November at the Ormeau Grounds in Belfast, with the northern province winning by one goal to no score. One thousand spectators watched the game and it is said the party that went on after the fixture lasted for a good three days. A couple of years later the newly-formed Munster Branch wanted in on the action and challenged Leinster to a game on Saturday, 24 March, 1877, to take place at College Park, Trinity College. Heavy snows prevented the game going ahead until the following Monday, but the Munster boys, who were mostly from the Limerick Club at this point, hung around in the capital for the game. However, their perseverance wasn't rewarded, as they went down by one penalty goal to nil. Still, at least Munster were in business. The fixture was repeated on 20 January the following year, with Leinster again winning by the same margin. It wasn't until December 1878 that Munster hosted their first ever interprovincial game, which was held at the Mardyke. Leinster were once again the opposition and home advantage did nothing for Munster as the visitors emerged victorious, this time by a much heavier margin of one penalty and three tries to nil. It wasn't getting any better.

Matches between the provinces took place in a rather haphazard manner until the 1946/47 season, when the Interprovincial Championship came into being. But, while an interprovincial champion was declared each season, there wasn't a huge deal made about the whole thing, apart from the international selectors using the series as something to base their calls on. It was this selection process that has caused Munster players and supporters to engage in many hours of heated debate over the years. There was a perception, and it probably existed until the mid-1990s, that any man from Munster would have to play twice as well as a lad from Leinster or Ulster to be selected for Ireland. It was something that successive generations of Munster teams fed off with gusto, the general plan being that they'd take out their non-selection for the national team on the boys from the other provinces when they next met them on the field. A sense of being hard done by was fostered in the province and it's something that persisted.

But if Munster rugby was hard done by, then the advent of the All-Ireland League in the 1990/91 season provided a real opportunity to redress those grievances. For if there was one aspect of the game that differentiated Munster from the other provinces it was the strength of the club scene. The passion and ferocity which characterised Munster Senior Cup and Junior Cup clashes around the province was legendary stuff. Losing was not an option. The Munster Senior Cup in particular was the pinnacle of the local scene. The competition was first run in 1886 and up until the early 1990s, and indeed for a few years after that, you were nothing in Munster club rugby unless you'd managed to tuck a Senior Cup winner's medal in your top pocket to wear as a badge of honour.

The passion of the Munster Cup stretches back to its very inception. The 1887 final between Limerick County and Queen's College, which was won by the Cork side, caused such a furore that a Mr Barnett, a player on the Limerick County team, wrote a damning letter to the 'Limerick Chronicle'. "I have never met with such discourtesy from a team, or to speak more correctly, from the captain of a team, than that which was shown to us by Queen's College. The game had scarcely started when it seemed that the College men had made up their minds to win by fair means or foul… had I been Mr Stokes, I would have withdrawn my team from the field and reported the matter to the Irish Rugby Union and get their opinion on the matter."

There were many finals played in similar circumstances, although most of them didn't prompt someone to write to their local paper. Even as recently as 1997, 12,000 crammed into Thomond Park on a Sunday afternoon to see Garryowen beat Young Munster by the skin of their teeth in a tense final which was typical of the showpieces that had gone before. The Munster Junior Cup was also well capable of drawing a more than respectable attendance to either Thomond or Musgrave Park.

Consequently, when the All-Ireland League started, it was no surprise to rugby people down south that the senior clubs from Limerick and Cork dominated the competition. That trend has continued over the last 16 seasons, with Munster clubs taking 13 titles. Rugby fans in the province also showed a desire for the new league. The climax to the league's inaugural season saw Garryowen take on Cork Constitution in a packed Dooradoyle, as close to 10,000 spectators crammed into the tiny ground to see the Temple Hill side claim the first ever title. Another game of note from those early days was the clash of Shannon and Garryowen at Thomond Park during the 1991/92 season. The fact that the game took place in mid-season made the estimated 14,000 attendance even more astounding.

There's little doubt that the All-Ireland League would still be the cherry on top of the Irish rugby cake had it not been for the events of August 1995. But as the world of rugby changed, the trends in Munster followed. The attendances at club games began to dwindle but only because the provincial team had taken centre stage once more, just as they had on that famous day in 1978.

But did Tom Kiernan realise exactly what he was about to create when himself and Vernon Pugh came up with the concept of the European Cup? Could he have foreseen that a television audience of more than 500,000 would tune into RTE for a final, or that Lansdowne Road would be sold out for a semi-final involving two Irish provinces? Did he have any idea that an Irish province would carry a bigger crowd abroad for the final than would attend the same year's Munster hurling decider in Thurles?

It's unlikely that he could have, but it didn't really matter. The important thing was the new arrival, the European Cup, was alive and kicking.

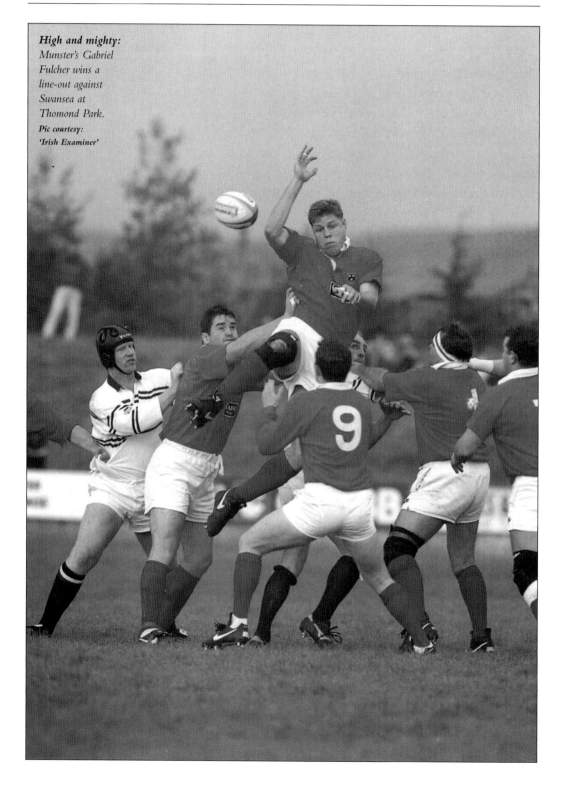

High and mighty:
Munster's Gabriel
Fulcher wins a
line-out against
Swansea at
Thomond Park.
Pic courtesy:
'Irish Examiner'

CHAPTER 2

IRISH DOUGH, FRENCH BREAD

1995/96

It wasn't often that the Thomond Park gates were open on a Wednesday afternoon in November. It would have been a common sight in spring when the pupils from St Munchin's, Crescent College and Ardscoil Rís would work their way across town to cheer on their classmates in the schools cup competitions but at the dawn of winter, it was a strange sight. However, the old rugby traditions were slowly unravelling. The move to professionalism three months earlier led to huge changes in the rugby landscape, and while opening Thomond Park for business on the first day in November 1995 was one of the smaller changes the sport would undergo over the next decade, the reason why they were open on that reasonably crisp afternoon would have far-reaching consequences.

Since Vernon Pugh and Tom Kiernan banged their heads together during the summer, the concept of the European Cup had not only been accepted by most of Europe's rugby unions (apart from England and Scotland), it had also developed into a living, breathing competition. Work behind the scenes had unearthed 12 teams to play in the first year of the tournament: Munster, Leinster and Ulster from Ireland; Toulouse, Castres and Begles-Bordeaux from France; Swansea, Cardiff and Pontypridd from Wales; Benetton Treviso and Milan from Italy; and Farul Constanta of Romania. Four pools of three teams were drawn, with each side earning two points for a victory and one for a draw. Teams were to play each other just once, with the pool winners qualifying for the semi-finals.

Munster were drawn in Pool 4 of the competition, alongside Swansea and Castres. The province would play Swansea at home and Castres away and although they'd have preferred to have had the French side in Limerick, it wasn't the worst draw in the competition. So on that first day of November, an estimated crowd of 7,000 made their way to the home of Limerick rugby, many dodging school and work, to see their province take on Swansea in their first ever Heineken Cup game.

Well before the game, Munster had helped to cast themselves in the role of underdogs. It was the only character they knew how to play. Swansea were one of the more progressive clubs in Britain and they'd already taken the necessary steps to establish themselves as a semi-professional outfit. Munster, meanwhile, were nothing of the sort.

Each member of the starting line-up had good, honest day jobs. Pat Murray worked in the Irish Permanent in Limerick City, Kenny Smith was a sales rep for Guinness, Mick Galwey worked for a business equipment company, Terry Kingston was a director of a computer systems company in Cork, while Peter Clohessy ran his own courier business. They worked the usual nine till five, or thereabouts, and then went training in the evening for their clubs. At that time when there was a Munster game on the horizon, the players' focus altered only slightly. As for payment in this professional era, players were compensated for their troubles. Following the introduction of professionalism, any individual player could ask their club for whatever fee they wanted – and they may even have gotten it – but with Munster in the 1995/96 season, the staple Heineken Cup payment from the IRFU was Ir£600 per match and nothing more. Nobody complained.

The game against Swansea was a lively one and there wasn't a lot between the semi-pros and the men who had work the next morning. Aled Williams, the talented Swansea and Wales out-half, kicked his side into an early lead but a Richard Wallace try, converted expertly by Smith, put Munster in front. Smith and Williams exchanged penalties before the interval to give the home side a 10-6 lead but then came the drama. A converted Alan Harris try after half-time had given the Welsh side a 13-10 advantage and Munster were struggling manfully to break them down. In the 78th minute, they cracked it. Swansea's defence out wide had been near-imperious all game long so this time Paul Burke decided to have a go up the middle. His slipped pass to the on-rushing Pat Murray was timed to perfection and the team's captain rounded the cover to cross the line. Smith converted and after some desperate defence in the closing minutes, Munster were home and dry at 17-13. Thomond Park had just swallowed the first of its victims in European competition.

*Middle man: Swansea's Alan Reynolds and Aled Williams get to grips with Mick Galwey during the first ever Heineken Cup game at Thomond Park. **Pic courtesy: 'Irish Examiner'***

Six days later the squad assembled at Shannon Airport. They made their way by car, three or four players in each, gear bags tucked away in the back, boots probably not even cleaned since their Monday evening training session. There were about 30 of them in all – the starting XV, five replacements, a five-strong management team, a few Munster Branch men, a handful of supporters and three members of the media. Not one of them knew much about Castres. In terms of geography, they guessed that it was nearer to Monaco than Paris but in rugby terms they knew even less. The management had attempted to get a video of their opponents in action but it proved to be an impossible task. They'd just have to play whatever was put in front in them.

They arrived in Castres that afternoon, checked into the hotel with the express warning that nobody was to make any phone calls from their room. Later that evening they had a bit of a run around on a local pitch. To their surprise they found that the following evening's game had been switched to a stadium 20km down the road in Mazamet, a town even smaller than Castres but one equipped with a flood-lit stadium. A switch like that would have caused uproar in the later days of the competition but back at the very beginning, there wasn't a whimper. Everybody was learning how to cope with the new era and there was bound to be a couple of teething problems along the way.

As kick-off approached in Stade Antoine Beguere, there were an estimated 6,500 home supporters in the ground, each keen to give the Munster team a taste of what it was like to play a competitive club fixture on French soil. Len Dineen, Limerick 95 FM's rugby commentator, has vivid memories of the scene. "It was completely different to what everybody had been used to," he remembers, "and that went for the players, management, committee men and the media. There were three of us in the back of the stand behind Perspex glass and God, were we lucky there was something between us and them (the Castres supporters). Every time a penalty was given against them by the Welsh referee, they'd turn around to us and shake their fists and make gestures. As if it were our fault or something. They were so passionate, it was such a unique occasion and nobody in the Munster party that day will forget it. A lot of us had experienced international matches against the French in Paris but club rugby, especially down in the south, proved to be something different entirely."

One of the main things that struck the players out on the pitch was the noise from the bands playing on the terraces. Most of them had experienced the Boherbuoy Brass and Reed Band on Munster Senior Cup final day at Thomond Park but this was a completely different kettle of fish. Nobody can quite remember the exact details, but there were three or four bands dotted around the ground, each pumping out music through every minute of action. Well, nearly every minute of action, as Kenny Smith recalls.

"Any time I placed the ball for a penalty, the bands would stop and the whole place would go so quiet," says the former Garryowen man. "It was actually eerie, it kind of made you appreciate how difficult things were for kickers who came to Thomond Park. But I knew in the back of my mind they wouldn't stay quiet. I just knew it. I can remember one penalty right in front of the posts, 40 yards out. I approached the ball and just as I kicked it, the bands started playing and a fog-horn erupted from somewhere in the stands. I think I hit the corner flag with that one."

Murray Kidd, the Irish coach at the time, supplemented that story afterwards. Beside where he was sitting in the stand was a man with a foghorn attached to a foot pump. Each time Smith approached a penalty, the man would suddenly perk to attention and his foot would hover over the pump. When Smith was inches away from the ball, he'd apply the pressure and laugh heartily if things didn't go so well.

Not that it bothered Smith all that much. He converted four penalties over the course of the game and as injury time arrived, the sides were locked at 12 points apiece. With the game almost over, David Corkery decided to put his head down and take contact rather than kick the ball to the stands. Unfortunately, his brave decision resulted in a turnover for Castres. They got their mitts on the ball, worked themselves into a nice position in the Munster 22 and centre Nicolas Combes bustled over for a converted try that broke the visitors' hearts. It was only afterwards that it dawned on everyone that a draw would have been enough for a place in the first Heineken Cup semi-finals. The first missed opportunity.

After the game the travelling party attended a reception at Castres' town hall. The mayor and a couple of local dignitaries were there and although proceedings went on until the early hours, the realisation that the Munster party had to face a 7am flight and a day's work once they got home quickly put the skids on the knees-up.

Swansea went on to qualify for the semi-finals from Munster's pool but were easily brushed aside by an excellent Toulouse side. Leinster played Cardiff on the other side of the draw but the Welsh side proved to be far stronger on the day and the final was set for the old Cardiff Arms Park on 7 January, 1996. A crowd of almost 22,000 turned out at the famous venue for an epic game, as Christophe Deylaud won the game for Toulouse with a penalty in the dying seconds of the second period of extra time. It wasn't the biggest or brashest occasion European sport had ever witnessed but it was a confident first step for a competition that quickly got into its stride.

Three and easy:
Steve McIvor, Ben
Cronin and David
Corkery celebrate
another try in the
demolition of Wasps.
Pic courtesy:
'Irish Examiner'

CHAPTER 3

HOME
TRUTHS

1996/97

One year on from the dawn of professionalism and things were still very uncertain at the top end of Irish rugby. The IRFU hadn't settled on an agreed course of action for the professional game; the Union was torn square between paying the country's elite players, and letting the rest fend for themselves, or going the whole way and initiating a complete professional structure in all four provinces. Hindsight may make their procrastination back then appear foolish but few could have predicted the manner in which the professional game would develop over the next decade or the profound impact the Heineken Cup would have on that process. What was decided upon for the 1996/97 season was that a core group of 34 players – those who caught the eye of Irish coach Murray Kidd – would be contracted on a full-time basis and be paid IR£30,000 per annum. Of that group, those who remained in Ireland would receive the added bonus of a free car. The players would also be paid £3,000 for each international they played and a bonus of £1,000 for every victory.

The bad news for Munster was that Peter Clohessy wouldn't be part of it all. The prop from Young Munster had been banned for 26 weeks for stamping on his French opponent Olivier Roumat during the 1996 Five Nations game between the sides in Paris and was sidelined until the start of 1997. With most interprovincial rugby taking place before Christmas, Clohessy was of no use to Munster but in September 1996, having contemplated retirement, the prop signed a six-month deal with the Queensland Reds to play in the Super 12s the following January. He would be back with Munster in time for the 1997/98 season.

At least Munster had some decent back-up in that area. Paul McCarthy, Ian Murray,

John 'Paco' Fitzgerald and Noel 'Buddha' Healy were all better than average props, and when the names of those players about to receive international contracts were eventually confirmed by the IRFU in the summer of 1996, there was some more good news for the province. Dominic Crotty, Brian Walsh, Brian O'Meara, Eddie Halvey, Mick Galwey, Anthony Foley and Steve McIvor were all handed contracts and would now be able to devote themselves to rugby full time. The rest of the Munster squad, meanwhile, would be paid on a game-by-game basis and would have to fit in training whenever their jobs, and the rest of their lives, allowed.

"I was in charge of security for Doc's nightclub in Limerick at the time and things did get tricky," says Noel Healy, former Shannon and Munster prop. "The nature of my job suited the rugby far better than what some of the other lads were at. I mostly worked at night, Thursday, Friday, Saturday and Sundays, and I could devote the rest of my day, and my week, to training. We trained in the morning in the gym, usually the very early morning, about 7am, and then in the evening we'd have a rugby session out on the pitch. You'd be very tired from the whole thing but it was just so important for all of us. I mean for me, getting a Munster cap was like getting an Irish one. I played for Shannon for years and won lots of All-Ireland League titles and even though the club meant the world to me and to everybody who played for them, playing for Munster was the ultimate. They were my Irish caps."

Drive on: *Anthony Foley powers through the Milan defence during Munster's 1996/97 Heineken Cup opener at Musgrave Park.* **Pic courtesy: 'Irish Examiner'**

The second running of the Heineken Cup was a far bigger operation. There were now 20 teams in the competition, including English and Scottish outfits who had opted out the first time around. The sides were divided into four pools of five teams, with the top two teams from each pool qualifying for the quarter-finals. Once again, Munster were drawn in Pool 4 of the competition with Milan, Cardiff, Wasps and Toulouse lobbed in alongside them. Again, it was a pool that the province could see some way out of.

Munster got their campaign under way with a home game against Milan on Saturday, 12 October at Musgrave Park. Typically for the time of year, the conditions were awful. Rain and wind meant Munster were playing the elements as much as the opposition. The home side decided to play with the wind in the first half and reaped the benefits. Brian Begley scored all of his side's 17 points during the half; his tally consisting of four penalties and a fine try which Brian Walsh and Mick Galwey served up to him on a plate.

Milan failed to score against the wind but the worry was that a 17-point advantage may not have been enough given the atrocious conditions. But Munster played the second half expertly, controlling the ball well around the fringes and generally playing the game anywhere but in their own 22. Federico Williams, the Milan full-back, did cross for a try midway through the half but further penalties from Killian Keane and Begley sealed a hard-earned 23-5 victory for the home side.

It was a nice way to start the competition but things were about to get an awful lot tougher in the away fixture against Cardiff. For one, the Welsh side were leading the way in the Principality since professionalism had dawned and secondly, the game was being played on the Wednesday after the Milan match. Not only would the players be tired, they'd also have to return to work prior to the Cardiff fixture. All those ingredients contributed to a good solid thrashing at the Arms Park, although Munster did make a decent game of it in the first half. The key moment came as that half ticked into injury time. With Munster 18-17 ahead in a fairly hectic contest, they lost a line-out on halfway and Rob Howley made a searing break from deep. The scrum-half chipped over Richard Wallace and as both players chased to the line, the Munster man failed to kick the ball dead and Howley pounced.

"That try was a real killer for us," Munster coach Jerry Holland admitted later. "Instead of turning round with a lead, we were six behind. We had played very well

Pass master:
Steve McIvor
sets up a move
against Milan.
Pic courtesy:
'Irish Examiner'

and were really getting into a rhythm." There was little or no rhythm after the break and Cardiff scored 24 unanswered points as the Munster side began to tire. With one win and one defeat chalked down, Munster's chances of qualification for the knockout stages now looked unlikely. But while there was hope, they'd keep going.

Three days later London Wasps arrived in Limerick with their bevy of international stars in their ranks. Canadian international Gareth Rees was at out-half, Samoan Inga Tuigamala in the centre, while Scottish international Damien Cronin was their totem in the second row. And then there was the English contingent, Lawrence Dallaglio, Chris Sheasby, Andy Gomarsall, Will Green and Nick Greenstock, to name but a few. Munster, for their part, started with 12 players from Limerick, Cork and Waterford, while Killian Keane and Steve McIvor, both from Dublin, were practically Limerick men at this point following their spell at Garryowen. The only true outsider was centre Sean McCahill, Sunday's Well's New Zealand import.

The rain began to splatter before kick-off, the final ingredient needed for any Munster giant-killing expedition. And not only did the home side manage to slay Wasps, the aristocrats of English rugby, they gave them a good trouncing. "It was one of those special days," remembers Healy, "one that anybody who was there will remember. The rain came down before kick-off and although it was our third game in a week, we were well up for this one. An English team against Munster at Thomond Park? There was no question of being tired. Even if you were wrecked, you'd summon the strength from somewhere to beat them."

It started in the way so many victories had been conceived in the good old days. Killian Keane launched a huge garryowen into the elements and Wasps full-back, Jon Ufton, failed to gather the ball. The Munster pack gathered round and with Anthony Foley steering operations, the juggernaut rolled its way over the line. The die for the day had been cast, the result decided from that very moment.

Dominic Crotty, the new kid on the block from UCC, set up Mick Galwey for the second try before half-time and just after the break Keane sealed the result as he collected his own chip over the Wasps defence for try number three. A few minutes later Ben Cronin galloped from 30 yards out to score an intercept try that sent the Thomond Park crowd into raptures. Before the end, and with the English champions looking like a bunch of amateurs cobbled together for the afternoon, Richard Wallace and Crotty dotted down two more tries. To compound Wasps' woes, referee Didier Mene awarded a penalty try to Munster before the end after the visitors failed to cope with a number of scrums on their own line. This completed an excellent seven-try performance by the hosts.

Caught up in the delirium afterwards and by the emphatic nature of Munster's victory, team manager Colm Tucker commented: "It was back to 1978. This has to go down as one of the truly great Munster performances, especially bearing in mind the circumstances."

Two down:
Ben Cronin
congratulates
Mick Galwey
after he scored the
second of
Munster's seven
tries against
Wasps.
Pic courtesy:
'Irish Examiner'

The men in red had just played three games in eight days but somehow they kept their very best until the last of the series. Typical Munster.

The win kept the province's chances of qualification for the knockout stages just about alive but matters improved the following weekend when Wasps, somehow, thrashed Toulouse 77-17 in London. That result meant that a victory in the south of France would put Munster through to the quarter-finals. It was an enticing prospect. Such was the interest in the game, RTE decided to screen it live but it was a video nasty that everybody present at Stade les Sept Deniers would have preferred to have left there. What happens during a Heineken Cup thrashing in France, stays in France, or something to that effect.

"Lads will regret that game for lots of reasons," Noel Healy recalls, "but my regrets were a bit different. In the build-up to the game I was so looking forward to playing against Christian Califano. No disrespect to any of the other players I'd propped against but this was the biggest challenge of my career. He was a top scrummager, one of the best in the world. You know, I always felt that I could have played for Ireland, there was no question about it in my mind. I'd been playing the game seriously for years before I picked up an injury when I was around 30 and I took a bit of time out after that. Then I said I'd go back and play a bit of junior rugby, then it became senior rugby and it rolled on from there. By the time I played my first game for Munster, I was 36 years of age. When I finished, I was 40."

He continued: "There were times during that spell where I knew I was better than other props around the country but my age always got in the way. There were occasions where I knew I should have been playing for the Ireland A team but they'd pick a younger guy just because he was younger. But this game against Toulouse and Califano was the one where I would be able to test myself against one of the best props in the world and you know what happened? I pulled a biceps early on in the game and I had to come off after 15 minutes. Fifteen bloody minutes. We had just two scrums in that time and while both of them went well, you can't judge yourself after two scrums. I didn't want to come off the field that day but the joke I pull out every now and again is that we were doing well until I came off the field. That was the turning point."

However, the facts don't tally with Healy's assertion as his side were actually 17 points behind after just 13 minutes of play. To their credit, they managed to keep Toulouse at that score until half-time, and added three penalties of their own along the way. But after the interval, the sluice gates opened wide, with Emile Ntamack acting as lock-keeper. By the end of the game Munster had been totally outclassed, conceding nine tries in one of their most comprehensive Heineken Cup defeats.

But it's still Mick Galwey's words of encouragement to his team that are best remembered.

Ntamack's first try on 68 minutes brought the home side over the 40-point mark and Galwey gathered his troops under the posts as they waited for the conversion to be taken. "Let's try keep it under 50," were the second row's immortal words. But the more famous ones were uttered four minutes later in the same spot after Stephane Ougier and Marcel Marfaing had both crossed for tries. "Let's try and keep it under 60 lads," was the captain's earnest call. They only just missed out on heeding Galwey's plea, as the home side eventually won 60-19. While the rallying cry may not have appeared comical at the time, even the most tired man under the posts that day would have to laugh at it now. They'd gone into the game hoping to secure a quarter-final spot and came out of it just about clinging onto their pride.

On trial:
Declan Kidney's first season as Munster coach was on a part-time basis

CHAPTER 4

PROS
AND CONS

1997/98

There are many strange place names dotted through Munster's Heineken Cup history but Lower Hutt isn't one that immediately springs to mind. In case you've never had the privilege, Lower Hutt is a town about 20 minutes outside Wellington in New Zealand, a tough, gritty kind of place where All Blacks Tana Umaga and Piri Weepu were brought up. It was here that the Irish players on the infamous development tour of 1997 stayed on one of their many stopovers, and it was also here that the IRFU, probably desperate for some good news from the trip, announced that former All Blacks captain Andy Leslie would be Munster's new Director of Rugby.

Leslie was a popular figure who achieved some success in the 1990s as Garryowen coach and his appointment was widely welcomed. The only problem was that the IRFU had made the announcement before Leslie had agreed to take the job. Sure enough, a few days later it was established that he wasn't taking the post – so much for the big Lower Hutt announcement. The fact that Leslie wasn't even the IRFU's first choice for the job added to the Union's embarrassment. Earlier that summer, former Wales coach John Bevan had agreed to join Munster but then changed his mind. Like Leslie, he didn't cite a reason for his about-turn. The search for Munster's first full-time, professional coach was turning into a farce.

Having travelled down the foreign route twice, and been left at the altar on both occasions, the IRFU decided to play it safe and the search began to focus on home talent. Declan Kidney wasn't a name that everybody in the province would have known, but having won eight provincial schools titles at senior and junior level for Presentation Boys Cork (PBC) in the space of nine years, his credentials were impressive. He was appointed head coach, with Niall O'Donovan, who was Shannon coach during the 1995, 1996 and 1997 All-Ireland League successes, rowing in as his assistant. Initially both were employed on a part-time basis and although it was never officially stated, there was little doubt that the pair would have to prove themselves over the coming year if they were to get full-time contracts. They were on trial.

The new coaching team were at a slight advantage to those who had gone before them. For the first time in the history of Irish rugby, a formal contract system was agreed for the provinces. Each province would have 10 players on full-time contracts, men who could now eat, sleep and drink rugby 24/7. The other 20 in the provincial panel were handed part-time contracts worth £7,500 each and a variety of appearance fees for different competitions. In essence, this was a compensation payment for any lost earnings the part-timers might incur. It wasn't an ideal system by any stretch of the imagination but at least some sort of professional structure had been cobbled together.

The 1997/98 Heineken Cup was the most ambitious yet. There were still 20 teams participating, now divided into five pools of four teams, but the key factor was that each team would play each other twice, home and away. Munster's opponents for the year were Harlequins, Cardiff and Bourgoin. In the space of three years, the number of guaranteed games in Europe had increased from two to four to six. The Heineken Cup was starting to look something like a real competition.

Munster kicked off proceedings with a trip to play Harlequins at The Stoop, a fixture which was most noteworthy beforehand because Keith Wood was about to come up against many of his friends and former club mates. But while there was some talk of that afterwards, particularly an altercation between Wood and Mick Galwey during the game, the issue was almost forgotten when the two teams shared 11 tries in a thrilling 48-40 victory for the Londoners.

Munster were 20-3 down in the first 20 minutes and it looked like their poor domestic form had followed them into Europe. The Interprovincial Championship in August had been a serious disappointment, with the men in red managing to record just a single victory over Connacht, while going down to both Ulster and Leinster. But the Heineken Cup was different, and while things were not looking too good in The Stoop, Munster didn't roll over and play dead. Anthony Horgan and Alan Quinlan both scored tries to leave the visitors 23-18 down minutes before half-time, and it might have stayed that way to the interval were it not for the fracas between Wood and Galwey. The incident saw the hooker leave the field injured and the Munster second row was sent for a spell in the sin bin for his handiwork. With Munster down to 14 men, Rob Liley scored a try before the half-time whistle and Harlequins were 12 points to the good and looking likely to cruise home from there.

But again, Munster didn't cave in. Tries in quick succession from Eddie Halvey and John Lacey left the scores tied at 30-30 on 52 minutes and it was only then the difference between the sides became apparent. Jamie Williams, Will Carling and Huw Harries all scored tries for Harlequins in the final half an hour as the home side's fitness shone through. It would become a familiar theme, as was proven the following weekend when Munster travelled to play Cardiff at the Arms Park.

Like the game the previous year between the sides, Munster took a bit of a battering, 43-23 this time, but at least their performance had moved up a notch. However, they got off to yet another slow start. The loss of Shane Leahy through illness before the kick-off didn't help their cause, and they were 12-0 down inside the first 10 minutes. The visitors finally kicked into gear in the second half. Tries from Alan Quinlan and John Lacey kept Munster hanging in there around the hour mark and although Lacey grabbed another before the end, Cardiff had already killed the game off with two quick-fire tries from back row Steve Williams.

"Both Harlequins and Cardiff were just that little bit further down the road than us," explains full-back John Lacey, who along with Alan Quinlan, Ronan O'Gara and Anthony Horgan had made his Munster debut at The Stoop. "When the game went professional back in 1995 the English, Welsh and French clubs latched onto the concept pretty quickly, not just the financial side of it but also the physical element of it. If we're being honest, certain teams were almost professional before things changed in 1995. In the case of both Harlequins and Cardiff, I don't think there was any difference between us and them when it came to pure rugby ability but their preparation was far better than ours.

Cardiff blues:
Munster's John Kelly fails to evade the tackle of Jonathan Humphreys

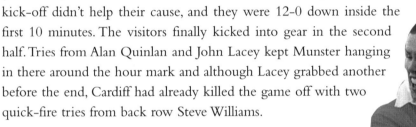

"At the time I was working as a rep for Statoil and I had a part-time Munster contract. I was training before work, then doing my actual job for eight hours before going back training in the evening again. Neither job, the rugby or the Statoil one, was being done properly in a situation like that and there would have been a fair few other lads in the same boat. No matter what anyone says, that was why we struggled that particular season."

With the Heineken Cup pool stages of 1997/98 being played on six successive weekends in September and October, there was no respite for Munster and the fixture against Bourgoin in Thomond Park followed the Cardiff defeat. It was a chance, at last, to play a game on home soil and to get a much-needed victory under their belts. Bourgoin, the Challenge Cup holders, arrived in Limerick having beaten Cardiff at home and lost to Harlequins away. But in a nervy game of poor quality the home side scraped home in the last five minutes thanks to another John Lacey try – his fourth in three games. "It was not a great match, but it was a huge win for us," said Niall O'Donovan afterwards. "It was a must-win situation and the players responded. We found ourselves with big deficits after the early stages of the matches against Harlequins and Cardiff and ended chasing the matches. We were determined we would not be in a similar position this time."

So the dream of reaching the knockout stages was alive, but not for too long. Cardiff travelled to Musgrave Park needing a win to stay in contention and earned what has become one of the rarest Heineken Cup achievements – an away victory against Munster. It was another high-scoring game but, yet again, a poor opening quarter from the home side let them down badly. Indeed, if you took the opening quarters from the two Cardiff games and throw them in with the defeat to Harlequins, Munster had conceded 49 points while scoring only nine. On the flip side, in total they'd outscored their opponents 86-79 in the final hour. It didn't take a rugby genius to work out where things were going wrong.

In Musgrave Park, Nigel Walker and Lee Jarvis scored early tries to rattle Munster and although they were 21-20 ahead thanks to tries from the outstanding Alan Quinlan and John Kelly, who was playing in his first game for the province, Cardiff proved too strong in the scrum and too disciplined overall. Tries from Jarvis, his second, and Jonathan Humphreys sealed a 37-32 victory for the Welsh side and a little badge of honour to go along with it. "We were lucky, we got out of jail a bit," Cardiff coach Terry Holmes said afterwards. "For the coaches, it was a nightmare, but as a game of rugby, it was magnificent. There was some superb rugby played. Munster were unlucky. They could have just nicked it."

That close call left Munster completely out of contention for an automatic spot in the quarter-finals and the slim chance they had of qualifying through a play-off all but disappeared in their second last pool game against Bourgoin at Stade Pierre Rajon. The province went down 21-6 in a stop-start, niggly kind of game. But at least they learned a few lessons, which they would use to their advantage in future campaigns.

Playing catch-up: Rhys Ellison carries the fight to Cardiff

"It was the small details which kind of showed how innocent we were at this level of competition," says Lacey. "Back then there was no such thing as chartering a plane for a match. If we were going to France, we had to go through London and there was usually a bit of a wait involved."

But if the travel arrangements were inconvenient, they sometimes had their lighter moments. "I can remember us bumping into the Stade Francais team at some airport one weekend, both of us on our way back from fixtures," Lacey recalls. "Of course we got onto the Claw (Peter Clohessy) straight away, saying Olivier Roumat was looking for him. Both of them shook hands in the end because they were getting such a ribbing from their teammates."

Dealing with the atmosphere in French club grounds was also a challenge for the new lads in the Munster team. "Most of us had never played in France before and Bourgoin wasn't the best place to be eased into it," Lacey maintains. "It's the closest atmosphere to Thomond Park I've ever experienced. The crowd are right on top of you and they're in your ear the whole game long, even if you can't understand them. I remember this one guy shouting at me and I kind of gestured back at him. The next thing he was actually trying to get on the pitch to get after me. It was crazy stuff. Nothing can prepare you for an atmosphere like that. The other thing that took some getting used to was the French food. I'll never forget the night we were sitting

Pace king: *Alan Quinlan makes a break against Harlequins at Thomond Park in Munster's final pool game*

in the hotel in Bourgoin waiting for dinner when the waiters started bringing out these tiny cooked chickens. John Hayes would have eaten the whole lot on his own. We were starving. Later most of the lads headed down to McDonald's to fill themselves. That's the way it was. Everything we learned in Europe we learned in those first couple of years in the competition."

Munster's final game was against Harlequins at Thomond Park and that, at least, finished on a bright note. Eight thousand supporters created a raucous atmosphere against the cosmopolitans from London. In that kind of a throaty, hostile environment, the visitors didn't appear to have the stomach for the fight and although Munster's margin of victory at the end was only seven points, it didn't do their overall display any kind of justice. Eddie Halvey and Rhys Ellison scored first-half tries to give the home side a rare early advantage and although Jamie Williams crossed for a try for the visitors, Munster's outstanding defence held firm in a final quarter where Harlequins were surprisingly placid.

However, while it was good to win the final pool game, there was a sense that Munster had left a play-off place behind. As things turned out, one more win would have earned Munster a quarter-final play-off game against eventual finalists, Brive.

So that was that, the provincial season done and dusted by November. Declan Kidney went on to lead the Ireland Under-19 team to victory at the World Cup in France later in the season, guiding the precocious talents of Donncha O'Callaghan and Brian O'Driscoll to become world beaters, but the lessons of the provincial campaign must surely have preyed on his mind through that winter and spring. Given the absence of any sort of support structure, it was always going to be a difficult first year for the new management team. As Kidney stated at the start of it all, himself and Niall O'Donovan were building things from scratch – even down to going out and buying "rubber bands and paper clips for the office".

Clawing through:
Peter Clohessy barges through the Harlequins defence

However, rubber bands and paper clips weren't the most pressing issues facing the management team; the fact that only a handful of their players were full-time professionals was still their primary concern. But there had been a number of positive aspects to the season. The team appeared to be more than capable of scoring tries and they showed admirable spirit and determination to bounce back in the games where they went behind early on. As John Lacey had intimated, Munster were as good rugby-wise as any side they faced; they just needed to put the other aspects of the operation in place.

New kid on the block: Mick O'Driscoll burst onto the scene to make an impressive Heineken Cup debut against Neath at Musgrave Park in late September

CHAPTER 5

BREAKING THROUGH

1998/99

The 1998/99 season was stick-your-neck-out time in Irish rugby. The IRFU finally decided that they were going to go at this professionalism lark with full gusto and the provinces were allowed to contract 21 full-time players for the first time, with a number of part-time contracts also made available. On top of that, the Union decided to appoint Declan Kidney and Niall O'Donovan to Munster on a full-time basis, the duo having apparently passed the previous year's 'trial'. Both were given three-year deals, with Kidney taking leave of absence from his teaching job at PBC to become Munster's Director of Rugby. Things were starting to come together.

The structure of the season also had a more professional look about it. For the first time in the history of the Interprovincial Championship, each side would play each other on a home and away basis, giving the provinces six games in the competition, as well as the six pool fixtures they were guaranteed in Europe. Their success, or otherwise, would determine whether they played after Christmas or not. In a summer where the IRFU mandarins must have been claiming serious overtime such was the level of ideas coming from the top brass, it was also decided that the Interprovincial Championship would adopt the Super 12's points system; namely four points for a win, two for a draw and a bonus point awarded for either scoring four or more tries, or for losing a game by seven points or less. It was progressive stuff, designed to encourage and reward attacking play in a rugby country that hadn't exactly been renowned for taking risks or being overly ambitious with the ball.

The only negative piece of news concerned the Heineken Cup, or the European Cup as it would be known for the 1998/99 season following the withdrawal of the headline sponsor. The English clubs, along with renegade Welsh sides Cardiff and Swansea, would not be taking part in that season's competition because of a financial dispute with the organisers and it did take away from the status of the competition, particularly from a Munster point of view. For Kidney's side, there was nothing like playing an English team at Thomond Park, especially a side with an exaggerated opinion of themselves, but at least there would be a far greater prospect of qualifying for the quarter-finals for the first time. That was the silver lining.

The season didn't start all that well for Munster. They lost to Leinster and Ulster in the first segment of the Interprovincial Championship and their victory over Connacht on the first day of the season was far from convincing. But at least they had the European Cup to focus on. This time the teams were divided into four pools of four, with the top two sides in each pool earning a place in the quarter-finals. Munster were drawn in Pool 2 with Padova, Perpignan and Neath, a tricky if negotiable draw from the Irish side's point of view.

The Italian side were first on Munster's hit list, with 2,000 turning up at Musgrave Park on 19 September to see the home side win 20-13, although it was a far from vintage performance. An Eddie Halvey try helped the home side to a 10-3 half-time lead against the wind but Declan Kidney's side performed poorly in the second period when they would have expected to kick on. John Kelly did score a try on 57 minutes to secure the win for Munster but, overall, the side's back play was poor and came in for much criticism afterwards.

That criticism obviously hit hard because the same team produced an entirely different performance against Neath at the Cork venue seven days later. Munster beat the Welsh side 34-10 and there was much to admire in their efforts. Barry Everitt had a fine game directing operations from out-half but it was still the impressive pack that laid the foundations for victory. A young lad by the name of Michael O'Driscoll made his debut in the second row alongside Mick Galwey, and as well as those two, hooker Mark McDermott could also aim at Alan Quinlan and Eddie Halvey in a line-out operation that was near-perfect on the day. Predictably enough, Galwey crossed for a try in each half and thanks to Mick Lynch's early try in the second half, Munster were home and dry pretty early.

By this stage, there was a new order in the Munster front row. Paco Fitzgerald, Paul McCarthy and Ian Murray had retired, and while Noel Healy was still toughing it out around the fringes of the squad, new blood was needed. Enter John Hayes. The man from Cappamore in County Limerick had played his first game of rugby as a flanker for Bruff at the age of 19 and now, six years later, he was well on his way to establishing himself as Munster's first choice tight-head prop. It was a remarkable story but like a lot of these things, it didn't happen by accident.

After his Bruff experience, he joined Shannon and then headed off to play for a couple of years in New Zealand, for the Marist Club in Invercargill on the southernmost tip of the country's South Island. Two years later he returned to Ireland and to Shannon, twice the man in every sense of the word. "He obviously had a bit of fondness for the grub out there because he came back a full size and a half bigger," recalls Mick Galwey. "We tried to throw him up in the line-out during one game and he broke Noel Healy's finger who was lifting him." He'd played a few games at prop in the southern hemisphere and that's where Niall O'Donovan decided his future lay with Shannon. Hayes was gradually eased into the front row, playing there in the final half an hour in AIL games for his club. And having been brought on in the 1998 Irish summer tour to South Africa to gain a bit of international experience, O'Donovan and Kidney felt he was ready for Munster action at the start of the following season. He started the games against Padova and Neath and already his performances suggested that he had the potential to make the number three jersey his own for some time to come.

The same could be said of the other new face that was about to come into the team. Peter Stringer had been involved in the Munster set-up the previous year, sitting on the bench on a number of occasions, but his full European debut came in the away match in Perpignan. The very fact that Declan Kidney was willing to throw a 21-year-old novice into such a hostile rugby environment spoke volumes of the esteem in which he held his former pupil at PBC. Stringer may have been one of the smallest professional rugby players in Ireland, and probably Europe, at the time but the speed at which he got to the breakdown, and the pace of his pass once he got there, marked him apart from Munster's other two scrum-halves at the time, Tom Tierney and Brian O'Meara. For the high-intensity, fast-paced rugby that Kidney clearly wanted to develop, Stringer was the ideal number nine.

With all his confidence in the player, though, Kidney must have been asking himself whether he'd actually done the lad a favour by starting him as Munster trailed Perpignan 29-3 by half-time at Stade Aime Giral. Twenty-six of those points had come in the final 13 minutes of the half, with Perpignan scoring four tries in that period, and Munster looked like they were going to get a right thrashing. Things didn't improve immediately after half-time as the home side scored a fifth try within three minutes of the restart, but that's when Munster's grit and pride started to kick in. They started to retain possession and made far fewer mistakes in the process. The scores followed, with tries from Barry Everitt, Mick Galwey and a penalty try sandwiched in between, making the final score line a far more respectable 41-24.

"We received a lesson in possession in the first half," said Declan Kidney after the game. "It was like little boys against men for 40 minutes. We were doing the second thing before the first. They broke through easier than I expected and that was worrying. There was a players' talk at half-time and we simply added that it was important not to turn over possession. We showed a bit more patience, not looking to score off first phase. On a positive note, we learnt from the first half and didn't let the lessons last 80 minutes."

The following weekend they advanced that lesson a little further by drawing 18-18 against Neath at The Gnoll. Overall it was a poor Munster performance, one where they again struggled to hold onto the ball, but a 75th-minute Mick Galwey try, converted by Killian Keane, left the visitors 18-11 in front and seemingly safe. But they lost their concentration in the last few minutes, allowing Patrick Horgan to stretch over the line from close range to bring the Welsh side within two points. Luke Richards added the conversion and that was that, Neath had stolen a point from a game where Munster should have grabbed both of them.

There was a buzz of excitement around the camp for the visit of Perpignan. For one, the province had just won the Interprovincial Championship the previous weekend thanks to three victories in a row and secondly, the game against the French side was to take place on 31 October, 1998, the 20th anniversary of the All Blacks game. Thomond Park was ready for the occasion, a plaque was to be unveiled at the side of the ground's main stand and the Munster players who transformed themselves from mortals to legends over the course of that special afternoon were going to be introduced to the crowd at half-time. Poor old Perpignan, the pool leaders, would have to deal with all that outpouring of emotion. But the French side got a reprieve. In the days before the game, heavy rainfall turned the Thomond Park pitch to mud and on the morning of the match, it was decided to switch proceedings to the sturdier playing surface at Musgrave Park.

But the 1978 anniversary celebrations still went ahead in Cork. At the pre-match function Graham Mourie, the All Blacks captain of 20 years earlier, recounted how a friend asked him a few weeks before his trip why he was going to Ireland. "To attend a dinner to celebrate Munster's victory over the All Blacks in '78," was Mourie's answer. "And what will your role be?" his friend asked. "I think I'm the entrée," the big Kiwi replied.

Perpignan proved to be the main course that particular afternoon. There had been some talk around the start of the 1998/99 season that the province would be much better off playing all their home European games in the cauldron of Thomond Park, but the ferocity and bravery of Munster's display at Musgrave Park against Perpignan didn't back up that particular theory. In the conditions, it turned into an awful slog of a game but Munster had the pack to grind out a victory. Peter Clohessy scored the try that effectively won the game on the half-hour mark, popping up to finish off a move cleverly engineered by Tom Tierney, Eddie Halvey and John Hayes. But the story of the game was Perpignan's tactics, most notably their tendency to use the boot excessively at the ruck. Referee Steve Lander sin-binned three players from the French side for various infringements over the course of the game and at the final whistle, the Perpignan players walked off the pitch without shaking hands.

Steady as she goes: *Eddie Halvey on the charge against Perpignan*

The victory assured Munster of a quarter-final spot with a trip to Padova still to come the following week and although they could have switched off and treated the Italian trip as a bit of a jolly, that was never going to be allowed under Declan Kidney – especially when there was at least one more goal that the coach wanted from the season. Before their trip to Stadio Plebiscito, Munster had played eight away games in European competition and had one solitary draw to show for their often courageous efforts. But that sorry statistic was put to bed in Italy as Munster bagged five tries in all – David Corkery, Brian Walsh, Eddie Halvey, Killian Keane and John

Kelly the scorers – as the doughty Italians were comprehensively beaten. It was yet another milestone reached. Not before time, either.

The draw for the quarter-finals pitted Munster against French side Colomiers, with the French side coming out of the hat first to earn the home draw. In their first foray into the knockout stages, Munster were facing a daunting task. Colomiers were a tough, forward-orientated team who weren't afraid to get physical when the need arose and they battered Munster from the first minute. They gave the visiting front row an awful time of it, while their line-out operation was top notch. Their forwards denied Munster any kind of ball and the 23-9 final score line was a thoroughly fair reflection of the way the game panned out.

While not aggrieved with the result, Munster were far from happy with the way they'd been treated by the French side. At the end of the game some players were manhandled by a number of home supporters, while the spoiling tactics employed by Colomiers came in for some criticism from the normally placid Declan Kidney, as did the performance of referee Nigel Whitehouse. "I think the referee would have

Emotions run high: Peter Clohessy and Anthony Foley give referee Nigel Whitehouse a piece of their minds during the controversial match against Colomiers

to assess himself on how he controlled that game," the Munster coach said. "Nobody is saying we deserved to win. We're very disappointed because we didn't win enough possession and didn't do much with what we had. But we did attempt to play rugby and they stopped us from doing so by whatever means they saw fit. It was really very frustrating and you could see that there was a lot of frustration out on the pitch."

But if Colomiers managed to defeat Munster, they didn't get the better of the next Irish side they met in the the competition as Ulster comfortably overcame them in the final. While Munster certainly didn't begrudge Ulster their triumph, the ease with which Harry Williams's side outclassed Colomiers in front of a packed Lansdowne Road made the southern province's defeat to the same side two stages earlier even more difficult to take. But that wasn't the end of the drama that season.

In a leaked IRFU fitness report at the end of April, Munster's professional players came in for heavy criticism. The document was authored by IRFU fitness advisor Craig White and while the report was quite broad in its criticism of Ireland's rugby players, there was a special, or not so special, mention for Munster. Apparently the province's fitness regime was the poorest of the four professional sides and a number of other players from around the country had, on an off-the-record basis, expressed their unhappiness at what Munster players were being allowed to get away with.

The following Monday, the Munster squad trained together in Limerick and the issue was discussed for 10 minutes. There was genuine anger at the contents of the report, and especially the way it had been brought into the public arena. Although there was no official response to the assertions in the report, the matter was certainly filed away in the subconscious by both players and coaches to be retrieved and used at a later date as a ready-made motivational tool. A comment from Cork Constitution coach Packie Derham summed up the Munster reaction to the affair. White may have been looking for athletes but "down here we've got rugby players", the former hooker stated.

Back in the red:
*Keith Wood
returned to
Munster as one of
the most admired
and highly-rated
players in world
rugby*

CHAPTER 6

LONDON CALLING

1999/2000

It was the first Friday in September and the Munster squad were in jovial mood, having a few pints and singing a few songs. They had good reason for this little knees-up, too. The province had just beaten Ulster, the then-European champions, for the first time in 19 years in Belfast and while the game had been played at Queen's University and not Ravenhill, that didn't bother anybody unduly. The important thing was that they'd broken their northern hoodoo and got their season off to a successful start in one fell swoop.

So while they were having the craic in the Belfast pub, their new team manager Brian O'Brien was cajoled into exercising his vocal cords. O'Brien had been brought into the fold towards the end of the previous season's campaign to replace Jerry Holland and was proving a very popular appointment. His knowledge of the game was encyclopaedic. He had lined out for Shannon, Munster and Ireland during his playing days and also acted as a selector for his club and province. What he didn't know about Munster rugby wasn't really worth knowing. On this particular night, however, the Munster squad were only interested in knowing about his singing voice.

So up he got and sang a number from Carmen Jones, Oscar Hammerstein's musical adaptation of George Bizet's famous opera Carmen. He'd bought the LP back in 1954 and while the beat and rhythm of the entire album had tickled his fancy from the very first time he placed the needle on the groove, one song had always got his blood pumping. 'Stand Up And Fight' told the tale of a boxer called Husky Miller and his dogged determination not to be knocked to the canvas, not to give in. O'Brien liked the song's sentiment and by the end of his first rendition, so did the Munster squad.

Chorus of approval: *Munster manager Brian O'Brien leads the Munster squad in a rendition of 'Stand Up And Fight'*

"It's a simple song," says O'Brien, "it basically tells you not to bloody give up no matter what pressure you're under. People caught onto this very fast, identified with it and they've made it their own. I've been asked to sing it on so many different occasions at this stage. And if people are asking me to sing it, it's obvious that they love the song… they're not asking me to sing it because of my voice."

Seeing the reaction of the players to those stirring words, Declan Kidney had the presence of mind to print the lyrics off the following week and hand them around after training. Where once they'd launched into a medley of 'There Is An Isle' and 'Beautiful Beautiful Munsters' after games, now they'd have their own tune.

The song wasn't the only new element in the Munster dressing room for the season. Previously the province made do with home-grown talent, guys who were playing for local clubs, but the summer of 1999 saw Declan Kidney and Niall O'Donovan's first proper recruitment drive. First to sign on the dotted line was Keith Wood, although his arrival wasn't so much a signing as a homecoming.

The Killaloe-born hooker had been one of the first players to move to England once professionalism had been given the green light by the IRB mandarins and across the water, Wood had been transformed from a raw youngster with plenty of bustling ability to one of the most admired and highly-rated players in the world game. His return from Harlequins would only be for one year and Wood's motivation was two-pronged. Firstly, to ensure that he prepared properly for Ireland's 1999 World Cup campaign and secondly, to help Munster in their quest to go that little bit further in the Heineken Cup.

Wood's arrival was a big boost to the squad and it certainly grabbed the headlines, but the capture of two other players was just as significant. The first was Mike Mullins, a New Zealand centre who had been struggling to

Foreign shores:
New Zealand centre Mike Mullins, whose father hails from Limerick, was one of three pre-season signings

make a name for himself in the backwaters of English rugby with Waterloo and West Hartlepool. With his wife and daughter still living in the southern hemisphere, it looked odds on that Mullins would be returning home, but after moves to Connacht and La Rochelle fell through, he was offered a Munster contract by the ever-alert Kidney. The fact that Mullins's father hailed from the Young Munster end of Limerick city, and he was therefore eligible to play for Ireland, made his signing easier for the IRFU to digest.

The other man to put pen to paper was John Langford, a giant second row from Australia. He'd played three times for the Wallabies, and was a regular with the ACT Brumbies in the Super 12 competition, but his arrival at Munster was just one of life's fortunate accidents. "I was supposed to join Leinster," says Langford. "I'd spoken on the phone to them a couple of times towards the end of the season and everything looked positive and I was convinced I would be moving there. Then it all went quiet on their end for a while. I got a little worried, rang them up and they said they were having second thoughts about me because they'd persuaded Mal O'Kelly to come back from London Irish. Now that might have been all great for Mal O'Kelly but I'd already told the Brumbies I was leaving so I had a bit of a problem. So I asked them, 'What am I supposed to do now?' There was a bit of humming and hawing at the other end of the phone and the guy I was talking to said maybe I should give Munster a call, they might be interested in me."

They certainly were, although Langford did have one more unusual encounter before he finalised his move. He was to meet Brian O'Brien at Heathrow Airport for a brief chat and as the two recognised each other at the arrivals hall, the Munster team manager extended his hand towards the second row. Langford offered his forward in preparation for a handshake but O'Brien bypassed it and went straight for his stomach to see how much fat he was carrying. After all, he would have to check if this six foot five inch Australian would be able to stand up and fight for the cause.

———————————●———————————

The 1999/2000 European Cup season – with the English teams back in the fold following their financially induced hissy fit – saw Munster drawn in a tricky pool, though it wasn't the sternest challenge they'd faced. Colomiers made up the French entry in Pool 4 and although they had lost in the final to Ulster the previous May, and had given Munster a physical battering along the way, they were hardly one of the superpowers of continental rugby. If anything, their star was on the wane as they struggled to compete with the deep pockets of Toulouse, Stade Francais and Perpignan.

Saracens and Pontypridd completed the line-up in Munster's pool. Pontypridd were an outfit with a rich tradition but club rugby in Wales was in transition and the Principality's talent was still spread too thin for any of their sides to really compete meaningfully with the English and French. In contrast, Saracens were a team that were symptomatic of the professional era. They were owned by Nigel Wray, a businessman who approached the game with a whole new perspective, and although many of his off-field marketing ideas had proven very successful, his multinational and highly-paid team had yet to really click on the field. They appeared to be a quality side on paper but without the real heart to put their bodies on the line when it mattered.

Just a month after Ireland's shock World Cup exit to Argentina in Lens, Munster began their campaign at home to Pontypridd at Thomond Park. The Interprovincial Championship had gone well, with Munster winning the competition with three wins out of three, and the visit of Pontypridd was eagerly anticipated. Munster duly started their European campaign with a victory, but it was a poor game of rugby. A Gareth Wyatt try helped the visitors to establish a 10-6 lead in the first quarter but Munster soon put their game faces on, scoring 26 unanswered points in the final hour, a tally that included tries from Alan Quinlan and Killian Keane.

Next up was a trip to London. Saracens had made Vicarage Road, the home of Watford Football Club, their home since 1997 and along with the away fixture against Colomiers, it promised to be the biggest challenge Munster would face in the pool stages. Despite the fact that Munster had played just one game away in England in European competition – the 48-40 defeat to Harlequins in 1997 – beating an English side on their home turf was always going to be a mental test as much as a physical one. Good Irish teams had a habit of losing in England, consequently the Saracens game wasn't just about Munster being technically better than the opposition, it was also about the visitors being cocky and confident enough to win.

Long story:
John Langford, who came to Munster after a flirtation with a move to Leinster, wins a line-out against Pontypridd

Since coming into the job two seasons previously, Declan Kidney and Niall O'Donovan had put the province's first serious structures in place and the pair's professionalism off the field was beginning to yield performances and results. In the beginning, a number of senior players weren't necessarily convinced of Kidney's coaching talents but most squad members were impressed with the Cork man's way of going about his work.

"You always got the impression he wanted to make you a better person as well as a better rugby player," says John Lacey. "I remember one game back in 1997, Anthony Foley latched onto a loose ball but I was too slow in supporting him and the move broke down. He wanted me to concentrate better during games so for weeks and weeks he had me reading books to up my levels of concentration." Along a similar line goes the story of a young out-half at Dolphin who was unemployed during the time of Kidney's tenure there. The coach took him out of the first team and helped him to get a job, insisting that the youngster couldn't be expected to make decisions on the pitch during a game if he wasn't making any during the week.

Another factor that endeared him to the players was his unshakeable belief in Irish people and all things Irish. In the socially confident and expressive Ireland of 2006, that may be taken as a given by most but back in 1999 he was one of the few to constantly talk up the capabilities of Irish people, in all walks of life. "We have a brilliant natural resource with an awful lot of rugby players in the country," he told 'The Irish Times' back in 1999. "In fact, I think in the country overall we're unbelievable how many sports people we turn out for the size of us, yet we can be very harsh on one another..."

Kidney was also one of the first Irish rugby coaches to truly concentrate on the psychological side of the game. One team meeting in particular, the week before the game against Saracens, has passed into legend. The squad were sitting in one of the Thomond Park meeting rooms watching a video of one of Saracens' games that season and just as he pressed the play button, Kidney donned a fez hat (an item worn at games by the English side's fans) and started driving a remote-controlled car (that's how Saracens got their kicking tee onto the pitch) around the room. Everybody watched what he was doing, some started to laugh, and after a couple of minutes Kidney stopped and asked the players what had happened on the video screen. Nobody knew. The point had been made.

English breakfast: *Alan Quinlan, David Wallace, Jeremy Staunton and Mike Mullins celebrate the Saracens win*

So in the midst of the fez-wearing fans, the remote-controlled tee carrier, the majorettes and the sudden loud music from the PA system during the game, Munster took the field at Vicarage Road on Sunday, 28 November. It was to be an evening to remember. The visitors trailed 18-3 early in the game, by 21-9 at the break, and by 34-23 with eight minutes left. But they still emerged winners by a single point thanks to a Jeremy Staunton try which was converted by Ronan O'Gara on 77 minutes.

It was a monumental victory, one that Niall O'Donovan, who was the province's assistant coach at the time, believes to have been the turning point for Munster in the professional era. "We were dead and buried over there," he says. "I didn't see any way back for us at all. But to come back and beat them was a phenomenal achievement and everything started from there. We had a couple of hundred fans over with us that evening in London but before that we only had a handful going to away matches, friends and family and a few others. But that victory seemed to convince people that we were actually worth watching, worth following. Before that, people came to Thomond Park to watch the opposition, the Wasps and Harlequins of this world. After beating Saracens away from home, people started to come to watch us."

Turning point:
'People came to Thomond Park to watch the opposition, the Wasps and Harlequins of this world,' says Niall O'Donovan. 'After beating Saracens away from home, people started to come to watch us'

John Langford could also sense a sea-change following that game. "There were about 300 supporters over there at the time and I remember before the game having a look around the ground and seeing that there were signs everywhere saying it was a criminal offence for supporters to enter the field of play. But after the game they were all on the paddock, they didn't care about the threat and it was an amazing scene. It's one of the things that will always stay with me, a special moment."

Two weeks later Munster headed to Colomiers clearly buoyed by their victory at Vicarage Road, but with a specific goal in mind for their sojourn to France. "Everything we did in the Heineken Cup was built on something else, everything had a foundation," says Niall O'Donovan. "When me and Declan took over from Jerry Holland, the team were already used to winning home matches in Limerick and Cork. They'd beaten the likes of Wasps, Swansea and Harlequins at home and that had given the squad a certain amount of confidence. When we came in, we just wanted to build on the foundation that was already there. One of the main things we wanted to achieve was consistency. We didn't necessarily want to be the best Munster team in the history of the province, but we did want to become the most consistent. The province always had a history of getting big results one week and losing the next week but we wanted to ensure that cycle changed."

So after the high of Saracens, Munster wanted to avoid a potential trough against Colomiers. The French outfit had roughed them up a little in the quarter-final the previous year but this side were a more confident bunch after their victory in London. Within five minutes they were eight points to the good after Jason Holland – Midleton's Kiwi import who had made quite an impression since being co-opted into the provincial set-up early in the season – had finished off a move that involved Alan Quinlan, Mike Mullins and John Kelly, while Ronan O'Gara had earlier landed a penalty from close range. Tries from Jean Luc Sadourney and Jerome Sieurac on 24 and 28 minutes knocked the visitors back a little but two further O'Gara penalties before the interval gave Munster a 14-12 half-time lead.

Doubling up: *Jason Holland crosses for one of his two tries against Colomiers*

"I can remember sitting in the dressing room at half-time and thinking, 'Jesus, we have a chance here,'" says Mick Galwey. "It made a change from the other times we'd been in France where we'd be battered and bruised and counting our teeth, and talking about hanging in there and not letting the score get too big. But this time we had belief in what we were doing and the proof of the pudding came after that."

The tone for the second half was set by a Keith Wood try just four minutes after the break and on 58 minutes the game was all but finished as a contest when Holland crossed for his second try of the game. Marcus Horan even managed a fourth try for Munster before the end. The celebrations at the end showed how much the win meant to the team. Not only that, they'd now won two away matches in a row. That was the type of consistency that the management had been looking for.

A week after their minor miracle in France, Colomiers travelled to Musgrave Park on a dark, damp and windy Saturday afternoon. The conditions were almost an exact replica of the Perpignan game at the same venue the previous year and like that fixture, Munster adapted to their surroundings that little bit better and effectively mauled their way to victory. Keith Wood was the benefactor in chief of the superbly organised Munster line-out maul, scoring two tries, on 22 and 58 minutes, while acting as trailer to the whole operation. The other highlight in the 23-5 win was Dominic Crotty's try after 63 minutes, coming as it did off a well-executed backline move involving Ronan O'Gara and Mike Mullins. In the slippery conditions, it proved exactly what this progressive, confident Munster side were now capable of, aside from their ability to batter the opposing pack.

Mud bath: Ronan O'Gara cleans up after Keith Wood scores against Colomiers at Musgrave Park

After the game, which was played on the last Saturday before Christmas, there was a general buzz of optimism but Declan Kidney kept expectations firmly grounded, despite four wins on the trot. "We can be very harsh on ourselves here in Ireland in that if you lose it's all doom and gloom and if you win you can go over the top," said the coach. "It is important to remember that we may not qualify for the quarter-finals yet. If Saracens beat us then they have Colomiers at home. If they win the two games and beat us by more than a point then that puts them ahead of us unless we get something out of Pontypridd away. We will have to have a long look at the league tables after this weekend and then look at the Saracens game that might not only put us into the quarter-finals but give us home advantage."

As for double try-scoring hero Keith Wood, the Clare man had a special word for the Munster crowd. "I never underestimate the ability of the crowd to lift a side," said the hooker. "Some people say they never hear what goes on around them but I hear it all the time. We had it at Saracens with 10 minutes to go in the match when we were behind and struggling. Then there was a chant from a small group of Munster supporters in the crowd. In Colomiers a week ago there was another minor eruption of noise with people shouting for us and yes, it does make a difference."

With four wins out of four before Christmas, Munster were top of Pool 4 and in an extremely strong position to qualify for the knockout stages of the competition for the second year in a row. However, the visit of Saracens to Thomond Park could decide their fate. The London outfit had dominated when the sides had met at Vicarage Road and they were extremely disappointed to have lost the game by a single point. They simply had to beat Munster if they were to qualify for the quarter-finals and that very point was no doubt stressed to them by their owner, Nigel Wray, in the days before the game. He'd pumped an awful lot of money into the club and some return was needed.

The interest in the game was such that Thomond Park looked seriously overcrowded in the minutes before kick-off and that perception wasn't far from the truth. Each of the four terraces were almost swaying with the numbers packed into them and at one point, about 20 minutes into the game, eyewitnesses described how the car park between the stand and the Shannon clubhouse was thronged with people attempting to catch a glimpse of the game. Thankfully, nobody was injured on the day but the huge crowd present that afternoon – believed to be in the region of 19,000 – forced the Munster Branch and the fire department to downgrade Thomond Park's official capacity to 13,500 for all future games in the Heineken Cup.

But those who did manage to locate half a yard of space for themselves were treated to a mesmerising spectacle, a topsy-turvy game with a twist at the end. Saracens took

Civil war: *Cork-born Darragh O'Mahony, who scored an early try for Saracens, holds off the challenge of John Kelly and Mike Mullins*

a 17–8 lead into the break thanks to tries from Cork native Darragh O'Mahony and Mark Mapletoft but despite Mick Galwey's early try, the visitors looked by far the more comfortable side in the greasy conditions. Ronan O'Gara narrowed that gap minutes after the break and on 52 minutes Munster were a point in front thanks to a brilliantly-crafted Jason Holland try. A trio of charges from Keith Wood, Alan Quinlan and David Wallace put Munster on the front foot and O'Gara found space on the outside to release Holland for a score that shook the stadium. Over the next 20 minutes, O'Gara and Thierry Lacroix exchanged two penalties each to leave Munster a point up heading into the final few minutes but a series of concerted drives by Saracens, and a bit of a rolling maul, saw Mapletoft stagger over the line to put the visitors in front. Lacroix's conversion put six points between the sides and nobody could see a way back for Munster. The Thomond Park record looked to be dead in the water.

"Mapletoft scored under the posts and Jesus did he celebrate, I can still remember the look on his head when Lacroix was taking the conversion," says Mick Galwey. "We went under the posts for a bit of a chat and the whole crowd, all 20,000 of them or whatever it was, were completely silent. They were absolutely stunned, I'll never forget how quiet they were. I just looked at the lads and said, 'Ye all know what we have to do'. And they'd all been playing rugby long enough to know that it wasn't a penalty we were after, it was a converted try. We got up to their corner thanks to a couple of penalties and like all the important line-outs we had that season, it went to John Langford. Myself and the Claw were first around him when he landed back on earth and we worked our way over the line, we knew exactly what we were doing."

Keith Wood was the man finally credited with inching the ball over the line and as Thomond Park went wild, the realisation soon dawned on everybody that Ronan O'Gara would have to land the tricky conversion to earn Munster the victory. Mick Galwey handed him the ball – "there's nothing you can say to a man in a moment like that" – and the entire ground went into its traditional hush. Before O'Gara could start his run-up, Saracens attempted to charge the kick down but once they were admonished by the referee and order was restored, the nerveless Cork Constitution man stuck the ball between the sticks to give Munster a 31-30 lead. Thomond Park erupted once more.

"He had some balls," says Galwey, "it was a gutsy kick but amazingly there was still some time to play. They even managed to get into our half but John Langford used every inch he had in him to block a Thierry Lacroix drop-goal. The scenes at the end were amazing, I've never had my back slapped so much."

Neither had the rest of the team. It was a truly memorable day.

With qualification and a home quarter-final already secured, Munster travelled to Sardis Road to play Pontypridd the Saturday after their second Saracens late show keen to keep their unbeaten record in the pool stages intact and earn themselves an easier tie at Thomond Park in April. In a topsy-turvy game, yet another one in a season where Munster were fast gaining a reputation as entertainers rather than grafters, a disputed injury-time try from John Colderley and subsequent conversion from Brett Davey stole a 38-36 victory for the Welsh side. Munster were incandescent with rage at the decision, they clearly felt Peter Stringer had positioned his body between Colderley's shoulder and the ground, but they'd been chasing the Welsh side for most

Keeping the record straight: *Keith Wood celebrates with Alan Quinlan after his late try against Saracens at Thomond Park*

Conversion of faith: *Ronan O'Gara's last-minute kick sent Munster fans into raptures*

of the game and on the balance of play they couldn't argue with the two-point defeat. The result pitted them against Stade Francais in the quarter-finals, the club from the French capital who had negotiated a tricky pool comprising Leicester, Leinster and Glasgow to qualify for the knockout stages. Like Saracens, they were an outfit awash with money, flamboyant owner Max Guazzini bringing in the likes of Diego Dominguez, the Argentine who played for Italy, Brian Lima from Samoa and French stars Christophe Dominici and Sylvain Marconnet.

As well as the problems that Stade Francais would pose, Munster also had to contend with a 12-week break between the Pontypridd game and the quarter-final. The one bonus was that most of the squad were either involved with the international side or the Ireland A team – including new caps Peter Stringer, Ronan O'Gara and John Hayes – coached by Declan Kidney and Niall O'Donovan, and with both outfits doing well over the spring, most of the players were in decent form. There were no significant injury problems either going into the game, a near miracle for the time of year, and following a friendly against Leicester at Welford Road – a match Munster lost 25-17 but got rid of a few cobwebs – the Stade Francais fixture came into focus.

Switch in time: opting for Eddie Halvey ahead of Alan Quinlan against Stade Francais was the first of Declan Kidney's masterstrokes

There was huge hype around the tie and when the tickets went on sale 10 days before the game, a little bit of history was created as the first queues for Munster tickets formed outside the Limerick Sports Store and Gleeson's Sports in Limerick city centre and the Munster Branch offices in Cork. There were a couple of changes in the Munster side for the quarter-final. Jason Holland had to return to New Zealand due to a family bereavement and Killian Keane came in to replace him at inside centre. But while that switch was enforced, the second one certainly wasn't. Declan Kidney had decided to play Eddie Halvey ahead of Alan Quinlan in the back row and although it appeared to be an odd decision at the time, it was the first of the coach's famed masterstrokes.

Quinlan had been in decent form all season and alongside David Wallace on the open side and Anthony Foley at number eight, the Tipperary man had been an integral part of one of European rugby's most effective back-row combinations. Halvey, meanwhile, had opted not to take a professional contract that season and was an amateur player plugging away with Shannon in the All-Ireland League.

It looked a baffling call but as soon as the game kicked off, it made perfect sense. John Langford had given the Munster line-out some extra impetuous during the season, in both an attacking and defensive sense, but the addition of Halvey to the mix doubled the trouble for the opposition. Within a few minutes of the start, Halvey had already justified his selection by nicking a couple of Stade line-outs and it was clear the French side were struggling to deal with Langford, Mick Galwey and the Shannon flanker out of touch. Munster's line-out dominance laid the foundations for an exceptional performance.

With just 10 minutes on the clock, they were 12-0 ahead and it was just reward for their ambition. The game plan centred on running at Stade and keeping the ball in hand and four minutes in, Mike Mullins threw an overhead pass to Anthony Horgan wide left and the Cork Constitution winger powered over in the corner. Five minutes later Dominic Crotty ran through a neatly-engineered gap in the Stade midfield, brushing aside a couple of tackles on his way over the line. And that was essentially that. Ronan O'Gara kicked five more penalties and Munster cruised into their first ever Heineken Cup semi-final.

"We opted to play into the wind in the first half," recalls Mick Galwey, "and it worked perfectly for us. It was something we liked to do because it tended to focus the mind that little bit more. And once we got that early lead there was no catching us, we literally hit the ground running. A lot of the time the break away from the provincial team hindered our preparations a little, making us a little bit rusty in certain areas but there was another side to the whole thing. The break ensured that fellas were mad keen to pull the red jersey back on, hungry to get back playing with Munster and that day it certainly showed from the first whistle."

While the players sang 'Stand Up And Fight' in the dressing room afterwards, a new anthem was born in Thomond Park that afternoon. Midway through the first half during a break in play, with Munster in complete control of the game and the sun shining down, the crowd started into a rendition of 'The Fields Of Athenry'. Ronan O'Gara admitted afterwards that the song had given him "goose bumps all over" and that was a sentiment echoed by anyone that was in the ground that day. No proper explanation has ever been offered as to why the song was sung that particular day, but it struck a cord and was adopted as the anthem of the fans.

It was supposed to be a relaxing Sunday afternoon, a bit of a celebration. John Langford had just christened his first child, Conor, at St Mary's Church right in the middle of the Limerick city district known as The Parish, and there was a party afterwards out the road in Anthony Foley's house in Killaloe. Most of the Munster squad were there to wet the baby's head, but they were all a bit anxious. The draw for the Heineken Cup semi-finals was to be made that afternoon and they were waiting for the news to trickle through. Toulouse, Northampton and Llanelli were the other sides in the last four and Munster would gladly have taken either the English or Welsh team at home or away. They'd even have taken Toulouse at Lansdowne Road, but the only draw they wanted to avoid like the plague was the French side in France. And then the news came through. Toulouse away. Everybody thought some joker was having a bit of a laugh at first but nobody owned up to the prank. Munster had pulled the shortest straw.

The game was fixed for Stade Lescure in Bordeaux on Saturday, 6 May and the trip caught the imagination like no other. Around 3,000 fans put their hands deep in their pockets to shell out for the charter flights to the south of France, while others who didn't have the cash thought of more imaginative ways of getting to Bordeaux, including the two lads who made it from Limerick to Toulouse, and back, on motorbike. Despite the efforts supporters were going to in order to get to France, not many of them would have believed Munster were actually capable of winning the game. But, luckily, the mood in and around the camp was different.

"I personally believed we could win, certainly since that Saracens game," remembers Niall O'Donovan. "You see, we had a big advantage over all the other provinces at the time because most of our players were used to winning, they were accustomed to it. Since the All-Ireland League was founded, it was dominated by the likes of Shannon, Garryowen, Young Munster and Cork Constitution and these were the guys that made up our team at that point in time. They were a confident bunch and they expected to win games, they'd become used to it. Toulouse away was a difficult task but we knew how to win rugby matches and that's a fantastic habit to have."

Munster's preparations for the game were spot on. They expected it to be warm in Bordeaux and brought 500 litres of water over with them for the days before the game. Each player was ordered to drink three litres of water before kick-off on the Saturday and it seemed to pay off. While the Toulouse players were slumped in the shade of the tunnel at half-time despite being 15-11 ahead, Munster's players looked and felt an awful lot more energetic. They'd taken an early lead thanks to a John Hayes try but four penalties from Michel Marfaing, and one from Stephane Ougier, had edged the French side into the lead over the course of the half.

Bull run: *Peter Clohessy and Mick Galwey celebrate after John Hayes powers over for a try against Toulouse*

But Munster had a stiff wind behind them in the second period and that, along with Toulouse's body language, gave them a huge mental fillip when they came back onto the pitch. "When we came back from the dressing room before the start of the second half, Toulouse were still slumped in the tunnel and I just couldn't understand it," says Mick Galwey. "We'd been back to our dressing room, taken off our jerseys, put on fresh ones, used the jacks, got some water on board and went back out on the pitch, while they were still lounging around the tunnel looking exhausted. The minute we got back onto the pitch and into our huddle we spoke about how Toulouse had looked shattered and it did give us great confidence."

Two O'Gara penalties to one from Marfaing left Toulouse one point in front but even with Mike Mullins in the sin bin, Munster stood firm and didn't concede a score. It proved to be crucial. With the centre back in the fray, the province went about scoring their greatest ever try in the Heineken Cup. From a scrum just outside their 22, O'Gara put in a skip pass to Mullins, whose reverse pass found Dominic Crotty coming in on the angle. Jason Holland and John Kelly both carried the ball forward, with Anthony Foley also getting involved. With Stringer all the while flinging it out on a plate, O'Gara took it up next and then Kelly flung out a beauty of a pass for Anthony Horgan to beat Cedric Desbrosse, Emile Ntamack and Alain Penaud down the left wing. John Langford and Eddie Halvey secured the ball at the breakdown and

Different planet: Ronan O'Gara scores Munster's greatest ever Heineken Cup try against Toulouse

from Mullins's pass, Crotty ran direct at the ever-thinning Toulouse defence. The full-back offloaded in the tackle in front of the posts and O'Gara popped up on his shoulder to somersault between the posts for an amazing effort. From start to finish, the move had lasted 91 seconds. It was rugby from a different planet, wholly untypical of what Irish teams had produced in the past.

There was no stopping them from there. Within four minutes Holland had intercepted a loose Toulouse pass to sprint to the line and Munster were home and dry. "Jason was some man for an intercept," recalls Galwey, "I've never seen any man

Tears of joy: Niall O'Donovan, Declan Kidney and Brian O'Brien show what the victory over Toulouse means

better at timing his run. But we used to have great fun slagging him afterwards because as soon as he intercepted, he seemed to hit the quicksand pretty quick. He wasn't the fastest of lads and it looked like he was going in slow motion half the time."

Jerome Cazalbou did manage an injury-time effort for the French but it didn't matter one bit as Jim Fleming's next whistle signalled that Munster had qualified for the Heineken Cup final. Declan Kidney was hoisted high in the air by his players and the lap of honour in the spring sunshine was something to behold. Not only had Munster beaten Toulouse, they'd done it by playing a continental brand of rugby.

"The after-match scene was truly special," says Galwey. "We did a lap of honour and greeted our fans and when I got back to the tunnel an English reporter grabbed me and said he had Richard on the phone for me. I was thinking to myself who in God's name is Richard but it turned out to be Dickie Harris, as they called him in Limerick, on the set of some movie in Mexico congratulating us. And there I was thinking to myself, 'Jesus, he's in Mexico and he knows that we've beaten Toulouse, what in God's name are we after getting ourselves into?'"

It was a question all the squad would ask themselves over the coming weeks.

On the morning of 27 May, 2000, London was its usual busy self and any local walking around the city's West End, Covent Garden or any other spot you'd care to mention, wouldn't have had a clue that this was the biggest day in the history of Munster rugby. It was a city where any event could get lost. Many pockets of Munster fans had strolled around town that morning wondering whether the numbers expected in London for the final was simply media hype.

Thirty thousand was the figure that most newspapers had been quoting during the week and while it was an extraordinary number, the evidence was there to suggest that it could be true. Like the Toulouse game, the press had been filled with all manner of planes, trains and automobiles-type stories and every second person appeared to be knocking on the door of their credit union to release some funds.

But Munster fans must have wondered where the rest of their comrades were. Until they hit Earls Court underground station, that is, and they wondered no more. The station itself is an unforgettable kind of place, a crossover point for the Piccadilly and District lines, but anybody who wants to get to south-west London generally passes through this particular hub on the way. And there they were; hundreds of red-shirted Munster fans who'd worked their way to the station from all corners of the English capital. Most had flown over the night before and stayed in hotels, hostels or with family members. But Earls Court was their first collective meeting point on the way to their date with destiny and nobody felt they were alone in the English capital any longer.

Meanwhile, everything appeared to be going swimmingly in the Munster camp in the days before the game. There were no major injury problems for Declan Kidney to worry himself with and having arrived in London on the Thursday before the final, the squad seemed to have enjoyed being shielded away from the hype for a couple of days. But the benefit of hindsight has helped to cast a different light on Munster's preparations for the match against Northampton. Certainly nobody at the time felt there was anything wrong with what the squad was doing, but the passing of time has altered the views of a number of key members of the set-up.

In an interview given to 'The Irish Times' in 2005, Keith Wood admitted that Munster's choice of airport didn't help anyone in the run-up to the big game. "For some reason we didn't fly to Heathrow," said the hooker. "We flew to Gatwick, even though the game was in Twickenham, and we drove to the ground the day before the game and got caught in Friday traffic, and got caught on the way back. We spent the day in bloody traffic on a bus."

John Langford remembers another transport issue. "I think we got to the ground far too early on the day of the game," said the second row. "We mis-timed how long it was going to take, probably because of the traffic we'd been in the day before and we had far too much time to kill at the stadium. It was just a little thing but I hate being at the ground too long before kick-off and others were the same. It gives you too much time to think and looking back on it now, I think it affected everybody."

Not only did things not go smoothly on the day of the game, Niall O'Donovan now feels that they didn't handle the night before the final too cleverly either. "We allowed ourselves to get too emotional in the build-up to the final, particularly the night before the game," he admits. "We had a bit of a chat about the game and players started talking about how big the whole thing had become and how much they wanted to win. Guys probably got a bit too fired-up and emotional. Looking back on it now, we should have handled the build-up a whole lot better. But then again we'd come so far so quickly that year, it was a new experience for all of us."

With the electric atmosphere inside Twickenham light years away from that of your staid international game at the same venue, it was always possible that the occasion would get to the teams, and on the day it was Munster who took longer to settle. Two minutes in they were penalised for handling at a ruck and Paul Grayson stepped up to put Northampton into the lead. Even in the early exchanges it was easy to see that Munster were struggling at both the line-out and scrum, and that's why it was such a relief when Jason Holland landed a drop-goal after the Irish side's first spell of concerted pressure. Fifteen minutes later they went in front. Keith Wood made a burst up the right wing and from the ruck, O'Gara skip passed to Holland, who found Dominic Crotty and the full-back delivered a perfect pass to David Wallace who charged over the line. The out-half missed the convert but even though Grayson landed a second penalty on the stroke of Joel Dume's half-time whistle, Munster would have been absolutely delighted to take a lead into the interval.

Minutes into the second half, Dom Malone's break from inside his own half was just stopped by a desperate Eddie Halvey tackle, but a few minutes later Grayson knocked over his third penalty of the game to put the English side 9-8 in front with over half an hour on the clock. As the rain began to sheet down, Munster upped the tempo

No consolation:
'I broke down when I met my wife Joan and she handed me my daughter Neasa,' says Mick Galwey. 'I was in such a daze I brought her up with me to collect the silver plate we got for finishing runners-up'

but their efforts suffered a huge blow when Mick Galwey was sin-binned in controversial fashion. "I thought Dom Malone had tapped the penalty, knocked it on and I just went to play the advantage," says the Munster skipper. "But the referee thought I'd knocked it out of his hands. That was his call but I know I didn't. It was a huge blow and I felt it made a massive difference. We were going well at the time and if I'd stayed on, who knows what might have happened. But it was the loneliest 10 minutes of my life. It was the only place in the world you didn't want to be when your team were down by a single point and were chasing the Heineken Cup."

With Galwey back on the field and the score still unchanged, O'Gara missed a difficult penalty to put Munster in front and after a line-out maul was defended superbly by Northampton, the out-half had another kick bang on 80 minutes to win the game for Munster. "I'd played at Twickenham before with Australia and the one thing I did remember from my visit was that there was a gusty wind that blew around the ground," says John Langford. "I mentioned it to Rog the day before the game when we were having our captain's run."

Armed with that knowledge, O'Gara aimed his kick slightly to the right of the posts but that gusty wind took control of the ball and dragged it agonisingly past Northampton's left-hand post. It proved to be Munster's last opportunity on a devastating afternoon.

"The hardest thing to take after that game was the fact that we knew we didn't play well at all," says Galwey. "But we pulled ourselves together and went on a lap of honour around the pitch. Our supporters got up and cheered us and that made things even harder, it probably would have been easier for us to deal with if they started booing us. I broke down when I met my wife Joan and she handed me my daughter Neasa and I was in such a daze I brought her up with me to collect the silver plate we got for finishing runners-up. I haven't a clue where that is now, I just flung it at someone when I got back down onto the pitch. Arriving back at Shannon was another hard moment. There was a big crowd there to greet us and to be honest we felt as though we'd let them down, we didn't feel we deserved their plaudits. It was a tough couple of days to get through, but the world kept turning."

As the red-shirted masses drifted back towards Richmond Station, an upper-class, middle-aged English lady pondered aloud why all the Munster supporters were so down after the defeat. Usually, she stated, the Irish lost a game and then went on the beer afterwards to ensure that at the very least they had a decent night.

But this Munster journey was not simply about the craic. It was about winning.

Official complaint: *touch judge Steve Lander looks on as John O'Neill crosses for the try that never was against Stade Francais*

CHAPTER 7

TOUCHY SUBJECT

2000/01

It was never going to be easy for Munster to bounce back from the Northampton defeat. The loss had rattled the players' confidence, and there was a genuine fear that the side mightn't get to play in another decider. The road to Twickenham had been far too difficult a journey for anyone involved to take an early return to a Heineken Cup final as a given.

The departure of Keith Wood and Eddie Halvey was also unsettling. The pair were outstanding during the latter stages of the previous season's campaign but Declan Kidney would now have to do without them. Wood, the province's talisman, had returned to London and Harlequins, while the hugely-talented Halvey had signed on for London Irish.

But if there were questions aplenty for Munster to ponder as they headed into another campaign, then Kidney already had a few answers. "Everything starts from zero and we see how we go from here," said the Munster coach in an interview on the eve of the new season. "If we'd won the European Cup last season we'd still be doing the same thing. Like ourselves, Leinster, Ulster and Connacht are starting off from par. It's like a Thursday in golf. It's a completely different competition from last year even though you're playing against the same teams."

The coach even tackled the loss of Wood, the inspirational hooker who'd done so much to propel them to the final the previous season. "We have the Irish reserve hooker, Frankie Sheahan, to take Wood's place. He has had two years on the bench under Mark McDermott and Keith Wood, he'll have learnt from both of them, so the way I'm looking at it, it's an opportunity for him to show himself. There's no point in regretting Keith being gone. If I was to look upon it in any other way it would be a lie, what I've been saying to Frank over the last two years – telling him that his opportunity would come."

Mick Galwey was also upbeat. A pre-season tour to Scotland convinced the captain that Munster's 2000 Heineken Cup final appearance wouldn't be a one-off. "We all were a little worried that we mightn't get that far again," recalls the captain, "especially considering we wouldn't be a surprise to anybody anymore. I remember we went on a pre-season tour to play Glasgow and it was mentioned in the dressing room beforehand that our last game together had been in the Heineken Cup final and that it was important we got back on the road with a victory. We ended up beating them by 70 points or something like that and it was great, it proved to everybody that we were actually a good rugby team and that we'd learned a lot from the previous season. It gave us the confidence to go forward and believe in ourselves once again."

With the way things were shaping up, John Langford, the man who swore he was only going to be with Munster for one season, was enticed to stay on. "I had been planning to go home," says the second row. "I only had a one-year deal but the motivation to stay and finish what I had started with Munster was just too much. I think that was the motivation for everyone. I was worried during the summer that

Once more with feeling: 'The motivation to stay and finish what I had started with Munster was just too much,' says John Langford

because we had lost so narrowly the previous year, that we could have been down about it and struggled the following year. I spoke to Declan Kidney about the whole thing, we spoke about teams like Manchester United and how success only seemed to increase the desire for more. He wanted Munster to be like that and so did I. It became pretty clear that season that everybody wanted to push on further."

With a heightened expectation around the province, and an eager 13,000 crowd in attendance, Munster hosted Newport in their Pool 4 opener at Thomond Park. It was the

Welsh side's first foray into the Heineken Cup and they had a bit of money behind them too. Gary Teichmann, the former Springbok captain, skippered them from the back row and with Shane Howarth, the recent New Zealand convert to the Welsh cause, controlling things at out-half they represented a half-decent outfit. In fact, with a bit more experience in the competition they could have made a bit of history at Thomond Park. They controlled the game for long periods and were well capable of holding onto the ball and pinning Munster in their own 22 but when it came to turning possession into points, they were slightly naïve in their approach. A more experienced team might have put Munster away.

As it was, a rapid-fire start from Munster won them the game. Frankie Sheahan and Mick Galwey both scored tries from close in within the opening 15 minutes to ease the tension around the ground but going that far ahead so early proved to be a bit of a problem. "You can talk about performances and results and enjoying yourselves," said Kidney afterwards, "and now we're trying to do all three but it takes mental strength to do it. You're playing your first game in Europe, you're 15 points up in 15 minutes and I was thinking would he (the referee) ever blow the final whistle then, and that means it must be harder for the guys playing."

Home comfort: *Mick Galwey and Ronan O'Gara congratulate Anthony Horgan after his crucial try gave Munster a 20-6 half-time lead against Newport at Thomond Park*

It was difficult for Munster but having seen off some decent Newport pressure, Anthony Horgan crossed for a crucial try right on half-time and Munster went into the interval with a 20-6 lead. It proved to be enough in the end, but not before two clever tries from Ben Breeze, both scored out wide with the Munster defence completely outflanked, gave the home side something to think about. The final whistle was greeted with relief all around Thomond Park and afterwards the players celebrated the upcoming birthdays of Galwey and Mick O'Driscoll by plastering the dressing room walls with cake. Clearly, nobody had the stomach for food after such a close call on the pitch.

The following weekend Munster took a trip down memory lane. Their very first away match in the Heineken Cup had been against Castres and five years down the line they were returning to the part of the continent where their adventures began. In many ways it was apt, because Munster's performance at Stade Pierre-Antoine showed exactly how far they'd progressed as a team in European competition. They conceded two early tries to Philippe Garrigues and Albert Costes and when Alan Quinlan was sent to the sin bin before half-time with the visitors 20-6 behind, they looked to be in quite a spot of bother. But Munster refused to panic and instead nibbled away patiently at Castres' lead. Ronan O'Gara kept them in touch with his trusty boot and when Quinlan returned to steal a few balls in succession at the line-out, Munster at last had something to work off.

Roger and out: Ronan O'Gara seals the victory over Castres at the Stade Pierre-Antoine with a late try

Dominic Crotty gobbled up an easy try after an old-fashioned foot rush, while minutes later O'Gara set up Anthony Horgan for the province's second effort with a superbly-executed flat pass. With the game nearing its conclusion, the out-half stole the spoils for Munster with a try of his own after some neat link-up play between David Wallace, Jason Holland and Crotty. It was super stuff. Minutes later Gareth Simmonds' final whistle signalled Munster's third win on the trot in France. It was becoming something of a habit.

"That was the game that defined our season," says Galwey. "We showed some great composure away from home and the last five minutes stand out for me. We held onto the ball brilliantly, it was as though we were playing rugby league and we took the sting out of the game. We were clearly progressing as a team, we weren't just a blood and guts outfit or a mauling team. We were becoming a team capable of controlling a game in a difficult environment and the Castres win proved just that."

Ulster hands: Jeremy Davidson beats John Langford to win a line-out for Castres

Jeremy Davidson, the Ulster native and Castres captain, appeared to be equally surprised and impressed by Munster. "I didn't actually think they were capable of winning at half-time," said the Irish second row. "They were a totally different team in the second half and any team that wins here in Castres must be looked upon as a good one, more particularly in the circumstances that Munster found themselves at the break. It will take an exceptional side to beat them. Whatever else happens this season, they deserve the plaudits for this one."

The defeat appeared to leave the Ulster man downcast about his side's prospects for the rest of the campaign. "From our point of view it's not going to be easy. We have lost twice now and whatever happens we face an uphill struggle to qualify for the knockout stages. It is one thing to lose away but totally different to lose at home. Defeat in Castres was not on our agenda so I really don't know where we go from here."

The victory over Castres, and everything they'd achieved the previous season, put Munster in an odd position when Bath came to Limerick on 21 October. For the first time in their Heineken Cup history, they were firm favourites to beat a visiting English side at Thomond Park. It wasn't a situation that anybody in the squad were used to. Throughout the careers of these players, be it for Shannon, Garryowen, Cork

Constitution or Young Munster on one level, or Ireland, or indeed Munster, they'd almost been conditioned to view themselves as underdogs.

It was a psyche that went back to the very origins of Irish rugby. Back in the 1870s, the Leinster and Ulster Branches ruled the scene and when the IRFU was being formed in 1880, it was decreed that Munster would only be allowed full representation on the Union's committee if they managed to either draw or win against the sacred two provinces. There was such disrespect for rugby in the province that Leinster and Ulster wouldn't allow them proper representation at decision-making level unless they proved themselves worthy of it. By God, they'd show that high and mighty duo a thing or two and that's exactly what Munster did by beating Leinster for the first time later that very year. The belief that they were viewed as second-class partners in the Union engendered a persecution complex in the province from the very beginning. But by the 2000/01 season, things had changed radically. There was a maturity about the side and the set-up which was different.

"At that point in time we didn't want lads to be looking at matches in terms of being underdogs or being favourites," recalls Niall O'Donovan. "We were trying to get the players away from all that, to look at the game a little less emotionally. We needed to concentrate on things like how we were going to trouble the opposing line-out, or what was the best way to attack a certain team. The fact of the matter is that whether you're underdogs or favourites going into a game, you still need to prepare in the same way and I felt the players were buying into that mentality by detaching themselves a little from emotional things. Sure, there were some guys you'd want to fire up in the dressing room before a game because it made them perform better out on the pitch, but then again there were other fellas who couldn't concentrate if they were too fired up. We had to ignore whatever tag was being put on us by journalists and concentrate on getting things right."

This new mentality appeared to be working if the game against Bath was anything to go on. Munster led 6-3 at half-time thanks to two Ronan O'Gara penalties but an Anthony Horgan try just after the interval, with Mark Regan in the sin bin for stamping, changed the face of the game. It was some effort, too, as John Langford tapped a quick penalty inside his own half and eight phases later, with the help of some rapid-fire recycling, Dominic Crotty passed for the winger to cross in the corner. It was typical of the brilliance that this Munster team had moulded over the past couple of years; quick thinking and quick acting, all helped by quick ruck ball.

The game was still poised at 14-9 in Munster's favour with six minutes to go but as the visitors began to wilt, they were knocked to the canvas. First David Wallace careered between the posts following some great build-up play by both Anthony Foley and Jason Holland, while Horgan scored his second try of the game in injury time to give Munster a slightly flattering 22-point margin of victory.

"At 14-9 and 10 minutes to go, we were very much in there but I'm very disappointed at the way we folded at

Cleaning up:
David Wallace celebrates his try against Bath at Thomond Park

the end," said John Hall, the Bath forwards coach who'd got to know a lot about Munster rugby while coaching Garryowen for a couple of years in the late 1990s. "OK, the game was lost but that wasn't typical of a Bath side. As for Munster, I know a lot of their players and I can see now why they reached the final last year. They're a very good home side, they don't make many errors and they're very powerful up front. There's a lot of experience there and they played as a unit. I was not just impressed with their pack but also the backs. Mullins played well, so did O'Gara, and they looked more dangerous behind than we did."

With the platitudes handed out, particularly to a backline that had been much maligned over the years, Bath went about handing Munster a bit of a beating the following weekend at the Recreation Grounds. Beforehand, there was some doubt as to whether the match would actually take place at all as the picturesque venue down by the banks of the Avon River was severely flooded in a number of areas, but referee Nigel Whitehouse gave the go-ahead. The weather forced the cancellation of a number of ferries carrying Munster fans to the game and all in all it was a bad day for a side who had almost forgotten what it was like to lose.

A malfunctioning line-out was the visiting side's prime source of anguish. Mick Galwey left the fray injured after just 27 minutes and from there Munster had major problems securing their own ball out of touch. Because of that, the Munster backline had no quality ball to work with and their efforts were stymied from the beginning.

Washout: John Langford, John Hayes and Mick O'Driscoll show their disappointment after the defeat by Bath at the Recreation Grounds

Three penalties had Bath 9-0 ahead at half-time and although the tide of the game appeared to change when David Wallace crossed for a try three minutes into the second half, Bath regrouped and Munster continued to struggle. Ronan O'Gara, so usually reliable with his place-kicking, missed four out of four over the course of the 80 minutes and in worsening conditions, Munster never looked like scoring another try. Three more penalties for the home side in the second period edged them towards victory and handed Munster only their third defeat in 25 games.

Declan Kidney was, once again, calm and philosophical in defeat. "A day like this was always going to happen to us. But my overriding feeling is that we've won eight out of nine competitive games since the start of the season, we've played Bath twice and haven't conceded a try. I'm not going to be naïve enough to say we didn't make mistakes, we certainly did. But in the same way we didn't shout from the rooftops any time we won a match, I'm not going to panic because we lost one."

Despite the pain of defeat, and the pain of his knee injury, Mick Galwey remembers feeling almost complimented by the way the English side had won the game. "Tries were a big thing in the Heineken Cup but Bath scored six penalties that day and weren't even looking for anything else," says the captain. "I took it as a sign of how highly they rated us. We had got to a stage where even English teams on their home patch were just simply relieved to beat us. They didn't worry about anything else."

And there were further niceties in defeat from John Hall, this time for the Munster supporters. "It was a pleasure to play these two games. I think it's absolutely right that it came out 1-1 in the end. The Munster fans are really fantastic. The atmosphere when a kick at goal was being taken was something special, everything is quiet, and it's the way rugby should be played. And it's not just me, the young players, 21-, 22-year-olds, in our dressing room are saying the same thing."

The fallout from round four of the pool stages was positive for Munster, despite the defeat to Bath. Castres had beaten Newport in France on the same afternoon as Munster's defeat in England's West Country, so if the province were able to beat the Welsh side on their home patch, they would top the group with one game to go and a home quarter-final was then most certainly on the cards. It was a tempting carrot to dangle in front of a success-hungry team but the fractured nature of the Heineken Cup meant that Munster would have to wait a while to get a bite at it. The Bath game took place on 28 October but the Newport fixture wasn't to take place until 13 January.

In between, the second half of the Interprovincial Championship was squeezed in, with Munster once again claiming the title following an exciting 16-16 draw against Leinster at Donnybrook, and both sides met again in a physical friendly match in Cork early in the New Year. Leinster, clearly feeling they had a point to prove, won the game in front of 4,500 at Musgrave Park but the object of the exercise was to keep both teams primed for their final two Heineken Cup pool games.

The first of Munster's fixtures was against Newport at Rodney Parade. The Welsh side still had an outside chance of qualifying for the knockout stages, having beaten both Bath and Castres at home, but they needed to add Munster to that list if they wanted to progress any further. A couple of thousand travelling supporters still had enough money left after Christmas to make their way over for the game, and they were treated to a highly-entertaining spectacle, a game that had a little bit of everything and even better than that, a Munster victory at the end of it.

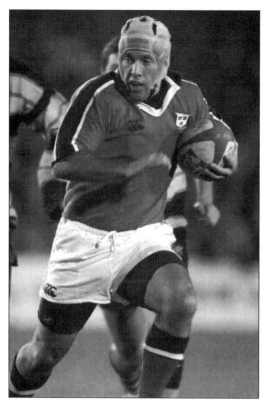

Power house: Mike Mullins goes over for a late try against Newport at Rodney Parade

Munster were 15-0 behind with just 20 minutes on the clock, as Newport's two Matts, Mostyn and Pini, scampered over for early tries. The visitors couldn't get their hands on the ball but all that changed once Mostyn was binned for taking out Anthony Horgan in the air and Ronan O'Gara crossed for Munster's first try after some sterling work by David Wallace. The out-half added the convert and narrowed Newport's lead to five points with a penalty on 36 minutes, but the Welsh side reasserted their dominance before the break with a penalty, drop-goal and penalty from the excellent Shane Howarth. As the Munster back row and line-out began to dominate proceedings, O'Gara knocked over four penalties to Howarth's one to put the visitors within two points of Newport. O'Gara was in fabulous form and when he landed a drop-goal on 75 minutes to put the Irish side into the lead for the first time in the game, there was only going to be one winner. In the closing minutes Mike Mullins and Anthony Horgan both crossed for tries to seal the deal and on the final whistle, Munster's travelling band of supporters danced with delight on the pitch as their heroes moved one step closer to the quarter-finals.

O'Gara was feted with the man-of-the-match award after the game having contributed 29 of his side's 39 points, and the out-half appeared to be maturing nicely into one of Munster's key performers. "I was striking the placed ball well, I was in the groove and once I got my set-up right, I knew they were going to go over," he said. "I have confidence in my own ability. You get knocked for certain things but I knew I was always capable of a performance like this. There were a few things to work on. My tackles were good tonight and my kicking out of hand was also good, even if I did have one or two slices. Now I've got to keep it at this level, there's an awful lot to play for personally this season. But, no, I'm not thinking as far

Welsh rarebit: *'There were thousands of our supporters on the pitch (after the victory over Newport),' says Mick Galwey. 'To see something like that away from home was fantastic'*

ahead as the Lions. Getting Munster into the quarter-finals is the priority and if you play well for Munster and for Ireland, then you're definitely in with a good chance."

"It's funny what you remember from games," says Mick Galwey. "When we were 15-0 behind I got the lads in a huddle behind the posts and reminded them that we hadn't got our hands on the ball yet, that we didn't need to panic. I also recall the Munster supporters singing, 'Who left the Claw out' at every given opportunity. Once the match was over, there were thousands of our supporters on the pitch and to see something like that away from home was fantastic. Every single one of us enjoyed those moments, even if it did take us half an hour to get back to the dressing room."

A victory over Castres at Musgrave Park the following weekend would guarantee a home quarter-final slot and on a damp Cork evening, 9,500 packed onto the terraces to ensure there were no slip-ups. It was a dour, dreary game of rugby and the only consolation was that Munster were in full control of proceedings throughout. Once Anthony Foley was helped over the line by his pack on 17 minutes, Munster never trailed Castres and the game was effectively over as early as the 24th minute when Dominic Crotty forced his way over in the corner following some intense Munster pressure. The rest was routine stuff and as the remainder of the pools came to a

Expectation, as well as interest, was high around the province heading into the game and Declan Kidney spent most of his week before talking up the worth of the opposition, explaining how they were the next big force in French rugby, but nobody was really listening. The supporters already had their eyes on bigger days ahead. As a result, the atmosphere in the ground that afternoon was odd, it was as though the normally passionate supporters had no fear whatsoever of the opposition, as though the fans had come to watch a demolition rather than a rugby match.

Thankfully the Munster team didn't feel like that. They were thoroughly focused on the job in hand and it showed in their performance. The fact of the matter was that they needed to be. Stuart Legg scored two tries for Biarritz in the opening 15 minutes as Munster struggled with the physicality of the visiting pack, but Anthony Foley squeezed an effort in between those two to keep his side within touching distance and over the next 40 minutes the hosts got their game together.

O'Gara kicked Munster into a 17-15 interval lead and just after the break, Foley got his second try to give them the all-important edge. Soon after, Denis Avril was binned for swinging an arm at David Wallace and Munster turned the screw, with Anthony Foley crossing for his hat-trick on 65 minutes. That left the home side 32-15 in front, but they fell asleep in the final quarter of an hour. Sebastien Bonnet intercepted a Mick Galwey offload to dash 50 yards to the line and although O'Gara landed a penalty to keep a gap of 13 points between the sides, Biarritz were back to within a score thanks to a Christophe Milheres try on 79 minutes. That made it four tries to three in favour of the visitors, not the norm at Thomond Park. The crowd's dismissive attitude to the French had been well and truly shaken by then but another O'Gara penalty in injury time, his 23rd point of the game, put Munster out of danger. Time to breathe again.

"I can't remember a harder match at Thomond Park," says Mick Galwey. "They had a huge pack of forwards and they really pounded at us, we really did struggle at times. The press and our supporters all thought they'd be a bit of a pushover in the days leading up to the game but we knew it was going to be a bruising battle. Even with a few minutes to go I was still hugely worried and we only began to relax when Ronan knocked over that late penalty. Afterwards, we all knew we had been in a game."

With most Munster players admitting, like Galwey, that Biarritz were as tough a side as they'd played in the competition, Declan Kidney went about trying to dampen down the hype surrounding his team. "The expectation levels for the Munster team are now way over the top," said the canny Cork man. "There was a lot of mental pressure on the lads today and they overcame that and all credit to them. In many ways coming here for Biarritz was like us going to Bordeaux for the Toulouse match last year. There isn't any reason why we can't be beaten here and all we can do is to make it as difficult as possible for all visiting teams. For them to score four tries was outstanding from their point of view. There were two very good teams out on the pitch today and we're just delighted to be through to the semi-finals again."

Racking 'em up: Ronan O'Gara slots over three of his 23 points against Biarritz

Probably just ahead of Ronan O'Gara, this was Anthony Foley's day. For a number eight to score three tries in a game is a rare feat, but to do so in a Heineken Cup quarter-final was something else entirely. The Shannon man's innate footballing intelligence shone through in all three of his efforts and there was an added bonus to go along with that achievement. Brian McGoey, the former Shannon scrum-half, had said that the first Munster player to score three tries in a Heineken Cup match would get free Dominos Pizzas for life in the city. Axel had just earned himself a decent crust.

It appeared that every force on God's earth was conspiring against Munster for the Heineken Cup semi-finals. Firstly, there was the draw itself, made at Dublin's Sugar Club in early February. Munster were to play Stade Francais at a neutral venue in France and if that wasn't bad enough, the ERC then decreed that the game would be played in Lille, not a venue in Paris. Those travelling Munster fans would have to splash out a little more cash to see their team in action.

Mother Nature then stuck her oar in. After Ireland had played their Six Nations games against Italy and France, the foot and mouth crisis struck Britain with local and international sporting fixtures badly hit. When the crisis first reared its head, the feeling was that one or two fixtures would be cancelled but as cases of the disease hit Wales, France and eventually, County Louth, the then-Minister for Agriculture, Joe Walsh, confirmed that no international sporting fixtures would take place until 30 days after the last case was found in either Britain or Ireland.

The Six Nations fixtures were originally rescheduled for the end of April and the first two weekends in May but even these rearrangements were postponed until the following autumn as the situation worsened. It left sports fans frustrated but it gave Munster a very real worry. If the game was going to take place, the province's players wouldn't have had a competitive fixture of any description for a full eight weeks. There was even the slight chance that Munster would have to forfeit their place in the last four if the ban was extended.

Mercifully, it never came to pass but that was where the good news ended. Aside from having a group of players who'd done nothing but play in a couple of AIB League games over the previous two months, Munster were also in the midst of a full-blown injury crisis. Alan Quinlan was definitely out with a broken thumb, John Kelly was struggling for fitness, while David Wallace was considered a huge doubt with knee ligament troubles. As if that wasn't enough, Peter Stringer, Dominic Crotty and Anthony Foley were all carrying slight knocks. The omens weren't good.

"The foot and mouth crisis hurt us badly," admits Mick Galwey. "We'd always been used to a bit of a break because of the Six Nations but this time nobody was playing any competitive rugby bar a couple of AIL games. It was a pity because having beaten France and Italy, the international team were in flying form and if the rest of the Six Nations had played itself out the way we all felt it would, most of our players would have been buzzing leading up to the semi-final. As it was, our competitive edge had been dulled and it was almost like starting the season all over again."

Eight days before the semi-final, Munster took on a Rest of Ireland selection at Thomond Park, the home side winning 24-22 in an entertaining game in front of a packed house. It had been a while since anybody had seen top-class rugby and it whetted everybody's appetite for the following weekend in France. There was a new face on view for Munster, too. Dion O'Cuinneagain, the former Ulster and Irish

Straight in: *Munster's new arrival Dion O'Cuinneagain gets friendly with the Rest of Ireland's Malcolm O'Kelly*

flanker, had been added to Munster's squad for the knockout stages by Declan Kidney and it proved a wise choice. The student doctor, who was now based in Cape Town, landed in Shannon Airport just four hours before the friendly game, but he came through his 20 minutes on the pitch unscathed and felt confident he could start the following week if the squad's injury crisis continued.

It was hardly the most positive way to head into such an important game but that didn't stop Munster's support. Whether it was the semi-final itself, or the fact they'd been so deprived of sporting action for months, about 10,000 fans splashed the cash to make their way to Lille. There was such a variety of possible ways of getting to the northern French industrial town that most were baffled by the choices put in front of them. Fly to Paris and then get the train to Lille? Or maybe fly to London and get the Eurostar to Lille? Or catch a flight to Brussels and work your way down from there? There were plenty of ways of getting there but not everyone was impressed with the place when they arrived.

Barring order: Munster supporters weren't too impressed with their French hosts when many pubs in Lille ran dry early on the Friday night before the Stade Francais match

Lille is an industrial city which bears no comparison to the likes of Toulouse, Perpignan and Bordeaux. To make matters worse, it's a long way from the heartland of French rugby and the locals didn't really get into the spirit of the build-up to the game. Indeed, they looked on the thousands of high-spirited, red-shirted fans with something close to bemusement. The visitors weren't all that impressed by their hosts either, especially when most of the proper pubs in the city ran out of beer early on the Friday night.

But at least things were going slightly better for the squad as matters on the injury front cleared up a little. David Wallace was, almost miraculously, passed fit to play, while a youngster named Donncha O'Callaghan was selected ahead of O'Cuinneagain at number six. Ever since he played a part in Ireland's Under-19 World Cup-winning team back in 1998, the Cork Con lock had been tipped to make it as a pro but his progress into the starting line-up had been delayed by the burgeoning second-row partnership of Galwey and Langford. The previous season, he had made three appearances off the bench but Kidney was in no rush to allow the youngest of the O'Callaghan clan to share the bragging rights with older sibling, Ultan, who had represented the province in the early days of the competition.

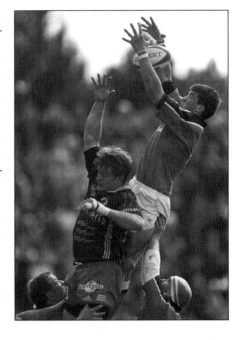

Leap of faith: *Donncha O'Callaghan wins a line-out against Stade Francais*

The only other change saw John O'Neill take John Kelly's place on the right wing and once kick-off approached, the clouds of pessimism that had been hanging around the squad and the fans over the previous couple of weeks suddenly disappeared from view. Game on.

From the first tackle it was clear that this was going to be a highly-physical encounter, one that was going to be dominated by the opposing packs. Both Diego Dominguez and Ronan O'Gara were in decent form with the boot and as the game inched towards half-time, the French side were 9-6 in front. But then disaster struck for Munster. Following a series of drives forward, Cliff Mytton, the Stade centre, got his hands on the ball and seared through a gap to touch the ball down under the posts. Dominguez added the convert and Munster were 16-6 down at the interval. Even the most optimistic travelling supporter would have found it hard to see how Munster were going to inch their way back into the game in the second half, but that's exactly what they did.

On 48 minutes O'Gara reduced that gap with his third penalty of the afternoon, and soon afterwards came the moment that defined the game. After putting the ball through a number of phases, Peter Stringer chipped a kick in the direction of John O'Neill and the winger put his head down to slide over the line right in the corner.

With no video replay facilities available at the venue, touch judge Steve Lander had to go with his initial instinct that O'Neill had touched the corner flag before touching down the ball and the try wasn't allowed. TV footage and a number of photographs would later prove that the Munster winger had finished the move off legally but there was nothing the province could do about it. After missing two difficult penalties on 62 and 67 minutes to draw Munster closer, O'Gara did manage two successful kicks to leave just a single point between the sides in injury time but Munster didn't have enough time to muster up one more opportunity. They'd lost by that single point.

"Can you imagine playing in a game like that," says Mick Galwey, "a really tough, tight game, and coming off the pitch to the sight of a photographer showing you a picture on his laptop of John O'Neill putting the ball down perfectly? Jesus we felt bad enough as it was, but knowing that John's try was legitimate finished us off altogether. As the incident was taking place, I looked at John's reaction and he jumped up straight away convinced that he'd scored. John wasn't the type of fella to make a meal out of something so I knew he'd got the ball down properly. I rushed straight over to Chris White to ask him to go to the video ref but he then told me there was none available. I was shocked, I just presumed there would be one because it had become the norm in the Six Nations at that point in time. I guess Steve Lander – or Stevie Wonder as we called him after the game – had to go with his first instinct but that didn't stop us from feeling sore about the whole thing."

Sorest of all from the whole episode was John O'Neill. A dedicated member of the Munster squad, the winger was distraught that his try wasn't allowed and his first questions centred on his own actions. "I was in bits," the Shannon winger said in the week after the game. "The place was like a morgue and your mind goes through a hundred and one things. I was wondering if I could've made it any clearer, should I have dropped the shoulder lower? But the refs at this level, I said, surely they get it right. Did I knock it on? What did I do wrong?"

The Cork native drove straight home after the plane carrying the Munster squad touched down at Shannon Airport, eschewing the opportunity to forget his troubles over a few pints with the rest of his teammates, but the players and supporters who hit the pubs of Limerick that night had a lot to moan about. The soccer pitch the game was played on wasn't suitable for rugby in the rain, the vast majority of the

Camera never lies: John O'Neill touches down for the disallowed try against Stade Francais

Talking point: Anthony Horgan consoles John O'Neill at the Stadium Lille Metropole

in the stadium. With regards events on the soggy pitch, there was a feeling in some quarters that one of Ronan O'Gara's 'missed' second-half penalties had actually bisected the posts and one particular TV angle seemed to prove as much. Then there was the sin-binning of Christophe Dominici for a stamp on Mick Galwey. Arthur Gomes came on to take the winger's place but nobody came off the pitch for a good two minutes. To add further insult, Dominici came back into the fray after just eight minutes on the sideline. There was enough there to complain about until well into the small hours.

A few days after the game Lander, to his credit, admitted his mistake. "I still have not seen the video replay but accept by what I have been told that it was a try," said the English official. "It's unfortunate, but officials have only a split second to make up their minds. As touch judge, I was fairly well on the spot as I thought. I felt that the ball had gone into touch in goal and that it wasn't a try. If I got it wrong, and it appears I did, I am sorry. All you can do on any given day is to react to what you see. I did not see the player get the touchdown. I was unsighted in that sense, and if I didn't see it being touched down then I was unable to confirm the score to the referee. In situations like that, when you know that decisions are proven wrong by television cameras which have the benefit of showing incidents in slow motion and from different angles, you would always be disappointed. As a match official, I have always gone out to do the right thing and to make all the right calls. Unfortunately, that doesn't happen all the time. There is always human error and that, I contend, is the essence of what sport is all about. I suppose, when things like this happen, I would have to ask myself whether I could have been in a different position, in a better position to make a call. Obviously I wasn't, but the call was made in good faith. In terms of disappointment in the Munster camp, I share that disappointment if proof was provided afterwards that it was a score. All I can say is that I have asked myself the question, from where I was, whether I could have done anything different. The simple and truthful answer is that I don't believe I could."

But whatever about the mistakes made by the officials, and the dodgy choice of venue for the semi-final, the fact of the matter was that Munster, for the second year in a row, didn't do themselves justice on a major occasion. "We didn't play well that day," says Galwey. "It's strange really because in all my years with Munster, I can never honestly remember a game where we played well and lost. When we hit form, we usually won games but the Stade Francais match was like the Northampton one the year before. We didn't do ourselves justice on the day and putting all the controversy

Captain's role: *Mick Galwey talks to the Munster players after the heartbreaking semi-final defeat*

surrounding John's try to one side, that's what hurt in the days after the game more than anything else."

To complete a lousy and forgettable day, the heavens opened just as the Munster fans left the ground and everybody was drenched to the skin. It seemed that the gods were also mourning Lander's decision not to award O'Neill's try. It was difficult to think of a more miserable end to a Munster campaign in Europe.

He came from a land
Down Under:
Jim Williams added
power and experience to
the Munster set-up

CHAPTER 8

ONCE BITTEN, TWICE SHY

2001/02

The summer of 2001 was all about the British and Irish Lions. Ronan O'Gara was the only Munster player named in Graham Henry's initial touring party to Australia and although David Wallace was called up later in the tour as injuries took their toll, it was a player on his way to Munster that really caught the eye. Rob Henderson had confirmed the previous April that he'd be making the switch from London to Limerick at the end of the summer and it certainly appeared to be an inspired piece of business if his Lions form was anything to go by. Henderson formed a centre partnership with Brian O'Driscoll on the tour that worked brilliantly over the course of the three tests, even if the Lions did eventually lose out in a fascinating series. All in all, Henderson looked like being a huge addition to the Munster set-up, and especially in an area where the province were in need of some additional quality.

While everyone was glued to events Down Under, Declan Kidney was working hard behind the scenes to sign a player who had missed out on making his mark on the Lions tour. Jim Williams was coming off the back of a couple of superb seasons with the ACT Brumbies and while he was the starting number eight for the Wallabies in the 2000 season, he was out of favour by the time the Lions bandwagon rolled into town in June 2001. Not making the series hurt Williams and Kidney didn't waste much time in offering him a new way forward on the other side of the world.

John Langford was a key man in persuading Williams to make the switch. The pair had been teammates at the Brumbies and when Kidney asked the second row to have a persuasive word in Williams's ear, Langford had no problem obliging. Sure why

Lions' pride: Rob Henderson was Declan Kidney's second high-profile signing

wouldn't he? Having initially come over to Munster for one season, Langford had to stay for a second because of unfinished business and when Munster lost in the semi-final to Stade Francais, he decided to extend his stay to a third year. There was no moving him. And what were Williams's plans coming over? The back row told everyone who'd listen that he'd stay for two years but after that he was definitely off home. There was nothing that could persuade him to stay any longer. But he'd learn.

The 2001/02 season was always going to be a bit of an odd one. The foot and mouth crisis the previous spring had disrupted the flow of the Six Nations and as a result, Ireland still had to play Scotland, Wales and England to complete their programme. The long and the short of it was that Ireland's top players would have quite an extreme season, especially before Christmas when they'd have to play in the newly-formed Celtic League, a patched-up Interprovincial Championship, the Heineken Cup, the November internationals, as well as those outstanding Six Nations fixtures.

The main point of interest in all of that was the advent of the Celtic League. The Welsh clubs and Scottish regions had already been competing in the Welsh/Scottish League for two seasons but the IRFU needed a proper outlet for their provinces in the professional era and they successfully managed to make a threesome of the Welsh and Scots affair. The first season of the competition, like many of the others, was wholly imperfect. There were 15 teams (nine Welsh, four Irish and two Scottish) divided into two sections, one of eight and another of seven, with the top four from each side of the league earning their place in the quarter-finals.

The season kicked off on 17 August with Munster beating Edinburgh away from home, and Declan Kidney's side, who were drawn in the group of seven, went on to win five of their further six fixtures in the league stages. That sequence was enough to earn them a place in the quarter-finals, where they beat Llanelli 13-6 at Thomond Park at the start of December, and they then batted aside Ulster 15-9 in a tight and tense semi-final at Lansdowne Road. That victory set up a meeting with old rivals Leinster in the competition's first final and it proved to be a fascinating afternoon at Irish rugby headquarters.

Celtic cross: Rob Henderson chases down Leinster's Brian O'Driscoll in the Celtic League final

Leinster played with 14 men for a good 55 minutes following Eric Miller's sending-off, and while you'd have backed Munster in those circumstances, it didn't turn out that way on the day as Matt Williams's charges held on to win. Tries from Anthony Foley and John O'Neill left Munster 15-9 ahead at half-time but with Nathan Spooner penalties chipping away at that lead, tries from Gordon D'Arcy and Shane Horgan edged Leinster to a famous 24-20 victory. A fierce rivalry was developing between the provinces and it was certainly advantage Leinster for now. The one consolation from a Munster perspective was that, at least, it hadn't been in the Heineken Cup.

Castres, Harlequins and Bridgend made up the Heineken Cup opposition for the 2001/02 season, and Munster kicked off their campaign with the visit of the French side to Thomond Park on 29 September. This was just one week after the international side's embarrassing loss to Scotland in Murrayfield and maybe there was still a little hangover from that defeat lingering in the air, because Munster struggled to put away a physical, if limited, Castres side. The respective boots of Ronan O'Gara and Romain Teulet were responsible for all but 10 points of the 51-point total in a 28-23 victory for the home side. Jason Holland's try proved the difference between the sides but Munster never looked comfortable.

"We met them twice last season and knew it would be much more difficult this time around," said Declan Kidney afterwards. "Castres are a very physical side, a very big

Tight call: *Jason Holland goes over for the decisive try against Castres at Thomond Park*

side and it takes a lot of effort to get the better of them. There were times when we made unforced errors and we may have taken the wrong option on occasions. We might have gone for a couple of more kicks at goal but I can understand how the guys might have felt. They wanted to score a try or two more and they went for it. But overall, I have to be happy with the victory. We won without Alan Quinlan or John Hayes and that helps sum up the strength of the squad."

The following weekend Munster were in London for an appointment at The Stoop with Harlequins. On their previous visit to the ground in the shadow of Twickenham, Munster had lost a humdinger of a game 48-40 but they'd come a long way since that innocent day and were now far better equipped to win Heineken Cup fixtures on the road. Before the game the hefty Munster presence at the venue watched David Beckham help England qualify for the World Cup with a late free-kick over Greece and when the rugby got underway, Munster too managed to work their way out of a sticky situation. A couple of early knock-ons from Anthony Foley and Jim Williams set the tone for a below-par Munster performance but they managed to take a 13-5 lead into the break after an extremely fortuitous Ronan O'Gara try. Things improved in the second half. Munster eased their way into the game thanks to an intercept try from Jason Holland – an intervention that was becoming his trademark – which sealed a 24-8 victory over a frankly disappointing Harlequins side. A better team might well have beaten Munster on the day, a point that was acknowledged afterwards.

"Munster played like Munster play all the time," said Keith Wood of the game against his home province. "Good defence, time after time, we make the mistakes, they score the tries. It's clinical, low-error cup rugby. Nobody does it better. We played great rugby at times but it was of no value to us. They played badly for 15 or 20 minutes and it was fortunate for them that they were playing with the wind because when they made a mistake, they could just hoof it away."

Munster's winning mentality was also lauded by Harlequins coach John Kingston, who'd previously been head-honcho at Connacht. "For Munster, and they'll try to tell you differently, the European Cup is the be all and end all of their season," he told the media afterwards. "If you ask Mick Galwey and Claw why they didn't retire at the end of last season, I think you'll find that's the reason. Having gone as close to

Old-timers: *Mick Galwey and Peter Clohessy enjoy the victory over Harlequins at The Stoop*

the holy grail as they have in the last two years that is why they're here. Therefore the pressure is greater in many ways and perhaps that showed in the first 20 minutes. But they are a battle-hardened side. I've watched them at first hand getting their arses kicked for various stages of matches and yet coming out smelling of roses. That says a huge amount for their character."

It was a clear sign of progress from Declan Kidney's side. Away wins for Munster had previously been of the epic variety. This one was purely routine.

The Heineken Cup resumed at the end of October. In between rounds two and three, Ireland had beaten both Wales and England to restore a bit of international pride following the catastrophe against Scotland, but a double-header against Bridgend was on the agenda for Munster and that was the sole focus as they aimed to stay on top of Pool 4. The Brewery Field isn't the easiest place for visiting teams to play but Munster made a decent job of it in the first half. John Kelly scored two fine tries as the visitors controlled the game and it would have been more had Anthony Horgan not knocked-on with the line in sight. As it was, Munster were somewhat shortchanged with their 13-6 lead and as their legs began to tire in the second half, Bridgend took advantage. Two penalties from Craig Warlow to one from O'Gara left the score at 16-12 heading into the final few minutes and Munster had

Taking it on the chin: Jason Holland feels the force of a Bridgend tackle

to defend desperately in the final moments to prevent the try that would have won the game for the Welsh outfit.

"We always found things difficult in Wales," says Mick Galwey, "and that Bridgend game was a tough test. I can remember us coming onto the pitch and the announcer saying, 'let's put our hands together for the five Munster players who helped to beat England last week'. It was an unusual kind of a thing to do and I thought to myself, 'hold on a minute here, we're being set up for a big fall'. But we put in a hell of a display to make sure that didn't happen, especially in the closing 10 minutes."

Again Munster had won away from home without playing that well but the plaudits for their efforts were beginning to build. "Some of these guys must have been out on their feet and I was amazed at their ability to keep going," said Bridgend's Robert Jones after the game. "They lasted the pace even though I thought they might not in the last few minutes. Now that they have won three matches and with two home games to come, you would have to fancy them to make it through to the quarter-finals. I reckon they're good enough for 10 points and a home quarter-final."

Munster's return leg with the Welsh took place eight days later at Musgrave Park. With Bridgend all but out of the competition following their defeat the previous week, this should have been a cakewalk for the home side but although they did win 40-6, they had to overcome an extremely physical and often dirty challenge from the Welsh side to do so. They chalked up four yellows and one red card over the course of the game but Munster simply concentrated on their rugby. "There were times when it could have boiled over but we were not interested," said Anthony Foley after the game. "We would have had a lot

Bridge too far: Gareth Thomas can only watch as Jeremy Staunton scores the third of Munster's five tries at Musgrave Park

more to lose than they would." It was a mature response from Munster and they got their reward with a five-try performance, Anthony Horgan, John Kelly, Jeremy Staunton, Jason Holland and Mike Mullins all crossing the line to supplement Ronan O'Gara's excellence with the boot. Phase two of the pool stages had, like the first phase, passed without a glitch and the competition was tucked away until after Christmas as the November internationals took centre stage.

And that's when Munster's season took a huge twist, despite the fact they weren't even playing. After Warren Gatland's side had put in a couple of decent displays in accounting for Samoa with ease and almost putting the All Blacks to the sword in a cracking encounter, the Kiwi was sacked and Eddie O'Sullivan, the then-assistant coach to the national side, was installed in his place. It was a highly-surprising route for the IRFU to take, especially since the only conditions put on O'Sullivan's appointment was that the Union were in charge of appointing his backroom staff. And that's where Munster's trouble began.

before, Munster were always going to be up against it in a fixture that meant so much to both sides. On a sunny afternoon in the south-west of France, it turned out to be an unbelievably close game, one that saw Munster trailing by just three points heading into six minutes of injury time. A David Wallace try, set up by a Ronan O'Gara break, had put Munster in the position to top the group by virtue of points difference and all they needed to do was hold out. But just as those added minutes were ticking to a close without any drama, Olivier Sarramea rounded Anthony Horgan on the left touchline and Castres stole the points, and top spot in the pool, in dramatic style.

"We were looking at a home draw in the quarter-finals five minutes into injury time and 60 seconds later we're looking at an away game," groaned Kidney afterwards, but the coach did later admit that his players weren't fully aware that they had done enough to top the pool after Wallace's try. It was an amazing oversight from a Munster point of view but it was done, the clock couldn't be turned back.

The pool stages were completed the following day and the draw for the quarter-finals pitted Galwey's men against the mighty Stade Francais, in Paris. It was a cruel draw, even if the manner of their defeat to the French in Lille the year before would undoubtedly motivate the team, looking for a win in Paris was a big ask.

The last-minute lapse had clearly cost Munster dear but an incident in the 58th minute of the final pool game made the defeat even more difficult to stomach. Peter Clohessy claimed he was bitten by Castres' Ivory Coast-born number eight Ismaela Lassissi as a scrum collapsed on the turn and while Munster initially felt they'd have to let the incident go due to lack of video evidence, even though the teeth marks on the prop's forearm were clear to see, they uncovered further television footage from French TV which showed the incident far more clearly.

"I can remember the scrum breaking up and hearing Claw roaring," recalls Mick Galwey. "At the break in play he showed me his hand and you could see the bite mark in his arm, it was as clear as day. Claw knew who bit him and he wasn't afraid to tell everybody either. We usually didn't cite players but in this situation we just felt we had to, there's no way you could let a fella get away with something like that."

A citing against the back row's actions was lodged with the ERC in the days after the game but Castres responded with a citing of their own against Clohessy for racial

Tooth for the battle: *Peter Clohessy carries the fight to Castres*

and discriminatory comments made during the game. The tit-for-tat nature of Castres' actions made the ERC disciplinary procedure look like an ass – not for the first time – and the hearing into both incidents took place on 17 January in Dublin. Just before they convened the French club withdrew the charge against Clohessy, which showed exactly how much credence it had, and Lassissi was then handed a one-year ban for the charge brought against him. It looked like some sort of justice had been done.

That was until the appeal and one of the more bizarre and appalling rulings in rugby disciplinary history. The ERC disciplinary committee overturned Lassissi's one-year ban at an appeal hearing on the Thursday before Munster's game against Stade Francais and their reason was simply extraordinary. The only new testimony at the hearing came from the Castres doctor, who maintained that in his considered view, the marks on Clohessy's forearm "were not consistent with a human bite". The ERC cleared the player on this new testimony. It was a whitewash.

And the banned played on: Ismaela Lassissi turns up for his ERC hearing for an alleged bite on Peter Clohessy

The Lassissi incident was a distraction but Munster put it to one side, they had other things on their minds. The previous season's semi-final defeat was a massive blow and while it was hardly Stade's fault that Steve Lander had made the wrong call, Munster couldn't go out and play Lander again. Beating Stade in Paris would have to suffice.

"They'd beaten us the previous year in Lille in that horrible game," says Mick Galwey, "and they weren't slow in rubbing it in to us either at the time. Then, the day before the game, we were due for our captain's run but they wouldn't leave the pitch and there was a bit of a schemozzle involving a few officials. But it was great in a way, because it pumped us up nicely in the day or two leading up to the game. There was no way we were going to leave anything behind us in the dressing room that day."

On a wild and windy Paris afternoon, Munster had the benefit of the near gale-force wind in the first half and they managed to use it cleverly. An early Ronan O'Gara penalty got them on the scoreboard and after Anthony Horgan scored a 19th-minute try having sidestepped two defenders off a flat pass from his out-half, the visitors were well in control. Almost immediately, Diego Dominguez got his side on the scoreboard with a close-range penalty but two further successful kicks from O'Gara, along with a cheeky drop-goal from the number 10, gave Munster a 16-3 interval lead. But would it be enough facing into the wind in the second half.

Seven minutes after the restart Christophe Juillet bundled his way over for Stade to reduce the gap to eight points and with penalties from Dominguez on 56 and 74 minutes bringing the home side to within a kick of Munster, it seemed only a matter of time before they grabbed the lead. But the Irish side dug into reserves of strength and discipline they probably didn't even know they had and in the final minutes, they kept their cool and shut Stade out.

"The discipline was awesome," said a battered and bruised Anthony Foley after the game. "We could not afford to give away any penalties in the second half against someone (Dominguez) who could kick them from his own 10-metre line. We played

On the run: *Nathan Williams fails to stop Anthony Horgan from scoring against Stade Francais*

as a unit. Everyone stepped forward and did what was required. We put up with the sly punches, the sly digs. We kept our cool, focused on what we wanted to achieve and produced our best performance for a long time."

While Foley rightly lauded Munster's discipline, Mick Galwey feels there was one moment of indiscipline that helped to mould the province's resolve. "In the previous year's semi-final," says the former skipper, "somebody in their second row caught John Hayes with an up-and-under in the scrum and his jaw was broken because of it. Then in the first half of the game in Paris, Hayes was hit in exactly the same way and he went mad. I'd never seen him get mad like that before, it wasn't really his style, but something obviously blew inside his head. Sylvain Marconnet tried to hit him as the scrum broke up, but Hayes responded with a punch that knocked him to the ground. I can remember myself and Claw having a look at each other once he punched him and we were both thinking, 'It's all going to kick off now'. But it didn't, that was the end of it. Marconnet was taken off a few minutes later in utter confusion and that was a big moment. It showed that we weren't going to be bullied and it geed up everybody."

One of the post-match highlights was Paul O'Connell's television interview. Over the course of the 90-second grilling, the Young Munster man used the word "unreal" 15 times and it was clear that the second row was blown away by what he and his teammates had just achieved. O'Connell had only been invited to train with the Munster squad in the summer of 2001, and while the Stade Francais game was only his second start in the red shirt in the Heineken Cup, it was clear the 22-year-old was a bit special. The squad already contained second rows Mick Galwey, Mick O'Driscoll, John Langford and Donncha O'Callaghan, but such was O'Connell's talent that he'd jumped to number two in the pecking order by the time the knockout stages came about. As a teenager, he'd excelled at both swimming and golf but rugby was clearly his calling and a superb display against Stade, a game in which he showed scant disregard for his own well-being, marked O'Connell as having well and truly arrived.

Unreal, as he would have said himself.

———————————●———————————

Three days after their Stade heroics, Welsh legend Gareth Edwards conducted the draw for the semi-finals. Llanelli and Northampton were pulled from the hat first, which meant that Munster would play Castres with only home advantage up for decision. As the province held its collective breath, Edwards pulled the name of the French side out first to consign Declan Kidney's side to their third away semi-final in a row. Having got over their initial shock, Munster went about campaigning to have the game played in Paris but the ERC decreed a few weeks later that the match would take place at Stade de la Mediterranee in Beziers. It was another odd choice of venue, just like Lille had been the year before, but they'd have to deal with it.

There was a 10-week break before the semi-final as the Six Nations took centre stage for a couple of months. Declan Kidney and Niall O'Donovan, along with Eddie O'Sullivan, had a difficult transition to the international arena as Ireland easily batted aside the challenges of Wales, Scotland and Italy at home, but lost heavily to both England and France on their travels. The good news, though, was that the Munster contingent had come through the tournament unscathed, all raring to have a crack at Castres. Of course there was a good deal of bad blood between the sides because of the Clohessy incident, but that couldn't be allowed to flow into Munster's thinking before the game. They were going to have to be a hell of a lot more professional than that if they were to qualify for their second final. Eight days before their trip to France, Leinster travelled to Musgrave Park for a warm-up game to aid Munster's preparations and the 6-6 draw in extremely wet conditions was a decent work-out for a team that hadn't played a match in 10 weeks.

Band of brothers: *the Munster team prepare for their friendly clash with Leinster at Musgrave Park*

One man who didn't play in that warm-up game was Peter Clohessy. The prop had suffered burns in his back garden while burning rubbish on 9 April and the initial feeling was that the Young Munster man wouldn't be back in time for the semi-final against Castres. "It was a serious enough incident," recalls Galwey. "He arrived into training one day with his face a bit scorched and his arm badly burned and we could all see it had rattled him a little. But I think he came to training looking for a bit of sympathy and by God, he was in the wrong place for that because we gave him an unmerciful slagging. That probably helped him recover a little quicker."

It was just as well that Clohessy made it back in time for the semi-final because even though conditions were perfect for running rugby on the day of the game in Beziers, it was the battle of the forwards that decided proceedings. Castres, whose pack were on top early on, worked themselves into a 9-0 lead with half an hour on the clock thanks to three Romain Teulet penalties but a chorus of 'The Fields Of Athenry' from the 8,000 or so Munster supporters in attendance appeared to wake the Irish from their slumber. After a maul was illegally dragged down, Ronan O'Gara got the province on the scoreboard with a penalty a minute before half-time, while barely 60 seconds later the out-half repeated the trick to reduce Castres' interval lead to just three points.

Foreign fields: a blast of 'The Fields Of Athenry' appeared to wake Munster from their slumber against Castres in Beziers

It must have been a blow for the French side because Munster owned the second period. O'Gara drew his side level with a penalty on 42 minutes and over the course of the next half an hour, as the likes of Mick Galwey, Paul O'Connell and Alan Quinlan began to dominate the forward exchanges, the out-half landed three further kicks to put Munster 18-12 in front. With a six-point lead, the French side were still within striking distance but John Kelly provided the insurance points with a try three minutes into injury time to seal the result

French toast: *Peter Stringer and John Kelly celebrate the victory over Castres*

for Munster. Shaun Longstaff did manage a consolation score for Castres before the end but it didn't stop the Irish province from qualifying for their second Heineken Cup final which would be played in Cardiff's Millennium Stadium.

"Another four weeks with this bunch is great," enthused Declan Kidney, who'd just seen his Munster career extended a little further. "Getting to 9-6 at the break demoralised them and lifted us. As a result, we started well in the second half, went a few points in front and closed it out from there. It was an extremely disciplined performance and a great result for our supporters who've had to go through so much pain in the past couple of years. Hopefully we can make up for it in Cardiff."

The only negative note of the day was the treatment of a number of Munster supporters after the game. There had been a strong police presence all around the pitch in Beziers for the match and once the final whistle was blown, a number of enthusiastic supporters had attempted to get onto the pitch. The French police were having none of it and instead of dealing with the intruders politely, many were wrestled to the ground unceremoniously. It all looked utterly out of place at a rugby match.

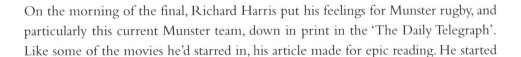

On the morning of the final, Richard Harris put his feelings for Munster rugby, and particularly this current Munster team, down in print in the 'The Daily Telegraph'. Like some of the movies he'd starred in, his article made for epic reading. He started

Out of touch:
Austin Healy and the corner flag stop John O'Neill from scoring against Leicester

Out of touch: Austin Healy and the corner flag stop John O'Neill from scoring against Leicester

Freddie Tuilagi put Tim Stimpson away up the left touchline and with Munster lacking numbers in defence, Geordan Murphy arrived on the full-back's shoulder to dance his way over the line. The conversion was missed, giving Munster a 6-5 half-time advantage but the province's support would hardly have been confident going into the second half. Not only did Leicester look more potent with the ball in hand, Munster's line-out was also misfiring badly, meaning that the province were struggling to get any sort of decent possession in attacking areas.

But once O'Gara kicked his third penalty on 49 minutes to put Munster four points up, it appeared for a brief moment that the Irish side might actually be able to grind out a victory, despite their deficiencies out of touch. However, Leicester weren't known as the best team in England for nothing and on 59 minutes Austin Healy produced a bit of magic, dummying his way effortlessly around O'Gara, for the game's crucial score. Stimpson added the conversion, and a penalty on 69 minutes, to put six points between the sides as Munster summoned every bit of energy they had left to put the Tigers under the cosh for the game's final moments.

John O'Neill came close but unlike the game against Stade Francais the previous year, he did actually touch the corner flag on his way to the line. O'Gara missed two penalties as the clock ticked down but in the final seconds Munster were given one last chance when they were awarded a scrum under the Leicester posts.

Every Munster fan in the stadium got to their feet. This was it, this was their last chance to snatch victory from the jaws of defeat. Before the front rows engaged, the move that could win the province the Heineken Cup was called. "We were going to go inside and outside off the back of the scrum and David Wallace was going to come through the middle," recalls Mick Galwey. "We'd used that same move once earlier on in the year and we'd scored from it. I'm not saying we were definitely going to score that day but we were in a great position to do so."

But while the Munster players primed themselves and went through the move in their heads, Neil Back knocked the ball out of Peter Stringer's hands before he could feed the scrum. None of the match officials saw Back's intervention and when the ball squirted out on the Leicester side, referee Joel Jutge must have thought that the Tigers had won the ball against the head. Most of the players on the pitch, and supporters in the stands, would have believed the same thing initially but they'd find out the truth later on and those in red shirts cursed Back because of it.

Peter Stringer chased after the referee, and then headed for the touch judge to ask if either of them had seen what happened, but his protests were in vain. The final whistle sounded seconds later and Munster had lost their second Heineken Cup final

Handy work: *Peter Stringer lets referee Joel Jutge know just what he thinks of Neil Back's late 'intervention' at the Millennium Stadium*

in the space of three years. Not that they could complain too much about their fate, Back's late act of skulduggery aside. Although they struggled in the line-out, the province had performed decently over the course of the 80 minutes but they'd been beaten by the better side. Two tries to none told its own story and while Munster could come up with a whole host of reasons why they'd lost to Northampton back in 2000, there were no excuses this time. Equally, there was no disgrace in losing to such a fine side as the Tigers.

"It was a fantastic game, a memorable occasion but I don't think we deserved to win," admits Galwey. "They scored two tries, we scored none and you can't argue with that. They were just a better team than us. Again, I'd say that we didn't play to the same standard we had throughout the year but maybe we just weren't allowed play to that standard by the opposition on the day. It was heartbreaking afterwards seeing all those fans but we didn't deserve to win, it was as simple as that."

Immediately after the game, Back insisted that he had no regrets about his actions, but a couple of months after the final, the open side changed his mind and began to show some remorse for his disruption of Munster's last scrum. "I know it upset my wife, Alison. If I thought there was any way of redressing it, I would consider it. It has tarnished my reputation. In making any judgement, I would hope people will evaluate me over my whole career and not label me on that moment. It happened spontaneously. I weighed the options up in a split-second and did what I did."

No going back: 'It has tarnished my reputation,' said Neil Back about his hand-in-the-scrum antics

Back's flip-flopping has only served to annoy Mick Galwey to this day. "After the game he came out and said he did what he had to do for Leicester to win the game but he was a bit smarmy about the thing, but I guess that's the kind of fella he is anyway. That's fair enough I suppose but then six months down the road he apologises and fuck me, I was thinking, stick to your word. We were trying to move on with our lives and get on with things and next thing he apologises and it brings you back to the whole thing again. I even thought less of him after that. I've met him a few times since, I'd salute him but I think he knows what I'm thinking."

Through gritted teeth: *'I've met him (Neil Back) a few times since,' says Mick Galwey. 'I'd salute him but I think he knows what I'm thinking'*

The following morning back in Limerick, Munster held a team meeting but it was more like a wake. The plan was to present Declan Kidney and Niall O'Donovan with a few gifts on their departure but it was an odd sort of occasion. Jerry Holland, who had returned as team manager at the start of the 2000/01 season, did the talking but everybody else was in sombre mood as they attempted to come to terms with a second Heineken Cup final defeat. "It was a pretty emotional day," remembers Niall O'Donovan. "Everybody was so down and I have to say it was very tough to say goodbye. We'd worked with most of those guys for six years, we'd been through an awful lot together and to leave without actually winning the Heineken Cup was unfulfilling. We'd come close on two or three occasions and even that day after the final there were players coming up to myself and Declan saying they wished they could have won it for us. It was a difficult way to say goodbye."

Mumhan phase: 'There was something down there (in Munster) that I just wasn't seeing and I thought to myself, I just had to go down to see what it was,' says Alan Gaffney

CHAPTER 9

MIRACLES DO HAPPEN

2002/03

It can't have been an easy scene for Alan Gaffney to deal with. Following the final defeat to Leicester, Declan Kidney and Niall O'Donovan clocked out as Munster's coaches and the team they'd nurtured since the IRFU reluctantly appointed them back in the summer of 1997 was now under new care. Gaffney had been confirmed as Munster's new leader back in April, and while most rugby fans would have recognised the name and face because of his time as assistant coach with Leinster, they would have known little of the Aussie's rugby roots.

Gaffney was a product of Randwick, the Sydney club with a well-earned reputation for playing the game with a bit of verve and style. A list of the club's past players reads as a who's who of Australian rugby – David Campese, Phil Kearns, Ewen McKenzie and the Ella brothers all wore the club colours at various stages. It's a proud club with proud traditions, none more so than the fact that the club's head coach is directly elected by the players. Alan Gaffney filled that role between 1989 and 1995, before going to work as an assistant coach with the New South Wales Waratahs for two years from 1997 onwards and then travelling across the globe to become Matt Williams's side-kick with Leinster in 2000. His CV was impressive, his pedigree and quality unquestionable, but even the man himself had to think long and hard when Munster came knocking at his door that spring.

"Matt Williams had been over with Saracens for talks and I was certain he was going to take the job at the time," Gaffney recounts. "The thing was that I wasn't going to go with Matt to London, I was happy in Ireland and particularly at Leinster so I began to think about my own future and what was in store. Now as it turned out, Matt came back and told everybody he was staying but nobody from Leinster came to talk to me about a new deal as assistant coach and out of the blue, a couple of days later, Munster got in touch. I had talks with them and was pretty much offered the job straight away but I did agonise over it. It was a very tough decision at the time. I was in a comfort zone at Leinster. I was coaching some very talented people in their backline and there was no drama there. It wasn't a chore going to work, I was working with some great players, not just your Dricos and your D'Arcys, Nathan Spooner was there and there were a few other top backs also. I thought to myself, 'Do I really want to be going out there and doing too many things?' But there was a mantra I've always used throughout my life as a coach and it's one I say to players again and again: 'never die wondering'. And with a mantra like that, I would have been hypocritical if I didn't take up the challenge. So all this was going through my mind and then Leinster came in with a new deal and an increased salary and that confused me even more. But I went ahead with my initial decision, although I have to say it was with some trepidation – a lot of trepidation in fact."

The success Munster had enjoyed was one of the factors which actually delayed Gaffney's decision. "To go down to Munster, who'd been in the final the previous year and who'd been in two finals and one semi-final over the previous three years, there was really only one way to go and that was down. There wasn't much room to work upwards and a lot of people told me that. There was trepidation about going down there and being a failure."

Red for dead: Dominic Crotty leaves another Leinster defender in his wake

Gaffney admits that during his two seasons with Leinster, Munster had been a sort of fascination for him. "I looked at Munster and I'd just admired them for so long. But despite my admiration, I was still looking at them as an outsider and saying, 'How in God's name do they do it, I just don't understand'. I'd coached in a number of games against them and they'd always come from nowhere to beat us. At Donnybrook one day we totally outplayed them and then Killian Keane kicked a penalty on 88 minutes to earn them a draw. It was baffling. Another day we were playing down in

Musgrave and I thought, we're on top here and then we got thrashed. I couldn't explain it. And I kept wondering how they were doing what they were doing. I just didn't see the quality in the team. I couldn't understand why they were getting to the finals in Europe. There was something down there that I just wasn't seeing and I thought to myself, I just had to go down to see what it was."

Munster's season began with a Celtic League victory over Llanelli at Stradey Park on 31 August but despite the changing of the guard upstairs, there weren't a lot of new faces on the park. Peter Clohessy had finally handed over the baton to Marcus Horan in the front row, while Dominic Malone, the Northampton scrum-half who'd won the Heineken Cup against Munster (and had been involved in the incident which had seen Mick Galwey sin-binned) had also joined as back-up to Peter Stringer. But Alan Gaffney's policy wasn't root-and-branch change, he'd planned something a lot more subtle than that in his first year in charge.

"The only plan I had was to make them a little bit more expansive," he recalls, "and when I say expansive I don't mean running the ball to the wings every time. I wanted us to be more expansive in the way we were playing the game, to get some of those forwards with enormous abilities into different areas and get them carrying the ball and to do a lot more. In doing that, I wasn't having a go at what had been done before at Munster, because the team had been enormous achievers in the way they'd been doing things and the guts of things were perfect. All we were trying to do was add that little bit more, just that little bit extra to get them up to the next level."

In the early months of his reign, Gaffney can remember getting a lot of criticism for what he was trying to do with the province. "I got a lot of stick for it, I can remember that. We were having an after-match thing in Claw's one night and next thing this very pretty girl walked over to me and asked me could she have a word. I said 'sure', and she asked me to come over to the corner with her. Now I wasn't having any wraps on myself, I was just wondering what the hell she wanted to talk to me about. Then, when we were over in the corner, she abused me from a height. She told me that I shouldn't have Munster playing running rugby and I just thought to myself, hold on there a second, this is something completely different."

Aside from putting a bit of width on Munster's game, Gaffney also wanted to add a bit more structure. Again, it wasn't that what had gone before was wrong, it was just the coach wanted to add another layer to what had been there previously.

"We decided, both myself and the players, that we needed a bit more of a structure. We were trying to get an outcome, we needed a performance to get that outcome but to get the performance, we needed to have a process. For example, if they do a long restart for us down the right-hand touchline, the question for the players is what is an acceptable outcome for us? Is it Ronan kicking the ball out on our 22 and it's their line-out? No, that's not an acceptable outcome. Is it Ronan kicking the ball to halfway? Yes. But how do we get there? There's no point in hoping that he can make it because he might have no angle. So we had to come up with a process, to be able to do certain things, to give Ronan the angle to reach halfway. That's what we went through those first few months and it took a while for us to get used to doing that. I think everybody bought into it but these things don't start working overnight."

Munster's Heineken Cup pool for the season looked quite reasonable when the draw was made during the summer, but a few things had changed over the first few months of the season. Perpignan were always going to be a difficult proposition, Viadana remained a handy prospect no matter which way you came at it, but, almost overnight, Gloucester were a different story entirely. When the draw was made, Munster were about to face a tough, passionate side who were capable of beating anybody on their day. The problem with Gloucester was that their days were too rare and infrequent, just as Munster's had been in the Heineken Cup's early days. Gloucester were almost a carbon copy of Munster a few years back. But things had

Consolation prize:
Peter Stringer crosses for Munster's only try against Gloucester at Kingsholm but it was to prove a crucial score

changed. A superb start to their Zurich Premiership campaign had seen the West Country outfit grow in confidence and Munster were facing the form side in European rugby in their opening Heineken Cup pool game.

It turned out to be a tough October day at Kingsholm. Munster played against the wind in the first period and they wouldn't have been too disappointed to go in 16–9 down at the interval after Marcel Garvey's try had edged the home side in front. But the hosts powered on as the game entered its final quarter. Jake Boer, the Gloucester captain, was mauled over the line by his colleagues in the pack and with a bit of breathing space to operate in, Ludovic Mercier and Boer, for the second time, rubbed a bit of salt into Munster's now open wounds. There was a late riposte from Munster when Peter Stringer went over for an injury-time try and while it looked to mean nothing at the time, it was to have huge implications later in the season.

"We were beaten up front and to be honest it was a comprehensive whacking," recalls Gaffney. "We were going through various things early in the season and we didn't have enough time to get things right in the Celtic League before the Heineken Cup started. But the worrying thing was that we basically handed them their tries. We made a lot of mistakes that afternoon."

Anthony Foley admitted as much after the game: "We were well in it at half-time. We conceded a fairly soft try, a turnover, a kick ahead and their man won the race for it. We were holding out well, playing to what our plan was, but they came at us in the second half. They got three tries and after that we were trying to get the try count back some way in our favour and eventually we did that. It was the only pleasing thing about the second half. This result means we can't afford to lose again in the group. That means beating Gloucester at home and Perpignan away as well as at home. It's another challenge, we're looking forward to it, and it starts next week."

So the pressure was on for the visit of Perpignan to Thomond Park. The French side only touched down at Shannon Airport four hours before kick-off and while their attitude may have been slightly lax, it didn't show during the game. They caused Munster plenty of problems and the home side were pretty lucky to be 17–14 ahead at the interval. John Kelly had scored a great try off a beautifully-timed Ronan O'Gara pass, while Alan Quinlan sailed around the front of a line-out to touch down for a simple try. But tries from Nicolas Couttet and Manny Edmonds, off an intercept, had kept the visitors in the game and Munster just couldn't shake them off.

Perpignan had two players, Renaud Peillard and John Daniell, sent to the bin in the first 20 minutes of the second half and it was then Munster turned the screw. Ronan O'Gara was spot on with the boot, knocking over two penalties, while John Hayes sidestepped a couple of tackles to flop over the line for the score that sealed the game for Munster. Julien Laharrague did score another try for Perpignan before the end but the home side, in front of a strangely quiet crowd, managed to hold on to win. Things were still going far from smoothly but at least they had their first win in the bag.

Viadana, strangely enough for an Italian side, came to Musgrave Park on the first Friday in December with a touch of confidence. They'd lost their opening two games at home to Perpignan and away to Gloucester but they had managed to score seven tries in the process and at the very least, they felt they could rattle Munster a little.

Record haul:
Anthony Horgan
touches down for
one of Munster's
nine tries against
Viadana at
Musgrave Park

On the night in question, they didn't even come close. Munster scored nine tries in total to win 64-0 in front of 6,500 in Cork. Anthony Foley set things in motion with a try off a line-out maul just three minutes in and from then on there was no looking back. The win was Munster's biggest ever margin of victory in the Heineken Cup and their joint-highest try tally in any one game. The first part of the double-header sorted out without any huge fuss, Munster travelled to Viadana for the return leg eight days later. It was a fun weekend over in the north Italian town for the couple of hundred Munster supporters who made their way out and not just because of the scenic setting. Alan Gaffney's side scored another nine tries against the Italians – with two tries apiece for Jason Holland, Frankie Sheahan and Alan Quinlan – although they did concede three tries this time around in a 55-22 victory. All of which set up the trip to Perpignan nicely.

On the same day that Munster dished out their second thrashing in seven days to Viadana, Gloucester had lost their first game of the pool stage away to the French side. The juggernaut had been halted. The result meant that Alan Gaffney's side were now top of the pool with six points and if they accounted for both Perpignan away and Gloucester at home, they'd qualify for the quarter-finals without any fuss.

So while Munster might have known what they needed to do to qualify for the knockout stages for the fifth year in succession, it was far from an easy task, particularly the visit to Perpignan. Munster had played at Stade Aime Giral during their 1998/99 Heineken Cup campaign, losing 41-24 in as hostile an atmosphere as they'd experienced in European rugby. If anything, this fixture was going to be even more difficult.

"I was forewarned about playing in Perpignan by John Connolly who was at Stade Francais at the time," says Gaffney. "I rang him up for a bit of information and he was telling me as they were driving into the ground for a league game, the supporters tried to turn the Stade bus over. So with that in the back of my mind, myself and Jerry Holland went down to watch them play live and to see what the atmosphere was like. We bought a couple of tickets the day before but we hadn't a clue where to go and the stewards weren't very helpful. So we just

Against the head: Mossie Lawlor reflects on the defeat to Perpignan at the Stade Aime Giral

sat where we saw a few spare seats and it turned out we were in the middle of the season ticket holders. People were coming in and stretching over us and kissing and hugging each other and Jerry said to me, 'just look straight ahead, keep looking straight ahead'. Then they started chanting, 'USAP, USAP, USAP'. And Jerry kept saying to me out of the side of his mouth, 'just keep looking ahead'. I was there to take notes and watch Perpignan. I had a pen and paper with me but they stayed firmly in my pocket."

When Gaffney and Holland returned to Perpignan with their team a few weeks later on the second Saturday of 2003, the Munster support was present in its usual numbers for the game but they didn't have an awful lot to cheer about. In fact, rarely can they have been so depressed leaving a venue. The home side won the game 23-8 and were utterly deserving of that margin of victory. Munster just didn't compete on the day and were thoroughly outplayed, especially in the second half when they had a bitter and strong wind at their backs. They trailed just 13-8 at half-time, an Anthony Foley try and an O'Gara penalty making up the visitors' tally, but without the injured Anthony Horgan, Paul O'Connell, Rob Henderson and David Wallace, Munster just didn't have the ball-carrying ability to trouble a brutish Perpignan pack.

"We played like busted arses in the second half," says Gaffney. "We were poor and we handed them points very easily. It was one of our worst displays. We knew we had to win both of our games to qualify for the knockout stages and we came off that field as dejected as we've ever come off the field, except maybe the game against Wasps. Everybody thought that was the end of our season. The trip home was an absolute nightmare. People still come up to me now and say, 'Alan, have you ever been as depressed as you were that day against Perpignan?' I don't think I ever have been so low. I was thinking, 'Jeez, I've come down here and totally stuffed up'. On the way back we started to work out what we needed to do to qualify and we were thinking, 'how do we even start worrying about this?' We were all but out."

All but out. Alan Gaffney's words describe the situation succinctly. Once the immediate disappointment of the defeat to Perpignan had lifted, Munster discovered that they needed to beat Gloucester by 27 points and by four tries more than the English side could manage if they were to qualify for the quarter-finals for the fifth season in a row. Twenty-seven points and four tries? They'd lost by four tries to one and 19 points back when the sides had met in October, and if anything, Gloucester had improved since then. It seemed impossible.

"I remember the first day back in training the next week coming up to the Gloucester game," said John Kelly. "Everybody was down, and we could have reacted badly and just buried our heads in the sand. But as a whole squad we stood together and said we'd give it a shot. "The session wasn't all sweetness and light, though. Those who attended can still remember a quiet mood about the place at the beginning, an air of depression still lingering in the air. But then the forwards started to scrummage, and scrummage and scrummage and when they brought the session to a halt an hour and 15 minutes later, everybody's dander was back up. They were going to have a right good go at Gloucester and everything else would look after itself.

Later in the week they set about their homework. It was maths first. They'd done the calculations on the plane back from Perpignan but they did them again. It was the same answer as before, it hadn't got any easier. A win by four tries and 27 points would allow them to leapfrog Gloucester and qualify for the quarter-finals. "We didn't bang on about the four tries and the 27 points, there was no point in doing that," Gaffney explains. "We just had to go out there and do the best we could. We had our processes in place, we wanted to go out and win the game and nothing else was discussed. Once you start talking about 27 points and all that, you put more pressure on the players and you can get distracted and we didn't want that. Jim Williams did know what we had to do and that was all that really mattered."

The permutations put aside, they began to work on their game plan. They'd already spotted a few Gloucester weaknesses. "We just had to take them on," Gaffney says. "We realised we'd been beaten up in the first game and we knew our forward pack was a lot better than what we showed that day. In certain parts of the pitch we believed Mercier was weak, we believed that Henry Paul could be tested under a high ball at full-back, we understood where Delport came in off the blind side, we understood that if we scrummaged right we could put them under pressure. That's why we worked so hard on the scrum coming into the game."

Their game plan nailed down, the tone of the pre-match meetings was important. Munster needed to get the right mix between blind rage and controlled aggression. If they delved too deep into either area, they'd struggle. Frankie Sheahan took care of pumping the blood, bringing in a couple of newspaper articles that had been heavily critical of Munster's efforts in Perpignan. He also unearthed an article written by Jeremy Guscott stating the Gloucester pack would blow Munster away. It was like a red rag to a bull, and not just John Hayes. Someone else produced a quote from Andy Gomarsall saying that he was actually looking forward to playing a game at Thomond Park. Nobody looked forward to playing at Thomond Park. The blood was boiling.

Then came the reasonably controlled segment of their preparations. Jerry Holland, Brian Hickey, Mick Galwey and Gaffney all started to talk about Munster's home record in the Heineken Cup and the importance of keeping it intact. It struck a chord with the players. Nobody wanted to be wearing a red jersey the day the first visiting side struck gold in Limerick. It also succeeded in moving the focus away from the four tries and 27 points, winning the game was the most important goal.

On the morning of the match, the rain poured down but Gaffney had a few distractions to deal with. At the Clarion Hotel, somebody handed him a piece of paper which was supposed to have been left in the back of a taxi by a member of the Gloucester backroom team. It, apparently, contained details of the visitors' game plan. Over the course of time, this famous sheet of paper has come to assume legendary status but in fact, it was one of the day's greatest myths.

"Somebody showed me a bit of paper," Gaffney admits, "but it was just Gloucester's generic way of playing the game. 'We'll kick right from this position, we'll do this from re-starts', but it wasn't a game plan and if it was, it wasn't very detailed. It was just one sheet of paper. This was about 11 o'clock in the morning and to this day, I'm serious when I say this, this is not a word of a lie, I read the first couple of lines and discarded it. It was just generic stuff, there was no detail at all in it. It was a nothing and if you think I was going to change our plans that late in the day, you'd be wrong. They can bang on about how that lost game plan cost them but that didn't cost them, a lot of other things did on the day but not that."

The other distraction for Gaffney was the match programme. It contained an article written by Heather Kidd, wife of former Irish coach Murray, stating that Munster "must score three more tries than Gloucester and beat them by more than 19 points". A confusing situation had just been made a hell of a lot worse.

"The guys did know what they had to do," Gaffney insists, "but then that article was written in the programme that was completely wrong. In the heat of the moment a lot of the team were thinking, 'Were we right or was the programme right?' We did know what we needed to do, we worked it out on the way back from Perpignan, but that article just confused us. That article, which I really hold people responsible for, was poor form. It wasn't just her, whoever proof read that programme was at fault too. For that to be put in there in an incorrect way was poor form."

But if some of Munster's players weren't totally sure what they needed to do to qualify for the quarter-finals when they took to the field, it didn't really matter. They just wanted to beat Gloucester and scoring a single point more than the English side would ensure that they did just that. In front of a raucous crowd who appeared just as keen to hold onto Thomond Park's glorious record, Munster looked pretty focused from Joel Dume's first whistle. Ronan O'Gara and Ludovic Mercier exchanged penalties early on but then the home side took control. They opted for scrums in situations where previously they'd have run the ball or kicked for touch and that gave them the early initiative.

The move for John Kelly's opening try came straight off the training ground. They'd identified that Thinus Delport drifted off his wing almost by reflex and Peter Stringer found his winger with a superbly-timed pass. The rest was academic. But while that first try was easy, the next one was a long time in coming. Munster huffed and puffed through the rest of the half, spending much of it in their own territory, but they upped the ante as the first half ticked towards a conclusion. Jeremy Staunton and Ronan O'Gara both had a dart at the Gloucester defence and just as they seemed to be running out of options, Jason Holland threaded a grubber kick in behind the visitors' line and Mossie Lawlor pounced for the try.

"That was the vital try," Gaffney maintains. "It was only when we scored that and went in 16-6 up that I actually felt the whole thing was on. But the important thing was that we kept doing what we were doing, that we didn't start to take stupid risks. If we started to panic, everything would be up in the air again."

But there was no panic and no risks. They stuck to the game plan and O'Gara kicked a penalty to make it 19-6. Then, Holland lobbed a cross kick in the direction of Mick O'Driscoll on the right touchline and the second row somehow grabbed the ball and fell over the line in one swift movement. O'Gara landed the convert and Munster were just one step away from glory. Or were they? Gloucester were awarded a penalty in front of the Munster posts, a number of the visiting players pumped their fists in the air, but Ludovic Mercier was completely oblivious to what the kick meant and he took the penalty quickly. Nothing came of it. It was a stroke of luck.

Munster regrouped and plugged away, battling for that all-important fourth try. Half the crowd and indeed, half the players on the pitch, thought that three tries would be enough but it wasn't and Jim Williams knew it. He directed O'Gara to kick a late penalty to the corner, Mick O'Driscoll grabbed the line-out and the subsequent maul was halted just short of the line. Jeremy Staunton had a go around the fringes but after he was tackled, the recycled ball fell to Jason Holland and he put John Kelly over. Thomond Park blew its top and while confusion still reigned, O'Gara knocked over the convert to leave the final score at 33-6. That was a 27-point gap and they had the four tries in the pocket. The miracle had just been performed in front of 13,500 ecstatic supporters.

There was still confusion in the crowd. Some thought they'd done it, others had been so baffled by the programme that they didn't know who to believe. But the

FIRST TRY

SECOND TRY

THIRD TRY

Miracle match: *on an unforgettable day at Thomond Park, Munster notch up the four tries and 27-point winning margin necessary to progress to the knockout stages. John Kelly (2), Mossie Lawlor and Mick O'Driscoll all crossed the try-line against Gloucester*

FOURTH TRY

behaviour of the players confirmed that Munster were in the draw for the play-offs. Most were carried across the pitch on the shoulders of supporters, fists pumping the air in delight. And while that sufficed for some fans, others weren't satisfied until they saw the team re-emerge from the dressing room to mount the Thomond Park steps and sing a few verses of 'Stand Up And Fight'.

"They came to Thomond Park not expecting to be beaten," believes Gaffney. "They came there as the runaway leaders of England. To be completely honest, the biggest mistake they made was not treating Munster with respect. They treated us with total disrespect and most of the players will say the same thing. It wasn't their spectators, they were absolutely fantastic before and after the game but their players showed us no respect whatsover. It played right into our hands."

Everybody was delirious afterwards, but as ever Anthony Foley was one of the most articulate. "Everybody had us written off," said the man of the match. "Nobody gave us a chance of getting through, but that's always the case with us, isn't it? I think we've lost three games (this season) and all three away from home and if you ask anybody, 'how's Munster's season this season?' they'll tell you it's not a great season. And yet we're in the quarter-final of the European Cup and with a Celtic League final to play. I suppose that's down to the standards we've set over the last few years. They're very high, which is good because every time we go out on the pitch we have to try and live up to them. At times that can get frustrating because anybody watching us against Perpignan last week could see things were not going our way and it wasn't our fault and we kept battling right the way to the end. These are the things that happen to teams away from home and they're hard to live with at times. But we felt it was a bit too early for people to actually bury us."

Nigel Melville, the Gloucester director of rugby, bore the look of a broken man afterwards but he was magnanimous in defeat. "After that Munster must never say never. Any team that did what they did under so much pressure in this game must not be counted out. I'm sure they will go from strength to strength in the rest of the competition because, if they have been down a couple of times, these guys are never out. They're a remarkable side, absolutely amazing."

As for the rest of the night, it was one of Limerick's most memorable, arguably up there with the celebrations that followed that famous victory back in 1978. "The whole scene in the city that night was so bloody special," recalls Gaffney. "It was one of the most memorable nights of my life. No question about that. For me, I think I was more relieved than anybody else in the whole city that night, just relieved that we'd qualified again, that I hadn't screwed things up."

The feel-good factor from the Gloucester game fed nicely into Munster's preparations for the Celtic League final against Neath in Cardiff's Millennium Stadium, even if there was a hint of doom and gloom when it became clear that Munster would be playing Leicester at Welford Road in the quarter-finals. Having come through their section of the league phase of the competition with six wins out of a possible seven, Munster then defeated Connacht 33-3 at Musgrave Park in the quarter-final, before accounting for Ulster by 42-10 in the semi-final at Thomond Park three days into the New Year. Although there was nowhere near as much excitement around the province for the final as there was for any Heineken Cup fixture, 15,000 Munster supporters still managed to make their way to Cardiff for the game. In the end there were more Munster than Neath fans in the Welsh capital for the match, despite the fact that Neath's supporters had only an hour to travel for the fixture. But then again, it only served to highlight Munster's burgeoning support base.

League of nations: Mick Galwey and Jim Williams raise the Celtic League trophy after the 37-17 final victory over Neath at the Millennium Stadium

Having lost three high-profile finals in the previous three years – two Heineken Cups and one Celtic League – this game was strangely routine for Munster. They were clearly the better and more organised side over the course of the 80 minutes and even though Ronan O'Gara had to go off early after his ankle took a bit of a raking at a ruck, Munster were fully in control. Four penalties from O'Gara before he departed the scene gave his side an early platform, while an Alan Quinlan try before half-time gave the visitors a 22-9 interval lead. From there, tries from Marcus Horan and Rob Henderson eased Munster home to the delight of their support. The final score line of 37-17 to Munster showed just how easy it had been for the province.

"I was amazed at the amount of people who came over," said Mick Galwey after the game. "We'd half, if not more, of the attendance and that's fantastic. It goes to show the supporters follow us through thick and thin, they always have done, and hopefully they always will. I think they like what they see, they see an honest team who give it everything. Sometimes we win and sometimes we lose but I think everyone feels part of this Munster set-up."

Despite a delayed flight back from Cardiff that night, there was still enough time for Peter Clohessy's bar to host the celebrations. After a number of disappointments in successive years, few could begrudge Munster the silverware.

———————◆———————

The build-up to the Leicester Tigers game contained all the usual stuff. There's nothing like a Munster team with a point to prove and the defeat in the final the previous May in Cardiff still hurt. "They didn't talk about it out in the open but psychologically it was on their minds, without a doubt," Gaffney maintains. "There was nothing pinned up on the dressing room wall, nothing mentioned about the Neil Back thing, at least it wasn't something they talked about in front of me."

There's no doubt the draw was a tough one. The English side were going for a third Heineken Cup win in a row, a feat that would mark them down as the kingpins of European rugby. They'd also lost just two games from 22 at Welford Road in the competition's history and even the most optimistic Munster fan must have travelled to Leicester in hope rather than anticipation. The great pity was that there were only a couple of thousand travelling over with tickets. The home side had the option of playing the fixture at the 28,000-capacity Walkers Stadium, home of the city's football club, but they decided in the end to stay on their own patch, where just 17,500 people could witness proceedings. Munster were hyped up for the occasion but this game wasn't going to be about raw, naked aggression. It needed to be about much more than that and on the afternoon in question, it undoubtedly was. Gaffney's side battered Leicester physically, before finally applying the finishing touch out wide late in the game.

The line-out was the key to this wholly comprehensive 20-7 victory. Donncha O'Callaghan and Paul O'Connell had superb games out of touch, and along with Alan Quinlan at the tail, they managed to steal 12 Leicester line-outs over the course of the 80 minutes. Normally, this didn't happen to Leicester on their home patch. This didn't happen to Leicester, full stop. But Munster's operation was so good that Sunday afternoon that Martin Johnson and Ben Kay, a pair who would go on to lift the World Cup with England the following October, just couldn't get a grip on proceedings. It was 3-0 to the visitors at half-time thanks to a Ronan O'Gara penalty but they were finding it difficult to work openings in the English side's blanket defence. Munster's lack of a cutting edge looked like it was going to be punished early in the second half as Steve Booth scored a try, which was converted by Tim Stimpson. However, a little bit of class swung the game the way of the visitors. It was typical high-octane, hot-paced stuff as Munster pushed forward and recycled the ball rapidly as the final 20 minutes of the game beckoned. O'Gara switched the direction of the attack from

blind to the open side and there, Frankie Sheahan, Paul O'Connell and Marcus Horan made a trio of telling incisions to leave Munster in front of the Leicester sticks. Then came the moment of magic as Stringer fed O'Gara and the out-half dummied his way over the line from close range.

Little and large: Peter Stringer steals through to score as Leicester's Martin Johnson watches helplessly

It was inspirational stuff. Munster fought hard defensively from there but they clinched victory with another well-constructed move. Rob Henderson made the initial break up the middle and after Mike Mullins and Alan Quinlan made ground up the left-hand touchline, Stringer popped up on the flanker's shoulder to finish off the move. Munster were home and hosed. As the final whistle sounded thousands of travelling fans flooded onto the pitch to celebrate with the team. Gaffney was a happy man but he still has a sole regret from that game, although it's just a small one.

"To this day one of the great things we could have done was to go for a pushover try with the last play of the game. We'd mauled them 40 metres at that point and Martin Johnson had come in from the side to give away a penalty. I know the game was over and we might have picked up an injury or something, but I'm sure we would have mauled them over the line and that would have rubbed the shit in after the previous year. Even now I still think to myself, maybe we should have done that."

Raising standards:
an ecstatic Donncha O'Callaghan is carried from the Welford Road pitch

The semi-final draw had been made back in February, before the quarter-finals had been played, but it was far from kind to Munster. In fact for the umpteenth time the draw had been downright cruel. The men in red had been pulled out of the hat alongside Toulouse or Northampton, and the English and French sides would be the ones with home advantage. Predictably enough, the home side emerged from their side of the draw with ease and the game was set for the 38,000-capacity municipal venue in Toulouse, or Le Stadium as the locals called it.

About 10,000 Munster fans made their travel arrangements to the south of France, once again using every conceivable route and mode of transport to get there. A quick calculation, and a conservative one at that, put their total weekend spend at about €5m (it was the first big trip in the new currency) and when looked upon in those terms, the exodus was truly amazing. Where the money was coming from baffled many but there were a number of different sources. The opening up of Europe's financial boundaries allowed Irish people access to the savings of the rest of the continent and whether it was through traditional banks, or the credit unions, Munster supporters had no problem in accessing cheap loans. The other source, mentioned a lot on this particular trip, was inheritance. Fathers brought their sons and daughters to Toulouse in the belief that it was better that everybody enjoyed the money together while all concerned were living rather than receive it in far more emotional circumstances a couple of decades down the line. So from Place du Capitole to Place Wilson, in the city of a hundred different squares that all looked the same, the Munster fans ate and sang whatever they had in their pockets, all in the name of their rugby heroes.

As you could have figured out from the buzz around the city that weekend, the atmosphere within the stadium was thoroughly unique, and the game didn't disappoint either. It was an epic encounter, maybe not in a pure rugby sense, but it pulsed from the very first minute to the last and the outcome hung in the balance just as long. You couldn't take your eyes off the pitch for a second. A downpour 10 minutes before kick-off made underfoot conditions slightly tricky but in playing the more controlled rugby, Munster found themselves 6-0 up thanks to a Ronan O'Gara penalty and drop-goal. Toulouse were struggling to get going, allowing a number of try-scoring opportunities to pass them by because of uncharacteristically poor handling, but a Yann Delaigue penalty just on the stroke of half-time left them just three points behind at the interval. After the restart, the Munster forwards were still doing the

Irish pride: Toulouse's Trevor Brennan tries to halt Anthony Foley's charge

business in the ball-carrying department, allowing O'Gara to land his second drop-goal of the game to restore his side's six-point lead.

Then, in the 53rd minute, came the substitution that changed the game and in essence, summed up the difference between the opposing squads. Jean-Baptiste Ellisalde came on for Yann Delaigue, with Freddie Michalak switching to out-half and the substitute taking over the scrum-half berth. It was one of six substitutes that the French side made over the course of the second half, while Munster would make just the one – Jason Holland coming on for Rob Henderson. Toulouse had clear quality on their bench, while even the most optimistic Munster fan would have to admit that Alan Gaffney's replacement options were thoroughly limited.

Whatever about the other five changes that Toulouse made, Ellisalde's was the most crucial. His snappy pass created that extra yard of space for the Toulouse backs to exploit and they thrived on it. Ellisalde and O'Gara exchanged penalties to keep Munster six points in front with six minutes of normal time remaining but the killer blow was struck soon after. The French side ran the ball through the phases and with Munster rapidly running out of defenders, Michalak skipped over in the left-hand corner. Ellisalde's touchline conversion dissected the posts and Toulouse were in front for the first time.

Tears for fears: Paul O'Connell takes it all in after the defeat by Toulouse

It was a tough blow to take but Munster didn't lie down. Twice they worked their way upfield and twice Ronan O'Gara attempted drop-goals from at least 40 yards out. Unfortunately, he was wide with both efforts. Chris White's final whistle signalled another heartbreaking result, another 'oh-so-nearly' story.

"I was really proud that day," remembers Alan Gaffney. "We went back to the team hotel and were pissed by the time we got to the airport. But while we were having a few pints, the lads weren't too down on themselves. We competed very well with the Toulouse pack and we were only a hair's breadth away from winning the game. The players got a great ovation from the fans afterwards, both sets of fans, and they totally deserved it. We were only a whisker away from winning and if we had, we'd have been playing Perpignan in the final at Lansdowne Road. You'd have had to fancy us for that but it wasn't to be. But that's how close we were to winning the tournament that year. And on that day, I was proud of everything the lads did."

Gaffney still has regrets, though. "There was one area where I take responsibility for. We didn't have a call if we wanted to get in position for a drop-goal. Ronan had two goes from about 40 yards out but we should have had a play where our forwards got us closer to the line. After that game we developed a call and a play to get closer to the posts but we didn't at the time and I hold my hands up for that."

So close: Mick Galwey consoles Alan Gaffney following the loss to Toulouse

The ultimate disappointment aside, it was some occasion, arguably the first day European club rugby had produced a sporting occasion to match European football, and Munster's fans played as much a part in creating that spectacle as their passionate, bouncing counterparts from Toulouse.

"I'm amazed and delighted that rugby is supported by the people of Munster as was shown here today," said Toulouse supremo Guy Noves afterwards. "The people of Munster - it's almost the Nation of Munster - it gave me shivers to see how they were supported today and that people will travel like that. I think we will see a huge party here tonight, it reminds me of the Toulouse-Perpignan matches in the past (when) it was almost nations supporting, peoples supporting the teams. I would like to have 12,000 Toulouse fans with us in the final like Munster had today."

Good darts:
Frankie Sheahan
successfully
appealed an
ERC ruling
which banned
him from the
game for
two years

That afternoon in Toulouse, Frankie Sheahan had an incredible game. The hooker had come through a rough patch, and some unfair criticism, the previous season as his darts at line-out time went astray in an Ireland team that was just coming together under Eddie O'Sullivan's new coaching regime. He paid for a couple of under-par performances with his starting place but far from getting him down, Sheahan simply redoubled his efforts and was in the form of his life by the time that Toulouse game came around. Little did he know that the aftermath of that clash would lead directly to the next challenge of his career. The hooker was selected at random to supply a urine sample after the game and he eventually did, although it took a couple of hours and a few bottles of water for the dehydrated forward to produce it. The sample eventually provided, he thought no more about the matter and joined the rest of his teammates in reflecting on yet another close call in the final stages of the Heineken Cup.

He'd probably forgotten about the drug test completely by the time he set off with the Irish squad for their tour of Australia, Tonga and Samoa at the end of May but he was in for a bit of a shock by the time he got to Perth. Word had come through from the IRFU that Sheahan had failed the drug test and in an instant his career was in jeopardy. The initial word trickling through was that it was simply an administrative error, that Sheahan hadn't ticked the box that stated he was an asthmatic but the issue proved to be a little trickier than that.

There had been an administrative error, namely that Sheahan hadn't been registered as an asthmatic, but the bigger problem was that the levels of the inhaler medicine – salbutamol – found in his sample was off completely off the radar. It aroused suspicion among the authorities and the long and the short of it was that Sheahan was handed down a two-year ban from rugby by the ERC at a hearing held in Dublin in July of that year.

Sheahan strenuously denied the charge and insisted that he was completely innocent, bar the failure to tick the correct form confirming he was an asthmatic. Sure, the levels of salbutamol in his urine were high but that was simply because the Munster hooker had come through a high-intensity match played on a balmy day. A few conspiracists in the media peddled the line that Irish society was just too innocent to believe that one of their own would cheat, but they were guilty of using the wrong case to prove a valid argument. Frankie Sheahan wasn't a guilty man and an appeal of his ban was successful in September of that year. The appeal cost the player close to a six-figure sum but at least he was able to head to the World Cup with Ireland later that September and put the sorry episode behind him.

And at least there was one positive result from another 'oh-so-nearly' season.

Black magic: *the capture of Christian Cullen was a major coup for Munster*

CHAPTER 10

STING IN THE TAIL

2003/04

Alan Gaffney had been expecting the question all night and here it was. Munster had just launched their new logo, complete with stag and three crowns, at the Bank of Ireland on O'Connell Street, Limerick, and the questions and answers session with supporters was in full swing. Then came the query, the one that everybody had been keen to ask since the rumours had started swilling around the province a few weeks earlier. Would Christian Cullen be joining Munster? Was it possible?

This was 2 July, a good six weeks since Munster's initial target had gone back on his verbal promise to join the province. Chris Latham, the Queensland and Australia full-back, was the man who'd given Gaffney his word. A strong-running, intelligent and pragmatic player, Latham appeared to be the perfect signing to augment Munster's game-breaking ability in the backline but on his farewell game for the Queensland Reds in the middle of May, his emotions got the better of him and with tears in his eyes, he decided to hang around in Brisbane.

"It wasn't until late on in the last game of the season for the Reds that it really hit me," explained Latham before Ireland played Australia in the summer of 2003. "It would have been the end of my Wallaby career and it would have been the end of my Queensland career. And I haven't won a Super 12 title yet. I've put a lot of work into getting to where I am today and Queensland gave me the opportunity. With all this on my mind, I probably would have went to Munster and wouldn't have been happy. If I had done that it wouldn't have been fair to Alan Gaffney and to the guys on the team. I upset Alan and that's the most disappointing thing that has come from all of this. I've tried to talk to him since but I've had no luck. He's a great bloke, he puts his whole heart and soul into what he's doing and having been coached by him and knowing him personally, I know how this would affect him.'

Gaffney, as Latham said, was fuming at the time but he had to move on, and that's exactly what he did. He needed a game-breaker in his side – he knew that from the manner of Munster's defeat to Toulouse – and had been promised the finance by the Munster Branch to get one. All he needed now was the right player to justify a salary of roughly €150,000 per annum. A call he received in early June from an English agent sent him in the right direction. The word was that Christian Cullen was actively seeking a move from New Zealand following a falling out with All Blacks coach, John Mitchell. Gaffney himself found it difficult to believe that the Wellington full-back would not make the All Blacks' 30-man squad for the World Cup in Australia but a move for Cullen had to be worth a try at the very least.

Garrett Fitzgerald, Munster's chief executive, handled the finances with Dave Monnery, Cullen's agent, and while on holiday in Sydney, Gaffney headed over to Wellington in the second week in June to meet Cullen and his father. It was there the seeds of the deal were sown. The thing that impressed Gaffney most about Cullen was that the All Blacks legend wasn't worried about the money, he was more interested in learning more about Munster and what role he would play in the team. The Munster coach left Wellington feeling that Cullen would join the province but his previous experience with Latham convinced him to take nothing for granted.

So on that early July evening in the Bank of Ireland, Gaffney mumbled a few words about Cullen and indicated that the potential signing of the player was something that could drag on for the rest of the summer, if not into September or October. Once bitten, twice shy and all that but he need not have been so pessimistic. The following afternoon, Fitzgerald fielded a call from Monnery and Cullen's agent confirmed that the deal had been done. The All Blacks legend would be joining Munster at the end of the New Zealand NPC season.

When everybody got a chance to take a deep breath, the signing of Cullen sent rugby fans in the province wild. A quick scan of Cullen's career statistics explains why. He was the All Blacks top try-scorer of all time, with an incredible 46 tries in 58 tests for his country. He was the top try-scorer in the history of the Tri-Nations. He was the top try-scorer in the history of the Super 12. He was New Zealand's most capped full-back of all time. Was there a bigger name, a bigger legend still playing rugby? All this and Cullen was only 27 years old.

The signing was exactly what Gaffney had been looking for but getting the player he wanted was something of a rare occurrence during his three-year tenure with the province. Not only had provincial coaches to deal with players and agents, new signings had also to be approved by the IRFU's Players Advisory Group (PAG) which oversaw the movement of professional players in Irish rugby. "We were trying to get good backs at Munster for a long, long time," recalls Gaffney. "It's such an arduous process and it all depends whether you get the approval of the Union's Players Advisory Group or not. A lot of it depends on who you are and who's supporting who at any one point in time. You pat me on the back and I'll pat you on the back, that sort of thing." Breyton Paulse was one player Munster lost because of this process, Gaffney maintains. "We tried to get him (Paulse) for Munster for the 2005 season but the PAG said you can't get a South African, so he goes to Clermont. That's all fine but then Munster sign Anthon Pitout. It didn't quite add up, it didn't make any sense at all. Paulse would have put bums on seats, he would have been fantastic for Munster and he wouldn't have been classified as an overseas player in Europe (because of a work permit agreement between the EU and South Africa). It was baffling."

There was one other key player that Gaffney set his sights upon and captured. Shaun Payne was a virtual unknown to Munster fans when he signed in the summer of 2003. A utility back from South Africa, Payne held an Irish passport thanks to his Sligo-born grandmother and although he may have been 31 when he signed, Gaffney had been aware of the player for quite a while. "We were fortunate to get Shaun, despite his age. I can remember him playing with Natal before they became the Sharks and I thought he was a fantastic player. He then went and played with Swansea, they went bust and I couldn't wait to get him."

The steps had been taken to boost Munster's heavily-criticised backline, and just in time too. The Heineken Cup had decided to adopt the Super 12 bonus-point system, meaning that scoring tries in Europe would become more important than ever.

Cullen was due to arrive once Wellington had been knocked out of the National Provincial Championship (NPC), somewhere around the end of October, but it wasn't a huge issue for Gaffney – the coach was without most of his top players anyway. The World Cup kicked off in Australia on 10 October and there were 11 Munster players in Eddie O'Sullivan's original squad, until David Wallace made it an even dozen when he was called up later in the tournament. However, there are positives in most things and the absence of Munster's stalwarts allowed Gaffney to blood a number of promising young players in the Celtic League. Denis Leamy looked a sound bet at open-side flanker and was in fantastic form until an injury in November halted his progress, while the likes of Eoin Reddan, Jerry Flannery, Frank Roche, Stephen Keogh, Trevor Hogan and Mossie Lawlor all got some decent game time under their belts while the internationals were doing their very best for their country on the other side of the globe.

In all, Munster played nine games without their international contingent, winning three and losing six, although it must be said that they did lose a fair number of those games by tight margins. Still, the Celtic League was hardly the priority. More worrying than the six losses were the injury blows Munster had to digest ahead of their pool matches in the Heineken Cup. At the World Cup, Alan Quinlan, who had been in fine form, dislocated his shoulder while scoring a try in the pool game against Argentina in Adelaide and had been effectively ruled out for the rest of Munster's season. Then, a couple of days before he was due to arrive in Cork, Christian Cullen damaged his shoulder while playing for Wellington in the NPC final. "I can remember watching it through the gaps in my fingers," says Gaffney. "The first call was that he was fine. But the people in New Zealand didn't want to pay for the operation or the insurance so he comes over here with a bit of a doubt. The deal was done before he came over, there was absolutely nothing we could do."

So as the deal couldn't be renegotiated, Cullen continued with his moving plans and travelled to Ireland to set up home in Douglas in early November. After a couple of days in his new surroundings, the full-back underwent a scan and the results revealed that he would need a "minor operation" on his shoulder to bring him back to full fitness. The prognosis was that Cullen would be out of action for a few weeks but that prediction was kind. It would turn out to be a fair few weeks.

With Quinlan and Cullen sidelined, Munster played their first game of the season with their recently returned internationals on 28 November when they took on Cardiff in the Celtic League at Musgrave Park. The fixture took place just eight days before Munster's Heineken Cup bow, but thankfully all elements in the equation appeared to click as the home side won 31-10 in miserably wet conditions in Cork.

It was hardly ideal preparation for the Heineken Cup but that's the way the cards were dealt. The province was pitted against French, Italian and English sides, with Bourgoin, Benetton Treviso and Gloucester providing the opposition in the pool stages. Munster went straight in at the deep end, courtesy of a trip to France. It was a difficult assignment, Bourgoin away was hardly the place to go with an undercooked side. They may have been one of French rugby's least fashionable outfits but Bourgoin was a damn tough place to get a result, as Munster well knew from their visit to Stade Pierre Rajon back in 1998. The game took place on a cold Saturday night, with a light fog shrouding the 10,000-capacity venue, but in a tough, provincial atmosphere Munster managed to edge their way to an 18-17 victory.

Ronan O'Gara scored all his side's points with six penalties, his effort on 71 minutes clinching the game for his hard-working side. The other point of note in the game was the outstanding line-out performances of Paul O'Connell and Donncha O'Callaghan. The pair nicked a number of Bourgoin throws at vital times in the game, while keeping a clean sheet on their own ball. Philippe Saint-Andre's side did

Kicking king: *Ronan O'Gara scores the fourth of his six penalties in Munster's 18-17 victory over Bourgoin at the Stade Pierre Rajon*

And they're off: Jeremy Staunton scores the try of the game, Munster's first, against Benetton Treviso at Thomond Park

score the only try of the game through Sebastien Chabal but Munster's cuteness around the park won them a game they could quite easily have lost. "I suppose we didn't play particularly well but we came here to do a job and we did what we set out to do," said Jim Williams afterwards. "It was always going to be difficult but I did feel that we controlled the game generally and took our chances when they came. We were disappointed not to score a try and equally disappointed to concede one. That was down to us because they scored their try off a succession of mistakes. Still, we never felt there was a time when victory was beyond us."

The Munster coach was happy with the result. "They hadn't been beaten at home for three or four years at that stage," Gaffney remembers. "To walk away that night with a win was superb, no matter how rusty we might have been. We thought things had got better when we were sitting in the dressing room afterwards and word came around that Treviso had beaten Gloucester. But we soon found out that the information was actually wrong so that was a bit of a let-down. But still, the win against Bourgoin set the season up nicely for us."

The following week, Munster hosted Benetton Treviso at Thomond Park. A walkover on paper, it proved to be just as easy on the pitch – although it did take the home side a while to ease into their stride. Jeremy Staunton scored the try of the game following a nice team move that flowed through the phases almost perfectly, while O'Connell and O'Callaghan both scored off rolling mauls as Munster flexed their forward muscle. From there, it was routine stuff, with Anthony Foley and Jason Holland both bagging a brace of efforts and Shaun Payne, on the wing for the injured Anthony Horgan, rounding off a fine individual performance with a try. There were 11,000 at Thomond Park to witness this rout and it sent them all off into the Christmas night with a little extra festive cheer.

The Heineken Cup draw until the previous couple of seasons, had always been something of a mystery. It had been held behind closed doors for no apparent reason and while nobody can doubt the integrity of the ERC, you'd imagine that if they were in the habit of pairing clubs together, Munster and Gloucester would have been top of the list for the drama they produced in 2002/03. Well they didn't need to meddle with the balls for the 2003/04 season as the two sides were drawn out publicly in Pool 5 and the European rugby fraternity licked their lips.

There was also a new ingredient to add to the mix. Back in 2001, Ronan O'Gara had been selected to tour with the Lions in Australia. Just 24 years old at the time, he was third choice out-half on the tour but he played in a few games here and there, most notably the fixture against the New South Wales Waratahs at the Aussie Football Stadium in Sydney. O'Gara came on for the last 20 minutes of the game and having attempted to clear out a ruck, he found himself on the end of the busy fists of Waratahs' out-half Duncan McRae. It was an outrageous attack on the Munster man, with O'Gara left in no position to defend himself as McRae pinned his hands behind his back. The result was an ugly bruising and swelling to O'Gara's face and a six-week ban for the Australian. It was the very least he deserved. So when McRae joined Gloucester from the Waratahs in the summer of 2003, his return match with O'Gara was talked up from the second the two sides were drawn in the same pool. Would McRae get his retribution from O'Gara's Munster teammates? Or even the Thomond Park crowd? Fortunately for the Australian, he started his PR campaign early and it appeared to work.

"I am still embarrassed by what happened that night," McRae said a couple of weeks before the game. "There was no excuse for what I did and I deserved the punishment handed out to me. I said sorry at the time, but I have never met Ronan and if I do get to meet him next month I would like to apologise to him in person. I will be the villain of the piece when we visit Munster, but I have to make sure that I am properly focused because the two games against them are going to decide the destiny of the group title. I cannot explain why I acted as I did and it is

The eyes have it: Ronan O'Gara shows the wounds inflicted by Duncan McRae of the New South Wales Waratahs during the Lions tour match in 2001

something I will always regret. Everyone in the game appreciates that things happen on the field which in hindsight you come to feel ashamed about."

But that was a sideshow to the whole thing. Having beaten Connacht 3-0 on 2 January, thanks to a Ronan O'Gara penalty on a wet and windy evening in Athlone, Munster travelled to Kingsholm utterly determined to make amends for their heavy defeat at the same venue 14 months earlier. The evening kick-off allowed both sets of supporters an extra couple of hours to get into the swing of things and the ground was rocking by the time the teams took to the field. It was an even enough opening period. Henry Paul and Ronan O'Gara both exchanged penalties in a low-scoring first half and when the Munster out-half edged his side in front six minutes into the second half, the visitors may have felt things were going their way. But the truth of the matter was that Munster were playing poorly, struggling to string more than a couple of phases together at any one time, while their line-out was also way off the high standards Frankie Sheahan and Co had set for themselves. All in all, Gloucester looked the far more dangerous side. Sure enough, Henry Paul - converted from full-back to inside centre since the previous season - eventually set up Gloucester's one and only try, the rugby league convert weighting a perfectly-executed grubber kick behind the Munster defence for James Simpson-Daniel to secure possession and touch it down. Paul added the convert, two further penalties and a drop-goal before the end and although Anthony Horgan crossed for a fine Munster try with six minutes to go, they didn't really trouble Gloucester's lead in the closing moments.

Old school:
'I was calling bad line-outs,' said Paul O'Connell after Munster's poor performance against Gloucester at Kingsholm

It was another bad day at Kingsholm and afterwards an honest Paul O'Connell explained why the performance in general, and the line-out in particular, was so poor. "We didn't perform and they did and yet we still had our chances to snatch something from the game, a bonus point or even a draw," said the second row, who was fast becoming one of the province's key figures. "That, or even a win, was on the cards when we got the try. But I made a mistake at a line-out on our line and it cost us. I called the wrong call and confused all the lads. The ball went over the top and we lost it and gave away a penalty. It's very hard to hear the calls on the Shed side. Teams analyse you so much in this day and age. It's very hard to get 100% from your own line-out. Unfortunately, we made a few mistakes and that was mainly down to me and not Frankie's throwing. I was calling bad line-outs. I have to take the rap for that this week and hopefully next week we'll have it sorted. A few bad calls and you're on the back foot."

Gaffney wasn't pleased by what he saw that evening. "It was shocking, a very poor performance. Looking at that game, once again they did nothing to beat us, just like the previous time. We were just poor. We showed no discipline, we had blokes binned and while it's OK to come off and apologise for what you've done, you're still down a man. They were a big team, guys like Boer, Buxton and Paramore were great players. They had a bloody good side but again they did nothing to win the game. And I thought oh no, here we go again because they were coming to Thomond Park the next week."

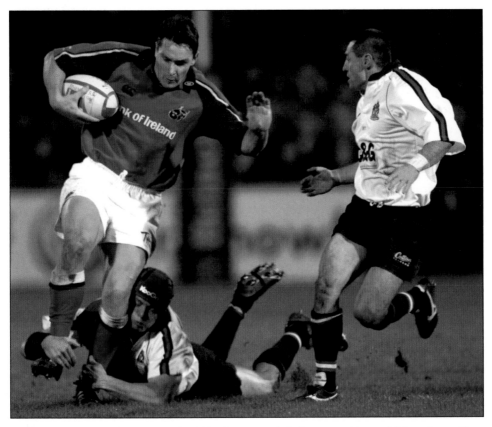

Red rag: *David Wallace tries to evade the tackle of Henry Paul of Gloucester as Duncan McRae, who would later make a hasty exit from Thomond Park, watches on*

155

Munster were on the back foot once more and, while there may not have been any four-try or 27-point margin to worry about, there was still something they needed to do to make qualification for the play-off stages possible. The introduction of the bonus-point system that season had changed the competition rules slightly and if Munster and Gloucester both finished on top of Pool 5 at the end of January, the match points earned in the games between the two sides would count first. As it was, Gloucester had four in their pocket from the Kingsholm win but if Munster could beat the English side, earn a four-try bonus point and deny their visitors a losing bonus point, they'd have five match points. It would give them a huge advantage heading into their final two pool games against Treviso and Bourgoin. Again, it wasn't something they banged on about in the dressing room beforehand but by the end of the 80 minutes they'd achieved their double goal, scoring four tries in a handsome and easy 35-14 victory.

"Gloucester gave us respect this time but we just bashed them," recalls Alan Gaffney. "We put it up to Henry Paul at inside-centre because I didn't believe he was a good player, we ran at Duncan McRae because I knew him and I knew he couldn't tackle. We were so disappointed coming out of Gloucester with a second defeat in a row but there was no trepidation in facing them. They scored early, that put us under pressure but as the game wore on, we just bashed them."

Jon Goodridge's early try did give Munster a fright but only that. Seven days on from their calamitous day at Kingsholm, the Munster line-out operation was the key to victory, earning a 100 per cent record off their own throw-ins and stealing four Gloucester balls over the course of the game. Chris Fortey, the English side's hooker, was sin-binned for taking Donncha O'Callaghan out in the air at a line-out and a few phases later Marcus Horan crossed the whitewash from a line-out maul. That was only the start of it. Before Fortey returned, Frankie Sheahan was credited with a second try following another maul and although three penalties from Paul had kept Gloucester in touch, Marcus Horan's try from a tap penalty in front of the posts bang on half-time gave Munster a 10-point interval lead. In a tight, busy and physical second period, Goodridge crossed for his second try to make the home crowd slightly nervous but a couple of O'Gara penalties, and a vital try from John Kelly 11 minutes from time, secured the victory and the bonus point for Munster.

On the final whistle, the scenes of the previous year's victory were repeated but there was no encore of 'Stand Up And Fight' on the steps. That would have to be kept for another day but there was one story outstanding, that of Duncan McRae. The Aussie had, at Kingsholm the week before, apologised to Ronan O'Gara for his assault on him back in 2001, but that didn't mean he was at ease heading to Thomond Park. "If you watch the video of the match, the final whistle goes and a millisecond later Duncan McRae runs across the screen to get to the dressing room," recounts Alan Gaffney. "He couldn't wait to get away from the crowd. Now Duncan's a good mate of mine from Randwick and I have to admit that assault on Ronan was totally of character and I think the pair of them sorted it out at Kingsholm. So I remember saying to Duncan after the Thomond Park game 'Come on, let's go out on the piss'. And he said 'Are you joking, there's no way I'm going out in this town. I'm even staying in Jury's under an assumed name'. I'm not sure how true that was, I never checked it out, but he really was genuinely terrified of what might happen to him if he bumped into a few Munster fans. All that night, when we were in the committee rooms at Thomond Park having a few drinks, he had Paramore and Buxton on either side of him everywhere he went. He thought he needed bodyguards to protect him."

After that impressive victory, Munster were the ones holding the whip heading into their final two games and they knew exactly what they wanted from their away trip to Treviso and the home game against an already eliminated Bourgoin. A bonus-point victory in both games would guarantee them top spot in the pool and not only that, it would more than likely be good enough to earn them a home quarter-final. Despite their 51-0 thrashing of the Italians at Thomond Park earlier in the season, Treviso were a different proposition at home. They'd already beaten Bourgoin at Stadio Communale Di Monigo that season and it was never going to be a walkover. So it proved. Munster trailed 10-7 at one point in the first half, after Walter Pozzebon and Mike Mullins had exchanged tries, but a line-out maul gave James Blaney, who was in for the injured Frankie Sheahan, his first

Tall tale:
Jim Williams wins a line-out against Benetton Treviso at the Stadio Communale Di Monigo

Munster try in Europe. Jim Williams repeated the trick for Munster just after the interval, with Manuel Dallan in the sin bin for Treviso, and a lucky bounce allowed Anthony Foley the opportunity to seal the victory and the bonus point for Munster. Jeremy Staunton scored a late try to leave the final score at 30-21 to the visitors and the mission was accomplished.

"We were poor, a bit lucky," admits Gaffney. "We went there thinking it was all going to happen automatically, especially after thrashing Gloucester, but it doesn't work like that. We gave the players a bit of a hard time afterwards, and so did the likes of Anthony Foley, saying we can't serve this shit up and expect to win the competition. We had a good crowd of supporters as usual on the trip – a couple of thousand at least – and while it was no chore for them to travel to Italy, they deserved much better."

Poor performance or not, there was one man impressed with what he'd seen from Munster on the day. "In my view, Munster would certainly be one of the best four sides at Super 12 level," said Treviso's Kiwi coach, Craig Green. "They have a great pack of forwards, good backs, a brilliant goal kicker and they finish off their chances very well. They made mistakes during the game but they kept their concentration. It takes a very good side to put bad moments in a match behind them. It's hard to say how well they would do, because the Super 12 is often played in a way to keep the public happy. Sometimes it's not just about winning games, it's about entertainment and refereeing tends to be a little bit below par. But yes, if you're talking about a team with the will to win and the ability to win, Munster would certainly be up there with the best in the southern hemisphere."

A glowing tribute from Green but it didn't lead to an improvement in Munster's performance the following weekend. With Gloucester beating Bourgoin away and earning a bonus point in the process, Munster knew they had to get a bonus point against the French to top the pool. And that's where the pressure came on. In the 'miracle match' against Gloucester, Munster had to score four tries and 27 points to leapfrog their opponents but because that goal was so outrageously difficult, everybody concentrated on winning the match instead. Against Bourgoin, both players and supporters knew that a victory with at least four tries was emminently attainable and therefore the pressure was on Munster right from the word go.

The home side started well and the first three tries came handy enough. Mike Mullins brushed off a couple of tackles on his way to the line early on, Paul

Small packages: *Peter Stringer sneaks through a crevice in the Bourgoin defence to score the third of Munster's four tries at Thomond Park*

O'Connell was driven over off yet another line-out maul and Peter Stringer showed superb opportunism on the hour mark to sneak through a tiny gap in the Bourgoin rearguard. That left 20 minutes to get try number four but it was a frustrating experience. Paul O'Connell and John Kelly both made poor decisions in promising positions but Munster got out of jail when referee Tony Spreadbury awarded a contentious penalty try on 74 minutes. It was an odd decision because although the Bourgoin scrum was clearly under pressure on their own line, the usual call would have been to award a penalty and start all over again. Instead the English whistler headed straight for the posts and awarded the penalty try.

"We were in a no-win situation in the sense that everyone expected us to get four tries no problem," said Ronan O'Gara after the game. "We were creating chances and not taking them and that can get in on a team a little bit. The crowd began to get restless and we just snatched at a few chances. There was an anxiety there and there was almost a cloud hanging over us in the sense that if we didn't get the four tries it would be like a defeat. I wasn't worried, just conscious of maintaining the intensity. When things weren't going to plan, that's where the experience this team has kicks in. It was a different pressure. It was all about the four tries."

While the Heineken Cup pool stages had been tipping along, Christian Cullen had been attempting to get his shoulder back to something close to working order. The 'minor' operation confirmed by the Munster Branch back in November had kept the full-back out of contention for a starting spot for all of December and January and it wasn't until the visit of the Ospreys on 27 February that the Kiwi star was finally declared fit to make his debut for Munster.

At last: Christian Cullen makes his Munster debut against the Ospreys at Musgrave Park

Musgrave Park was the venue for his long-awaited moment. It was a typically dark and damp Celtic League kind of night but a crowd of 8,000 turned out to see this little bit of Munster history. Cullen lined out, as expected, in the number 15 shirt and within 30 seconds he got his first touch of the ball, fielding a box kick from Ospreys' scrum-half Andy Williams with comparative ease. Over the course of the evening the Paekakariki Express looked a little rusty in his first proper game in almost four months, but one show and go from the former All Black in the first half gave the crowd a glimpse of what they could expect over the coming two and a half years. Munster lost by three points to the Ospreys that night but simply seeing Cullen in a red shirt for the first time sent most supporters home contented.

After the Six Nations – where Ireland missed out on a Grand Slam following a final-day defeat to England at Lansdowne Road – all eyes were on Munster's quarter-final clash with Stade Francais at Thomond Park. For once the draw for the play-offs had been kind and they were handed a home semi-final, against either Wasps or Gloucester, should they overcome the French. Tickets, needless to say, were like gold dust around the province in the week before the game and the hard-luck stories from those who couldn't get that special slip of paper, as well as the added revenue that could potentially be achieved, convinced the Munster Branch, with a little bit of a shove from the IRFU, to hold any future home quarter-finals at Lansdowne Road. It looked like the Stade Francais quarter-final could have been the very last one to be played at Thomond Park.

Despite the worry that the crowd at Thomond Park, to misquote Roy Keane, were getting a little 'prawn-sandwichy', there was a ferocious atmosphere at the Limerick venue on that Easter Saturday and those present were treated to two superbly-executed backline moves straight off the training ground, the first of which came after two minutes. Paul O'Connell was thrown in the air at a line-out but Frankie Sheahan threw to David Wallace at the tail. The flanker powered at the Stade cover and set up the ball for the backs. From there, Ronan O'Gara and Mike Mullins both threw delightful skip passes to outflank the 'four-up' Stade Francais defence and Christian Cullen, on his Heineken Cup debut, put Shaun Payne away in the corner. Nobody had expected Munster to go wide from the start, least of all Stade Francais but Alan Gaffney's surprise tactics had worked perfectly. O'Gara added the conversion and a penalty on six minutes, to put Munster 10-0 up. Then came their second trick. This time the move started close to the right-hand touchline, with O'Gara and Mullins both using the cut-out pass again. The centre's pass found John Kelly, who skirted around Ignacio Corleto and chipped the ball towards the line where Rob Henderson finished the move off. Ten minutes on the clock and with O'Gara's conversion, Munster were 17-0 ahead.

Naturally enough, the home side thought they had the match won at that point and relaxed a little. Corleto and Mullins exchanged tries before half-time to leave

Off to a flyer: Shaun Payne goes over for a second-minute try against Stade Francais at Thomond Park

Munster pretty comfortable at the break. Brian Liebenberg and Marcus Horan did likewise early in the second period to leave the home side 31-17 in front with 35 minutes still to go. However, the game was far from over and the home supporters were forced to endure a few hairy moments before the end. Christophe Moni crossed for a try on 72 minutes to make Munster tense up a little but two nerveless O'Gara penalties closed out the game for the home side. Thomas Lombard's late, late try was mere consolation for the French.

"We got ourselves into a bit of a hole in that game," says Gaffney. "We could have gotten ourselves in serious trouble despite a brilliant start. Diego Dominguez missed a handy penalty that would have put them within six points of us with 10 minutes to go but we saw it out with a couple of late penalties. We just lost our concentration, that was the only explanation. We were by far the better side on the day. I don't think they were in our league that day but they still could have sneaked it."

Munster had reached their fifth Heineken Cup semi-final in a row but there was a slight worry. Rarely, if ever, had a team come to Thomond Park and scored four tries against Munster. The province's defensive line was vulnerable and it was something that needed to improve.

The day after Munster's victory over Stade Francais, London Wasps blew Gloucester away at the Sixways Stadium and Warren Gatland's side earned themselves a date with

Whole different ball game: the semi-final match against Wasps tempted some well-known fans from far and wide to Lansdowne Road

Munster at Lansdowne Road on Sunday, 25 April. On paper, it was a mouth-watering prospect and the Munster fans certainly thought so. The sale of tickets was set for the Thursday after the quarter-final and despite the increased capacity of Lansdowne Road, there was an almighty scramble for them. The pavements outside Thomond Park and the Munster Branch offices in Cork were both, as usual, packed with people from early morning and the ticket fever even spread as far as Dublin. A certain amount of tickets were to go on sale at Ticketmaster in the St

Stephen's Green Shopping Centre and the IRFU headquarters on Lansdowne Road, and by 7am both venues had massive queues stretching back from their front doors. Munster mania had hit the capital.

From early morning on the Sunday of the semi-final, thousands of red shirts had taken over a little part of Dublin 4. From the Horseshoe Bar right down to the Schoolhouse Pub on Morehampton Road, everywhere was thronged with Munster supporters either calming their nerves with a few pints, exchanging tickets or meeting up with friends and family. Jury's Hotel in Ballsbridge was arguably the focal point of all this and at about 2pm that afternoon an interesting scene was played out. Warren Gatland, using the local knowledge acquired from his spell in charge of Ireland, had decided to base the Wasps squad right in the middle of all the hype and as they emerged from Jury's onto the team bus, thousands of Munster fans turned their heads and began chanting at the Wasps players. By the time the last player had jumped up the steps, a full blown 'Munster, Munster, Munster' could be heard right around Ballsbridge. It was a spellbinding noise, one that would have shaken most sides, but inside the bus one figure could be seen walking up and down the aisle. Lawrence Dallaglio, the London side's captain, was gesticulating like a traffic cop at an Italian intersection but his message was clear, not only would Wasps have to beat Munster on the pitch, they would have to quieten Munster's supporters too.

"That was a special occasion," recalls Alan Gaffney. "Going up to Lansdowne Road that day on the bus was one of the most emotional moments I had at Munster. Seeing all that red and everybody strolling through the streets. It was amazing. The guys had tears in their eyes that day." But despite the level of support, Munster's preparations for the game hadn't been going all that smoothly. The night before the game, David Wallace had been diagnosed with chicken pox and there was a severe shortage of back-row cover. Alan Quinlan was still on his way back from the injury he suffered against Argentina in the World Cup, and although he was nearing full fitness, the Munster management team felt they couldn't risk him in such a big game. So the next in line was Stephen Keogh, the inexperienced 21-year-old from Shannon. The youngster had been playing regular Celtic League rugby for Munster all season, and he also made four appearances off the bench in the Heineken Cup that year, but most of those took place when the game was already won and his experience of high-octane, big-game rugby was virtually zero. Still, there was no other option, Keogh would have to start.

By kick-off, the sea of red that had blanketed Ballsbridge beforehand had made its way inside Lansdowne Road. It was a breathtaking scene by the time Welsh referee Nigel Williams blew his first whistle. Six Nations games at the same venue just didn't compare – this was extra special. It was worth the queuing and not just for the spectacle. It was one of those epic games that passed in a blur. Ronan O'Gara had slotted three penalties by the 20th minute but Wasps had been doing a bit of scoring, too, thanks to a Josh Lewsey try and a conversion and penalty from Alex King. Then came a huge blow to Munster's hopes. O'Gara pulled a hamstring having been dragged into a ruck by a Wasps player and with no recognised out-half in their replacements, Jason Holland, an inside-centre by trade, was introduced from the bench to plug the gap. It was far from ideal.

"The critical moment of the game was Rog going off," says Gaffney. "He'd made a break or two, kicked for the corners well and slotted a few penalties, too. He was in fine form that day it seemed to me. You might say that Dutchy (Jason Holland) came on and landed five out of five place kicks at crucial times in the game but his kicking from open play let us down enormously. But we had no other cover, Jeremy Staunton was injured and we had nobody else to cover out-half." Holland did land a penalty three minutes after coming onto the pitch, immediately after Joe Worsley had been binned for slowing down the ball, but from the restart, his attempted

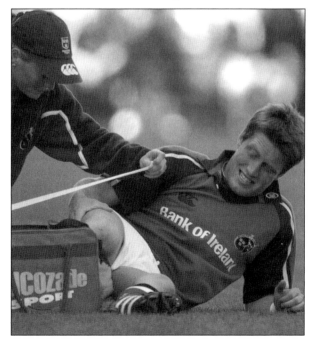

Critical condition: Munster physio Kirsty Peacock attends to Ronan O'Gara before the out-half was substituted against Wasps

clearance kick to touch was blocked down by Robert Howley and the Wasps scrum-half gathered the ball to set up Paul Volley for a try. Holland added another penalty before the interval to leave the score at 15-17 in the visitors' favour heading into the break but there wasn't much optimism around Lansdowne Road.

Without O'Gara, or another recognised out-half, there was no way Munster could survive in such a high-

Stretch in time: *Anthony Foley applies the finishing touch to score against Wasps*

tempo game. Or was there? Within minutes of the restart, it didn't seem so. Marc Van Gisbergen crossed the line for Wasps, despite his side still being down to 14 men but Holland slotted another penalty to reduce the gap to just four points. As the helter-skelter continued, Fraser Waters was then sent to the bin to cool down and in an incredible three-minute period while the centre was off the park, Munster turned the game on its head. A Cullen break and pass down the right found Keogh and when the flanker was stopped just short of the line, Anthony Foley popped up to apply the finishing touch. Almost immediately, Munster pumped a penalty deep into Wasps territory and the subsequent line-out maul saw Jim Williams credited with the try. Remarkably, Holland landed both converts from the touchline and Munster were 32-22 in front with 19 minutes left on the clock.

It was a strong position but things began to unravel when Donncha O'Callaghan was binned for infringing at a ruck and King landed the penalty to narrow the gap to seven. It was another crucial moment in the game. "It was the harshest sin-binning I've ever seen in my life," says Gaffney. "We'd committed one penalty on the ground,

Dutch courage:
Jason Holland
kicked five out of
five place kicks
after Ronan
O'Gara was forced
to leave the field
with a hamstring
injury against
Wasps

they'd committed eight and Donncha came in the side for a marginal penalty. It was only a marginal penalty and he gets binned. Jesus, it was an unbelievably tough call."

But Munster were hanging in there, somehow, with Christian Cullen making a couple of last-ditch, try-saving tackles on Fraser Waters. Then came another pivotal moment in the game. Rob Henderson was binned for coming in the side of a ruck and Munster were now down to 13 men. That period of the game infuriated Gaffney, for a couple of reasons. "When we had Rob Henderson sin-binned," remembers the coach, "Donncha was waiting to come back on from his spell in the bin and we stole one of their line-outs. All Dutchy needed to do was kick the ball to touch, put it dead and Donncha was back on. But he missed his touch, the next play developed and they scored down the left-hand side. It was a killer blow."

Gaffney's other point of contention concerned an incident before Henderson's binning. "In the build-up to Hendo's sin-binning, Paul O'Connell made a tackle down the left-hand touchline on Josh Lewsey and whoever was the next Wasps player in kicked Paulie in the middle of the back. Nigel Owens, the Welsh touch judge, puts his flag out having seen the incident but he put it down the minute Hendo committed his offence. Now that was sheer stupidity from Hendo's point of view. It was a rush of blood to the head. He only had to go back another half a metre and he was fine. But what the hell was Owens doing putting down his flag? If Hendo had to go, that player who kicked Paulie had to go as well. It was just pathetic."

Tom Voyce scored on the occasion that Holland missed his touch, with King adding the conversion to bring the sides level. And just when it looked as though extra time was likely, Trevor Leota scored in Munster's right-hand corner to seal the victory for the London side. Munster were dead on their feet and out of the Heineken Cup. The deathly silence around the ground on the final whistle aptly conveyed the feelings of the thousands of Munster supporters. It was almost as though they'd played every second of that game and they, too, were exhausted. There was a lingering sense of 'if only' about the place, and not for the first time. It was another Munster 'close, but no cigar' tale.

The Munster sqaud took their defeat on the chin afterwards but they were a little bothered about Wasps' spoiling tactics. "There's no doubt they were cynical and I said it after the match," explains Gaffney. "It's not something I've ever done before, I don't tend to complain after a defeat. But there's no doubt that they were cynical, they

Breaking through: '*He can do everything,*' *Anthony Foley said of Denis Leamy.* '*He's not one of these players you can't pigeon-hole. He's quick, he's evasive, he's strong… and he's a good lad to boot*'

CHAPTER 11

TIME FOR CHANGE

2004/05

If ever a Heineken Cup defeat hurt, it was the Wasps semi-final. The days, weeks and months after that excruciatingly narrow defeat produced a determination that had never been seen before on the Munster scene. Sure, all those other close calls – against Leicester, Stade Francais, Toulouse and the like – left an air of depression lingering about the place for quite a while, but it appeared that Lady Luck was the sole target of blame on those occasions. The attitude before the 2004 semi-final appeared to be that if they kept banging their heads against the door, it was bound to fall open at some stage. Times were about to change, though.

Just a couple of days, and sleepless nights, after that defeat to Warren Gatland's side, Jim Williams uttered the words that had been swilling around in his head since the final whistle that Sunday afternoon. In a frank interview in the Irish edition of 'The Sunday Times', the former Australian international outlined what Munster needed to do in order to eke that extra few per cent out of themselves on the big occasions. It wasn't the most politically correct point of view, but it's always difficult to tread carefully when a few home truths need spelling out. Williams really went for the jugular, blaming Munster's defeat against the English side on both the fact that they operated from two bases, Limerick and Cork, and that the province were bucking the trend by not investing in expert coaching. "I think Munster being based in Limerick and Cork is coming back to haunt us a little bit now," he told the paper. "I can't think of any other team in the world that is set up the way we are. I know the arguments for it and I know it has worked in the past but if you're asking how do we find the extra few per cent then this is an area we need to look at."

He didn't stop there, oh no. "Travelling is taking three or four hours out of your day. Sitting in the car after training makes the body stiffer and more tired. It can take a lot out of you. The Cork–Limerick road is not an easy one to travel. It could take anything from an hour and a half up to two and a half hours, and that's far too much valuable time lost, especially when you have a double session. You're getting home at five and six o'clock and, physically, you're stuffed. It's like a rolling effect. You don't train quite as well the next day or the next day. The danger is that other teams are going to pass Munster out. Everyone else is getting fitter and stronger and we need to keep up. Everything needs to move to another level."

Williams's words caused a heart flutter in the province, but the big question was what to do. The specialist coaching criticism wasn't a huge issue, the finance soon being made available to fund that avenue of improvement. But how could anyone hope to change the history, not to mention the geography, of the province? Munster had always operated out of both Limerick and Cork. They played their first ever inter-provincial game against Leinster at The Mardyke and through time, the provincial team had shared training and matches between Munster's two principal cities. Sure didn't those heroes from 1978 spend half their time in the weeks before the game

Jim'll fix it: *just a couple of days after the semi-final defeat to Wasps, Jim Williams spoke about how Munster could become more competitive, including a plan to change their training arrangements*

against the All Blacks on the road to or from Fermoy? The Australian's message may have been understood in an instant but the answer to this sensitive issue took a little longer to sort out.

By the time the squad, minus the internationals who'd been on tour in South Africa, came back for training in late June, they'd come up with something close to a workable solution. In a typical week of a Saturday match, the boys from Cork would travel to Limerick for training on a Monday at the University of Limerick, stay overnight for training on a Tuesday and then travel back home. The plan was to alternate the overnight stay between Limerick and Cork every second week but it didn't always work out like that because of the superior training facilities in Limerick. Then on Wednesday they'd have the day off and Thursday was spent in two groups. It wasn't perfect by any stretch of the imagination, but at least change had been initiated.

"It was something me and Jim Williams had been talking about for some time," admits Alan Gaffney. "Jim came out and said it after the Wasps game, and whether he should have come out and said it was one thing, because we were trying to go a bit softly, softly on the issue and his comments probably brought things to a head a little bit quicker than we would have liked. But there was no doubt that Munster had cost themselves too much time travelling between Limerick and Cork. There was always the argument from the old hard heads that training in both place makes you stronger, and they could be right. But to travel up and down to Cork for training sessions meant you were on the road for three or four hours and for me that was a waste of time, no matter what anybody else said. So we came to that compromise but there was a lot of opposition to it, a bit of resistance from the Cork brigade because we ended up staying in Limerick more than we planned. People wanted to go home but we didn't allow it. We had to be all in this together to see if it worked. The resistance came from the old guys who didn't want to change things, but these were guys who, from my point of view, didn't want to improve and were happy with the status quo. I don't think anyone should have been happy with the status quo. The fact of the matter was that we should have been operating out of one location, plain and simple. The person who eventually makes that happen will be a lot braver than me but I can promise you there'll be a lot of coaches who'll have gone to the bridge before that happens. But down the track it has to happen, I have no doubt about that, if Munster are to reach their full potential, they're going to have to."

The travel situation half-sorted, it was time to address the coaching problem and before the start of the season, Graham Steadman was added to the Munster brains trust. The new man's CV was typical of most union defence coaches. The 42-year-old was a former Great Britain rugby league international who served as head coach at Castleford for a couple of years, as well as assisting with Great Britain for a three-year period. He was from the same mould as Mike Ford, the Irish defence coach who'd done such a fine job with the national team, and his appointment assured a lot of people that Munster were taking Williams's words seriously.

⎯⎯⎯⎯⎯⎯⎯⬤⎯⎯⎯⎯⎯⎯⎯

Harlequins arrived in Limerick for Munster's Pool 4 opener on a wretched run of form in the Zurich Premiership, one that would eventually lead to their final day relegation from the top flight of English rugby. In the lead-up to the game it looked like being a routine assignment for Munster on their home patch, but it turned out to be anything but. On a wretched afternoon, where the drizzling rain was accompanied by a nasty breeze sweeping towards the Mayorstone end of the ground, it was never likely to be pretty. In the end Munster's extra power up front proved the difference between the sides, although the fact that the visitors lost three men to the sin bin didn't help their cause.

Back home: *Jeremy Staunton, on his return to Thomond Park, gets to grips with Christian Cullen*

Anthony Horgan crossed for Munster's opening try on 13 minutes, running onto a delicious pass from Ronan O'Gara to round the Harlequins cover, and after Jim Williams had scragged the ball from a Harlequins maul and released the alert Denis Leamy for the home side's second effort before half-time, the only issue appeared to be whether Munster would get the bonus point. But by the end they were happy to take the victory as Harlequins scrapped hard in the second period. Three penalties from Jeremy Staunton had kept them in touch throughout and they could have stolen an unlikely win in the final 10 minutes but Gaffney's side managed to hold on for a 15–9 victory.

"We pushed them hard that day," remembers Jeremy Staunton of his return to Thomond Park in the Harlequins side. "With a few breaks, we could have beaten them but as I well knew, Munster know how to just do enough for victory. For me, that was a big day, I was very nervous about it. You know, I'd never played in the number 10 shirt for Munster in the Heineken Cup in all the years I was there, and I always considered myself an out-half, not a full-back. So that day was my chance to prove that I could do a job there and I think I played quite well. In a game like that in the past, I would have went out there attempting to beat Munster on my own but I'd matured a little bit by that stage and I think people could see that on the day."

So while the returnee was reasonably happy with his efforts, most Munster supporters would have left Thomond Park that October evening not only soaked to the skin and with a potential head cold brewing, but also with a few doubts about their side's prospects for the season ahead. Munster were poor but, not only that, they had a tricky looking game ahead of them the following weekend against the Neath–Swansea Ospreys.

When the Welsh side decided to play the game at Neath's home The Gnoll, Munster were always likely to struggle to get a result. However, to complicate matters, they also had to contend with some old bad blood between the sides. It stemmed from a Celtic League game a couple of years before in Wales, a fixture where Munster were forced to field a young team due to international commitments. Sensing the visiting side's weakness, the Ospreys attempted to teach the kids a bit of a physical lesson and it didn't go down too well with the senior Munster players. They vowed never to be bullied by the Ospreys again and they aimed to put the record straight that day.

Typically, the Sunday game was a tetchy, nervy affair, one that was effectively won by the quick thinking of Peter Stringer at the back of the scrum. With Munster 12-9 behind in the opening minutes of the second half, the scrum-half shaped to move the ball left from a scrum five yards out but instead picked the ball from the base and darted right to sneak over the line. In a game that was essentially a kicking duel between Ronan O'Gara and Gavin Henson, Stringer's intervention proved decisive and gave the visitors a 20-18 victory. But that was only half the story.

The real drama happened in the following days. Richard Mustoe, the Ospreys winger on the day, had opened up Marcus Horan's forehead with his boot midway through the second half and was sent to the sin bin by Joel Jutge for his troubles. Having watched the video of the incident after the game, Munster decided to cite the player for the damage inflicted on the prop but were completely shocked when the Welsh side came up with a charge of their own. Elvis Sevelai'i, the Ospreys' Samoan centre, claimed that he had been racially abused by Marcus Horan during the game. The Munster camp, from the very second the citing was lodged with the ERC, denied the charge and were disgusted at the allegation made against one of the province's most polite, courteous and fair-minded players. There was never a doubt from anyone

Bloody disgrace: *Marcus Horan lies prostrate on The Gnoll pitch after receiving a boot on the head from the Ospreys' Richard Mustoe*

in Irish rugby circles that the claims were utterly false and on 10 November, a couple of days before Horan was due to play for Ireland against South Africa at Lansdowne Road, the ERC cleared him of the charge.

"In the case of Marcus Horan," read the ERC statement, "for an alleged remark made during the match to a player of the opposing team, the committee did not find it established that Mr Horan, or anyone else on the Munster team, had made the remark complained of. Therefore the committee dismissed the citing. Had the committee found the remark had been made, the committee would have regarded it as racist abuse and foul play. The committee went further and held that the alleged remark had not been made."

The last sentence showed what a dishonourable action the Ospreys had taken in citing Horan for something that clearly didn't happen and Munster weren't too sweet on how their Welsh opponents had acted. A Branch statement read: "We were always confident, and stated our belief from the outset, that Marcus Horan had no case to answer in relation to the charges levelled against him by the Neath-Swansea Ospreys. That confidence was justified by the ERC's decision and we are delighted that Marcus Horan has been fully exonerated. We are particularly pleased that the committee has ruled that in the case of the alleged racial abuse charge, the words were in fact not spoken by Marcus Horan. We are extremely disappointed that such a serious allegation which has cast a slur on the good name of Marcus Horan was only raised by Neath-Swansea Ospreys in response to Munster's citing of Richard Mustoe. We believe that the action taken by Neath-Swansea Ospreys has no place in sport."

Horan himself held his counsel for a couple of weeks but in an interview in the 'Sunday Tribune' after Christmas, he vented his frustration on how he'd been treated. "I mean what happens if I get accused of something like that again, will people believe me a second time?," the prop asked. "It's (making a claim) something that can be so easily done and it can cause so much damage. I know for a fact that a lot of the Opsreys players were genuinely disgusted by what happened and that was a good thing to hear. There are a certain few individuals in the club that are nasty enough and that's down to a personal thing, it's not down to the club as a whole."

A couple of individuals came in for particular criticism. "I haven't spoken to Elvis Sevelai'i since the incident and I actually wouldn't bother going near him or Shane Williams," said the Clare man. "They're the two guys who lied that day (of the hearing). They didn't have the guts or the balls to look me in the eyes when they were spouting lies so I don't think I would give them the time of day."

———————●———————

With Ireland having defeated South Africa, the United States and Argentina in the November internationals, Munster's players were on a bit of a high, if a little tired, following their break from provincial rugby. They didn't get much time to recuperate though as the province travelled to Castres, that favourite old destination of theirs, for a Friday night date with the home side at Stade Pierre-Antoine. Having not played together in red jerseys for a couple of weeks, the visitors were typically rusty and just didn't fire over the course of the game. A David Bory try in the first half effectively won the game for Castres and nobody could argue that Munster deserved anything more than the 19-12 defeat. Far from it, in fact.

"That was a shocker from our point of view," recalls Alan Gaffney. "The referee didn't help us that day, he was totally out of his depth in France. He couldn't handle the Castres crowd. Looking back at the video afterwards, you just couldn't understand some of the decisions he made. But we were poor, we were so disappointed. We created so many opportunities down the right-hand side where we created number after number after number, but our passing was pathetic. We got what we deserved."

Castres away:
Paul Volley races past Ronan O'Gara at the Stade Pierre-Antoin

But like Munster's trip to Wales, the real action kicked off again once the final whistle had been blown. All game long Paul Volley, the Castres number eight and former Wasps flanker, had been in Ronan O'Gara's face, both literally and metaphorically. The Englishman had clearly been assigned the job of rattling O'Gara as soon as he got possession and sure enough, every time Peter Stringer whipped the ball to his out-half, Volley arrived on the scene in the blink of an eye to put O'Gara under pressure. Of course all this was wholly legitimate, the flanker was merely doing his job, but Volley's other tactics designed to disrupt O'Gara certainly weren't. Every time the Munster out-half addressed a place kick, Volley stood 10 metres back and hurled abuse at him. Sledging is the general term for it and while it happens from time to time, it's generally accepted as a 'no-no' in the modern game.

Matters came to a head after the game when O'Gara and Volley were in the Sky Sports interview room under the stands at the same time. Predictably enough, it wasn't long before the pair were having a verbal cut off each other and as the kerfuffle continued, Paul O'Connell got wind of it and bounded into the room suggesting that Volley should pick on someone his own size. The situation fizzled out reasonably quickly but was certain to be resurrected the following week in Limerick.

Speaking to 'The Irish Times' in the build-up to Munster's home game against the French side, O'Gara spelt out what happened between himself and Volley in Castres. "I have no problem with the physical stuff at all. It was the verbal abuse while I was taking penalty kicks that disappointed me… What he said couldn't be printed. Just abusin' me like. The referee spoke with him and I don't know if he continued with it after that, I was focusing on taking my kicks. Ah, it's his job. That's all I have to say about it anyhow." The spat between the pair had been widely publicised by the media in the days before their second meeting and Volley must have known that he was in for a tough time from the 14,000 lucky enough to be in Thomond Park.

However, if the home supporters were expecting fireworks from the off, then they were disappointed as the men in red started slowly and Benjamin Lhande put Castres in front with a try after just five minutes. But the power of Munster's maul, something that had been missing the week before, soon kicked in and before the interval Anthony Foley and Denis Leamy had both crossed for tries off a couple of impossible-to-stop rolling mauls. After the break, both Paul O'Connell and Frankie Sheahan were credited with tries off further mauls and that weapon could have borne even more fruit for Munster had the television match official been able to see the ball being grounded on a further two rumbles. Right on full-time, Christian Cullen rounded off the rout with his first Heineken Cup try for the province.

"It was a real Munster performance - honest," declared man of the match O'Connell afterwards. "Axel asked for honesty before the game and that's what he got in abundance. That's what Munster is all about on days like this. Overall, it was as tough a game as I've played this year. A few of the boys are sore and on days like these the

High king:
*'It's like we
sense their
mood,'
said Paul
O'Connell
of the special
relationship
with the
Thomond
Park crowd
after the
victory over
Castres*

bumps can seem even worse if you lose. The fact that we won means they're not too bad. The performance is very satisfying. There was a lot of talk during the week from both sides and when you get out on the field, all the stuff you do in front of the media doesn't matter any more. You've got to produce the goods. We try not to antagonise people. We just go out on the pitch to do our best."

The Young Munster man then went on to describe the effect the Thomond Park crowd had on the team that evening. "There was a special atmosphere out there. I don't know what it is, the connection between ourselves and the crowd, it's like we sense their mood and they sense our mood. The intensity of the crowd matched the intensity of our performance and was a massive lift. You think of all the money they spend every year, so it was great to give them something to cheer about."

Anthony Foley also believed that Castres' behaviour the previous week had fired the Munster support up before the game. "Our supporters would have read the press and been a little angry coming to the game after what happened over there," said the captain. "The supporters brought that mood. You saw that before the game. They were really up for it. That feeds into what we're doing and when we are going about the business in the right way, they really get in there."

As for Paul Volley, he was predictably given a tough time of it. Every time the flanker went anywhere near the 'popular side' of the ground, the chant of 'Volley, Volley, Volley' rose from the masses. It was an eerie kind of a sound and on a bitterly cold evening, with mist rising from the crowd, it surely affected the cocky flanker. It turned out, however, that the former Wasps player and Ronan O'Gara had put their differences behind them as the game played its way out. "We shared a joke or two during the game and he was complimentary," said O'Gara after his 50th Heineken Cup appearance for Munster, a game where he also bypassed Diego Dominguez's European points record. "The boys said he was giving a bit of lip at the penalties but I wasn't aware of that. You've got to compliment the guy when he comes full circle. He was no angel last week but in terms of sport, it's nice that it should end like this."

It was even nicer that Munster finished 2004 on top of Pool 4 and in prime position to claim a quarter-final spot when the competition resumed in 2005.

———————

By this stage in the season, a new Munster forward was creating a bit of a fuss about the place. Denis Leamy had emerged onto the scene at the start of the 2003 season but he damaged his cruciate ligaments in a Celtic League game against Edinburgh that November and it put paid to his season. By the start of the 2004/05 season, however, Leamy was back at full fitness and, as a few of the Munster back-row players were enjoying an extended pre-season following the summer tour to South Africa, the man from Cashel got his opportunity to impress on the open side. With his huge paws, he grabbed every chance. Even though David Wallace was fully fit and rested by the time the Heineken Cup opener against Harlequins came around, it was Leamy who lined out, scoring an

Paws for thought: 'He's got the biggest pair of hands you'll ever come across,' said Anthony Foley of Denis Leamy

impressive heads-up try after a Jim Williams's ball steal. He was injured for the following two games against the Ospreys and Castres away, but returned with an impressive performance in an abrasive game against the French side at home.

The plaudits were starting to build at this point. It was difficult to see Leamy's weak point. He was a superb ball carrier, wonderfully aggressive in the tackle and had the ability to scavenge on the ground at the breakdown. Alan Gaffney was clearly a huge fan, but even Keith Wood, who was watching Leamy make his mark from across the water, was quoted as saying that the new kid would be well capable of playing at hooker should the need arise in the future. Even from a brief glimpse it was easy to see that Leamy was wonderfully versatile. Aside from Wood's assertion that he could play in the middle of the front row, it was clear that Leamy was equally comfortable in any position across the back row. This was, after all, a guy who'd played at number eight for Rockwell College in the Munster Senior Cup and even took his side's place kicks. "He can do everything," Anthony Foley said of the back-row prodigy. "He's not one of these players you can pigeon-hole. He's quick, he's evasive, he's strong, he's got the biggest pair of hands you'll ever come across, and he's a good lad to boot. He's quiet, unusually for a Tipperary lad. The Tipperary lads I come across are very loud and obstreperous, but Denis is the quiet one."

After the turn of the year, the Ospreys came to Limerick. It was the sides' second meeting in a few weeks, as a fortnight before that Lynn Jones's men were beaten 13-9 in a Celtic League match in Musgrave Park on an evening when Ryan Jones had been sent off in the first half for inflicting some damage on Donncha O'Callaghan. Typical of the games between these two, it was a niggly affair, another one that kept the needle between the sides alive. Before they headed back to Wales, some of the Ospreys players had a pop off Peter Stringer's abilities and their coach Jones sent out a warning shot with the Heineken Cup return match in mind. "They are not infallible," he commented. "They are not God's gift to rugby, they're just human beings like everybody else and they get things wrong if you apply a bit of pressure. Munster have had a good run in Europe and I'm sure they're desperate to do it this year but it's all to play for." Munster lapped up Jones's comments and answered him on the field. Surprisingly, there were very few fractious incidents over the course of the Heineken Cup clash but there was no shock in the fact that Munster recorded yet another European victory at Thomond Park. They won the game 20-10, thanks to tries from Anthony Foley and Christian Cullen in the first half, but having brought a 17-7 lead into the half-time break, there was a general sense of disappointment that the home side hadn't turned the screw after the interval and earned the four-try bonus point.

Ronan O'Gara was missing from the game with a knee injury – the first game he'd missed for Munster in Europe since 1999 – and although Paul Burke put in a more than competent display at out-half, the tries were not flowing. The midfield partnership was proving to be their biggest selection headache for Gaffney. Shaun Payne and Mike Mullins played there against the Ospreys, Payne and Rob Henderson had occupied those positions in the home game against Castres, while John Kelly and Henderson had started the Heineken Cup campaign against Harlequins in the number 12 and 13 shirts.

Touching the void: Paul Burke filled the hole left by Ronan O'Gara's enforced absence against the Ospreys

Sure, Munster were still winning games and were top of Pool 4 with just one fixture remaining, but their failure to secure bonus points was a concern. As it stood, Munster needed a bonus point from their trip to Twickenham to take on Harlequins if they were to have any hope of earning a home quarter-final. With the London side already out of contention for the knockout stages, it looked on paper at least to be an easy task but Munster's lack of creativity out wide made it a very difficult afternoon.

Just over 30,000 filled the lower tier of the stands, a record for a Heineken Cup pool game, but it was a frustrating afternoon for the thousands of supporters who winged their way over to London for the game. Mullins and Henderson were the centre combination for this 1pm kick-off but they produced little spark. Anthony Horgan scored a nice try on eight minutes wide on the right and despite a try from Ugo Monye 20 minutes later, Munster took a 12-10 lead into the interval after the outstanding Denis Leamy stretched over from close range after a spell of serious pressure close in. Two tries down, two more were needed for the bonus point but it never really looked like happening. It was a lacklustre display, one that had many worrying about Munster's prospects in the quarter-final.

It was a Tuesday morning at the University of Limerick (UL) bowl. Munster were taking a stroll through their lines in the sunshine a full five days before their quarter-final away to Biarritz but all was not going well on the injury front. All of the internationals had come through the Six Nations virtually unscathed but a couple of Celtic League fixtures had caused untold damage. The first to fall was Christian Cullen. After an injury-interrupted first season, the All Blacks legend had been looking good for the first time in a Munster shirt. In the games against Harlequins, Castres and the Ospreys at home, the full-back was in piping hot form as he and his teammates finally appeared to be on the same wavelength. His trademark runs from deep now appeared to be registering on the radar of those around him.

But on 5 March against Cardiff at the Arms Park, Cullen injured his left shoulder and was ruled out of the game for between four and six months. Munster got even worse news the weekend before they were due to play Biarritz. They were in Newport on a Friday night to play the Dragons in the Celtic League and during the game Ronan O'Gara damaged the medial ligaments in his right knee. He was effectively ruled out of the quarter-final by the time he reached the sideline at Rodney Parade. For a team that was struggling to put points on the board, the loss of their commander-in-chief was another serious blow to their ambitions.

So on that Tuesday afternoon at UL, Brian Lima ran out for his first serious training session with Munster. With O'Gara and Cullen out of the equation, the Samoan centre had been signed until the end of the season by Alan Gaffney to boost his side's backline options. The Samoan had been given the nickname "the chiropractor" for his ability to rearrange bones in the tackle and besides his defensive quality, there was a feeling that the 33-year-old had the ability to inject that little bit of unpredictability into Munster's game. He could also bash his way through a defence like few in world rugby. His arrival was a serious boost for players and supporters alike.

That was until later that Tuesday morning at UL. Having come through the full-contact part of the session without any problems, the Samoan damaged the quadriceps in his right knee while the backline were running through a few unopposed moves. He was treated at the side of the pitch by the Munster medical team and although Alan Gaffney stated afterwards that he was hopeful the player would still take some part in the fixture, he was ruled out by the time Thursday came around. It seemed that the gods were conspiring against Munster.

Four plus three equals one. Not a maths equation gone wrong, rather a Basque expression to sum up the four French and three Spanish provinces that make up the Basque country, that mythical patch of land tucked between the Pyrenees and the Atlantic Ocean. The city of Biarritz is right in the middle of it all and it's only in that context you can understand why the club decided to switch their quarter-final with Munster to the 32,000-capacity Estadio Anoeta in San Sebastian.

"What people have to understand is that when I go to San Sebastian, I cross no border," said the region's most famous son, former French full-back Serge Blanco. "It is the same for the 20,000-odd supporters who will come to see us play against Munster. As far as I am concerned Biarritz and San Sebastian are both in the Basque Country, so there can be no border or frontier to cross. And I am sure that of all people, the Irish will understand what I am talking about."

Technically of course, and despite Blanco's rhetoric, San Sebastian is in Spain and that explained why it took Biarritz a good three weeks to sort out the arrangements for the game. But when the news was officially confirmed in mid-February, the switch represented excellent news for Munster and their supporters. The 32,000 capacity at the new venue meant that over 8,000 tickets would go to the visiting side, an increase of 5,000 on the allocation Munster would have received had the game taken place at the Parc des Sports Aguilera in Biarritz. Almost as soon as the ERC had ratified Biarritz's decision to move the game, the Munster masses began working out ways of making their way to the Spanish, or rather, Basque city.

Just like many of their previous trips, San Sebastian wasn't the easiest spot in the world to get to but there were a couple of main choices; fly to Bilbao and spend the weekend in San Sebastian, or head to the south of France and hang around there until the day of the game. Many were enticed by the latter. The Biarritz authorities promised everybody a free bus ride to San Sebastian on the morning of the game and the

Basque glory: Munster and Biarritz supporters in high spirits in San Sebastian before the quarter-final clash

normally tranquil town was transformed for the weekend. Locals went around on the back of pick-up trucks all evening, singing and chanting good naturedly at the Munster folk who had all but taken over the town. The atmosphere was magnificent in both cities and with the sun shining down and everybody enjoying the local hospitality it must have been difficult for Munster fans to believe that anything could go wrong the following afternoon. The scene, both in Biarritz and in the picturesque streets and lanes of San Sebastian, seemed all too perfect.

The injury troubles forced Mike Mullins back into the Munster midfield alongside Rob Henderson, with Paul Burke, who'd played in the province's first European fixture back in 1995, back in the number 10 shirt. The reshaping of the backline, and the fact Munster were playing away from home, made them huge underdogs for this particular quarter-final, a position they were used to. Down the years, they'd gradually earned the respect of Europe's elite, who had learned the hard way not to underestimate the Irish outfit but this time around, it was patently clear that Biarritz felt they were going to win easily.

Orchestral manouevres in the dark: Dimitri Yachvili controls the Biarritz effort against Munster

The Basques were the new fancy boys of French rugby and had recruited heavily over the previous couple of seasons. The previous summer they had signed two of France's most high-profile players - Damien Traille, the no-nonsense centre; and the man who'd have you tongue-tied saying his name, Imanol Harinordoquy. But the pair were only the tip of a very cool iceberg, as the Biarritz squad included 16 other full internationals from four countries. Along with Harinordoquy and Traille, full-back Nicolas Brusque, flanker Serge Betsen, scrum-half Dimitri Yachvili, fly-half Julien

Peyrelongue and captain Thomas Lièvremont all played in the French team which beat England to win the Grand Slam in Paris earlier that year. Factor in wingers Jimmy Marlu, Philippe Bidabé and Philippe Bernat-Salles, the elusive Argentine centre Martin Gaitan, Romanian prop Petru Balan and the dynamic Samoan loose-head Kas Lealamanu'a and you start to appreciate Biarritz's galaxy of multi-national talent. It was little wonder that they expected to beat Munster at a canter.

And that's how the game started in San Sebastian, with the French side believing that the game was theirs for the taking and Munster doing nothing to dispute that assumption. By the end of the first half the visitors were 16 points down, following a try from Gaitan, and three penalties and a conversion from their main man, Dimitri Yachvili. Munster had been completely outplayed in the half and they just couldn't get their hands on the ball. With Leinster capitulating 29-13 to Leicester in their quarter-final the previous evening, it looked like another limp Irish exit was on the cards. But Munster came out in the second half a team transformed.

Second wind: *David Wallace's try shortly after the break gives Munster fresh hope*

189

Now they were the ones holding onto the ball and when David Wallace crossed for a try soon after the restart, the impossible seemed on. Players like Marcus Horan, Mike Mullins and Wallace were making clean breaks from all sorts of areas and the pity was that in the heat of the battle, they just didn't have the support runners to finish off a couple of those scintillating moves.

In the end, the only other score they mustered was a Paul Burke penalty and although still in the game at 16-10 as the clock ticked down, Yachvili knocked over one last penalty with time running out to ease the home side through the final moments of the game. They'd put up a brave battle but it wasn't enough. "I thought we got on top of their pack," said Anthony Foley afterwards. "It was a matter of building phases and we managed to do that quite a lot. Unfortunately, when things looked like going our way, we made mistakes, lost the ball going forward and that eased the pressure on the home side. At times we pushed the passes a bit and I suppose they deserve a bit of credit too for the way they put pressure on us. I hate losing and we obviously left ourselves with a bit too much work to do but I was proud at the way we fought back."

Looking back on the game, Gaffney believes that silly penalties were Munster's undoing. "We didn't play in the first half, we didn't play at all," he says. "And we gave away a lot of stupid penalties for dumb things. The one thing I'd stressed in the build-up to the game is that if you give Yachvili an opportunity, he's going to knock it over. But we gave away stupid penalties and that won them the game."

On that theme, Alan Quinlan opened his heart a couple of months later. "I sat in the stadium at the end of that game and just thought to myself, 'I can't take much more of this,'" the Tipperary man admitted. "I was so disappointed in myself that I got pinged for those penalties. The thing is you don't set out before a game to go out and give away penalties. I play quite abrasive rugby and even though I've tried to work hard on my discipline over the last few years, there's always going to be one or two given away on occasions and I've learned to except that and not beat myself up over it. But on that day I was so disappointed that I got caught. After I analysed them the next week with George Murray and Mervyn Murphy (Munster and Ireland video analysts respectively) there was probably one that was a penalty and the others were 50/50 calls. It was just one of those things. I was in the wrong place at the wrong time and I went to snatch for balls that were probably borderline still in the ruck. I was asking myself at that point, why did I have to be involved in those

Emotional moment: *Biarritz players and supporters show their joy, and relief, at the final whistle while Peter Stringer and Frankie Sheahan begin to come to terms with another Heineken Cup knockout defeat*

moments in play, why wasn't I out on the wing, why was I near that ruck, why did I think that ball was out? My discipline was quite good last season, I was calm before the game, I suppose I was just in the wrong place or the wrong time."

Aside from the discipline issue, Gaffney also felt his side played far too narrow in the first period. "There were times in that game where we were playing within a space of about 15 metres and it just got us into so much trouble. In the second half we used the entire width of the pitch and we caused them so many problems. We scored a try, Marcus Horan was stopped short, somebody else knocked on close to the line. But at least we tried to play the game in the second half. I shed tears after that game because I knew how close we'd been. When you look back at the season, a bonus point against either the Ospreys at home, or Harlequins away and we'd have had a different quarter-final. We may not have won that either but you never know."

So the thousands of Munster fans made their way back home from Biarritz and San Sebastian, through whatever complicated route they got there in the first place, all the time wondering were they ever going to win this damn competition.

The morning after that Leinster and Leicester quarter-final, the day of Munster's game with Biarritz, it was reported that Declan Kidney, the then-Leinster coach, would be confirmed as the new Munster coach in the not-too-distant future. The rumour certainly caused a stir in rugby circles. It later emerged that Declan Kidney had told the powers that be at Leinster, and captain Reggie Corrigan, a full 10 days before that Leicester game that he would be applying for the Munster job. And of course you could take it at that point that if he was applying for the gig, he must have been pretty certain that he was going to get it.

But what about Michael Bradley? From the very minute Alan Gaffney announced he was to become Eddie Jones's assistant with Australia, the Connacht coach, who was a former Cork Constitution, Munster and Ireland scrum-half, had been odds-on favourite to replace him at Munster. But for some reason he didn't get the job. Kidney was to be the man again, even if he was employed at the time by Munster's great rivals.

Silver lining: Alan Gaffney parades the Celtic Cup after his final game in charge of Munster

Kidney left Leinster almost immediately after the news emerged that he was on his way back south and on 8 April, it was confirmed that the man who'd led the province to two Heineken Cup finals in the past, would now be charged with finishing the job. He was handed a three-year contract by the Munster Branch.

But with Kidney on gardening leave for a couple of months, Alan Gaffney had enough time

192

for one last hurrah before he crossed hemispheres. The Ospreys had won the Celtic League but the Celtic Cup, in what would prove to be that competition's final year, was a decent note for Gaffney to finish off his Munster career. His side had beaten a stubborn Edinburgh outfit in the quarter-final at Thomond Park and snatched a 23-17 victory over Leinster at Lansdowne Road thanks to a late Anthony Foley try. That set up a final against Llanelli at the same venue and Munster put on some show for their coach's final match in charge. Anthony Horgan, Ronan O'Gara and Mike Mullins all crossed for tries in a comprehensive 27-16 victory, and Gaffney paraded the trophy around the four corners of Lansdowne while saying goodbye to the Munster supporters who, once again, had turned up in droves for the occasion.

Gaffney would undoubtedly have preferred if it were a different trophy he was holding, but it wasn't to be. That would have to be somebody else's job.

Meeting of minds:
*the relationship
between Munster
players and supporters
is one of the reasons
the province has
performed so well*

CHAPTER 12

BEATING THE BLUES

2005/06

There was no fanfare, no ticker tape parade through the streets of Cork, not even a press conference to formally confirm Declan Kidney's return as Munster coach for the start of the 2005/06 campaign. In keeping with the way he'd always gone about his business, Kidney just crept back into his old role almost unnoticed and quietly went about organising himself for the coming season.

He was probably relieved to get back to familiar territory following a tumultuous couple of years. When he formally relinquished control of Munster at the end of the 2002 season, Kidney must have been looking forward to helping Eddie O'Sullivan steer Ireland towards the 2003 World Cup in Australia. But the fact of the matter was that the two men didn't gel professionally, mainly because Kidney had been foisted upon O'Sullivan by the IRFU. The Union may have had no problem replacing the unfortunate Warren Gatland with O'Sullivan, but they still didn't have enough confidence in their new man to allow him to appoint his own backroom team.

As the years with Ireland wore on, the relationship between O'Sullivan and Kidney became increasingly tetchy and when the IRFU confirmed that the head coach would be granted an extension to his contract until after the 2008 Six Nations, it signalled the beginning of the end for the former Munster coach. In handing O'Sullivan a contract extension while offering nobody else in his coaching team a similar deal, the IRFU had all but confirmed that Kidney would be surplus to requirements when his contract finished at the end of the 2004 season.

Kidney must surely have seen that bullet coming but he handled himself with great dignity right up until the end of his contract. The IRFU then attempted to create an

Body language: Declan Kidney returned to Munster after a difficult spell with Ireland coach Eddie O'Sullivan

odd post for Kidney entitled 'Performance Manager of Age Grade Rugby', but if the role was as clumsy as the title, he was right to turn it down and look elsewhere. He was initially linked with the vacant position at Ulster but after Mark McCall was appointed at Ravenhill, Kidney joined up with the Newport Gwent Dragons. It was an uncomfortable looking situation for a man so dedicated to his family and although he was prepared to commute over and back to Rodney Parade, a solution presented itself when Leinster sacked Gary Ella and Kidney was installed as head-honcho at Donnybrook.

While it may have been a slightly easier commute to work, Kidney never looked fully at home in a Leinster tracksuit. He talked the talk and walked the walk but his way of doing things grated with a number of high-profile Leinster players. He did manage to lead them through the pool stages of the 2004/05 Heineken Cup with six wins out of six, but their tame quarter-final exit at the hands of Leicester – after he'd already indicated to some members of the Leinster set-up that he was applying for the Munster job – was embarrassing and there was little doubt he was on his way as soon as he could engineer as dignified an exit as possible. Was it just pure luck then that the IRFU decided not to extend Alan Gaffney's contract at the end of that season, leaving the way open for Kidney to return to Munster? The answer to that may never be known but he was no doubt delighted to return and put a troubled couple of years behind him.

Kidney's first task was to reorganise his backroom team. Brian Hickey had been employed as forwards coach by Alan Gaffney over the previous three seasons and although many expected him to make way once Kidney arrived back on the scene, his services were retained by the returning Director of Rugby. Graham Steadman would remain on the staff, too, but his role would now be on a part-time basis following his appointment as successor to Mike Ford as Irish defence coach.

Therefore the only major addition to the coaching staff was a familiar face. Jim Williams had been brought to Munster by Kidney back in 2001 and once he confirmed that the 2004/05 season was his last as a player, the coach went about persuading the wily back row to take up a coaching role with the province. Williams briefly considered an offer from Japan to extend his playing career for a further season but Kidney's persuasive powers swayed the Australian. He was confirmed as the province's 'continuity coach' before the start of the season, although he would work on an awful lot more areas of the game than simply keeping the ball alive.

On the playing front, James Storey, Eoin Reddan and Gordon McIlwham had been released but there were a couple of new faces on the scene. Trevor Halstead, a beefy South African international centre, had been trailed by Alan Gaffney for a good part of 2005 and once he settled back behind his desk, Kidney gave the green light for the signing to be completed. Mick O'Driscoll, meanwhile, had decided to return home to Cork after a successful, if injury-interrupted, couple of seasons with Perpignan and his arrival provided yet more competition in the second row, where Paul O'Connell, Donncha O'Callaghan and the ever-improving Trevor Hogan were fighting for two positions.

The other summer signings were South African winger Anthon Pitout, former Great Britain rugby league centre Gary Connolly and Italy international prop Federico

Proper order: *Italy international Federico Pucciariello was added to Munster's league of nations before the 2005/06 season*

Pucciariello. Nobody knew much about Pitout, although it was rumoured that he had also been on Toulouse's most wanted list, while the signing of Connolly surprised many supporters, not least because the player was 34 and had limited experience of playing union. Pucciariello, meanwhile, had a reputation as a thoroughly decent prop, comfortable on either side of the scrum, and although he had represented the Azzurri at international level, the 31-year-old was Argentine by birth.

The signings of Connolly and Pucciariello added two new members to Munster's league of nations, a far cry from the early days when Sean McCahill was the only man with a strange accent.

———————————————●———————————————

Munster's Celtic League season began with wins against the Borders and the Ospreys at home, but the calm and ease of Declan Kidney's return to the province was interrupted the following week in Limerick. On the evening of Wednesday, 14 September, after the gates of Thomond Park had been locked for the evening by Munster Branch officials, two hooded men entered the ground over one of the perimeter walls and proceeded to dig about 300 holes in the pristine playing surface. The damage was noticed as soon as the ground was opened later that evening to host the launch of that season's Munster Senior Cup.

Pitch battle: the Celtic League clash with Llanelli was switched to Musgrave Park after vandals desecrated the Thomond Park turf

The Gardai and those involved with Munster rugby were baffled by the incident and nobody could come up with a decent motive for the desecration of one of the city's most famous landmarks. The IRFU's consultant agronomist, Eddie Connaughton, visited the venue the day after the incident but the verdict wasn't all that bad. The turf expert recommended that the pitch would have to be closed until 22 October so as to give time for the repairs to take root, with turf from the in-goal area being used to replace some of the divots dotted throughout the pitch. The closure period meant that just one Celtic League game –

the visit of Llanelli – would have to be switched to Musgrave Park but at least all would be well at the venue by the time Castres came to visit in the Heineken Cup.

Munster won that switched Llannelli game by a single point, although they did suffer a serious blow when it was confirmed that Paul O'Connell would be out of action for up to two months because of a thumb injury picked up during the game. But aside from the loss of their inspirational second row, the province's Heineken Cup build-up was going well, particularly the Celtic League clashes with their Irish neighbours. Connacht were the first to be put to the sword at the Galway Sportsgrounds, with Gary Connolly scoring two tries on his debut in a 44-19 victory, while the following weekend in Cork, the home side were in terrific form as they disposed of a supposedly rejuvenated Leinster, 33-9. Everything was tipping along nicely for Munster's tough pool opener away to Sale two weeks later.

The 3,000 or so Munster fans who managed to get a day off work to nip across to Sale for the province's Heineken Cup clash did so with a fair share of optimism. The Manchester side were top of the Guinness Premiership, sure, and although their coach, Philippe Saint-Andre, had recruited heavily during the summer, most Munster fans felt that Sale were a mere flash in the pan, a typical English team who'd run into a bit of form and now believed they were world-beaters.

However, on the night, Sale proved they were as good as the press had intimated, even if it was primarily down to an extraordinary performance from Sebastien Chabal. Rarely has one player dominated any Heineken Cup match like the French number eight did in Stockport that night. His display over the 80 minutes was something to behold and in many ways it was as though he was cut from Munster cloth. Nothing seemed to deter him – he played like a one-man ball-carrying machine at times. If the number eight wasn't knocking Shaun Payne head over heels in the tackle, he was lifting Federico Pucciariello skywards and setting Jason Robinson on his way for what proved to be the match-winning try. He was the difference between the sides and when he commented after the game that Sale weren't "in this competition for fun", you knew he, at least, wasn't kidding.

Although they eventually lost 27-13, the peculiar thing was that Munster – who had been buoyed by a visit from Roy Keane the previous evening – were in a pretty strong position to win the game after half-time, despite Chabal's influence. They were 13-12 up with 50 minutes on the clock, but then things started to unravel. It all happened off a single scrum, seven metres from their own line. With Frankie Sheahan in the sin bin, Munster were shunted backwards towards the try-line and as the greasy ball squirted loose, scrum-half Tomás O'Leary – who was selected ahead of Peter Stringer – failed to secure possession and his opposite number Sililo Martens pounced to score a critical try. Sale never looked back from there, as Munster struggled in the final half an hour.

"They capitalised on a couple of mistakes and that was the bones of it," said Anthony Foley after the game. "We worked extremely hard to get all of our scores out there but then we went and gave away a couple of soft tries and you can't do that in European rugby. The sin-binning didn't help things either. They have a top pack and it's difficult enough to hold them when it's eight on eight. But eight on seven is near on impossible as we saw. You need to have a full deck when you're playing a team like Sale and I think that point was proven tonight."

However, while the loss was disappointing Ronan O'Gara was reluctant to put this particular game in the same category as Munster's losses at Kingsholm in previous seasons. "This isn't anything like what happened to us in Gloucester," said the out-half. "Yeah, the result puts us under immediate pressure, which is hardly a new experience I suppose, but it was promising for good spells in Sale. The problem was we didn't make the most of them (the scoring chances). At half-time I was fully confident we were going to go on and win the game, and when I kicked the penalty to go 13-9 up early in the second half, we were happy with the way things were going."

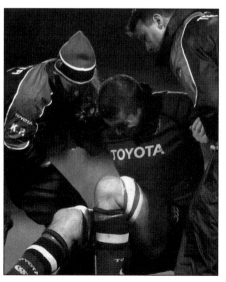

Not again: the luckless Alan Quinlan is helped to his feet after suffering knee ligament damage against Sale

If losing the game wasn't bad enough, Munster also suffered two serious injuries. With 20 minutes to go, Alan Quinlan went down following a challenge on the touchline and the diagnosis was that the luckless flanker would be out of action for at least eight months with knee ligament damage. Then, to compound Kidney's

200

woes, it was confirmed in the days after the game that Frankie Sheahan had damaged his neck in the latter stages of the game and would be out of action for an indefinite period.

Bonus prize: John Kelly goes over for Munster's fourth try against Castres at Thomond Park

But as history has shown, there's nothing like a defeat to get Munster going and poor Castres were given a proper hiding the following weekend at Thomond Park. With Jerry Flannery in for Sheahan at hooker and Denis Leamy switching to number six to allow David Wallace back into the team at open side, the hosts ran riot. Paul Volley was greeted with his now familiar chant from the 'popular side' of the ground but even the English flanker was surprisingly quiet on an evening when the Munster pack ruled supreme. The maul was the home side's weapon of choice – as it had been when the sides met the season before – and within 20 minutes, both Donncha O'Callaghan and Flannery had crossed for tries.

On 25 minutes, Gary Connolly chipped through for Anthony Horgan to secure Munster's third and at that point it was only a matter of figuring out when, and not if, the bonus-point try was going to come. It eventually arrived in the 65th minute thanks to Ronan O'Gara's perfectly-weighted cross-kick for John Kelly to collect on the touchline. And although the visitors bagged a try earlier and had Munster under a bit of pressure, Trevor Halstead put a nice gloss on the score line as he slalomed between two Castres players to give Munster a comfortable 42-16 win. As a statement of intent, this was powerful.

"Had we lost this game, it would have been mathematically very difficult, if not impossible, to even qualify from the group," said Declan Kidney afterwards. "All we have done by winning is to stay alive. The bonus point is helpful, but will only be helpful in the long run if we win our matches. Things have changed in this competition with the bonus-point system. It's more complicated than it was. If I had been offered a choice before this, I would have settled for the win. You can't afford to chase bonus points without first establishing a solid platform for victory."

Ireland's November international series was nothing short of a disaster. With Paul O'Connell and Brian O'Driscoll on the sidelines, Eddie O'Sullivan's side were convincingly beaten by both New Zealand and Australia, while the victory over Romania was secured with close to a full-strength team. The critics rounded on the coach, not the players, after the trio of fixtures passed but the Munster contingent involved in the international squad – which now included Jerry Flannery, who got his first cap against Romania – could hardly have been bursting with confidence on their return to the provincial set-up.

In many ways it showed when Munster travelled to Rodney Parade to play the Dragons. A travelling support of about 3,000 made their way over to Wales for the game and although they must have been cheered by a pretty comprehensive 24-8 victory over the home side, the lack of ambition in Munster's game plan was worrying. It was a strange game. Early on, Mossie Lawlor and Ronan O'Gara opted for and landed drop-goals in front of the Dragons' posts, but on both occasions Munster were on the front foot and a more patient approach would surely have seen them cross for a couple of tries.

That view could be dismissed as mere conjecture but it was given some credence when Denis Leamy bundled his way over for Munster's opening try before the interval after another impressive display of forward power. But the visitors just seemed happy to win the game and to forget about the bonus point, despite the fact that they were in full control and running proceedings. On the hour mark, Marcus Horan wormed his way over for a try following another destructive line-out maul but the all-out assault for tries three and four never happened. It seemed a bizarre way to approach matters, especially in such a tight pool and particularly for a Munster team that had never lacked ambition in any game or at any venue in the past.

"Our one and only aim out there was to win the game," insisted Kidney afterwards. "The Dragons are a quality side and we knew that if we were to succeed out there, we'd have to deny them possession. We did that but even though we were 17-3 ahead at one point, I still felt we didn't have the game sewn up." It was strange because Kidney must have been one of the few people in the ground who doubted Munster's superiority. But at least the Dragons were set to visit Thomond Park the following weekend and all would be put right then. Well, that was the theory, but it didn't turn out anything like that. This time the Welsh side adopted a more direct approach and that shift in tactics caused Munster all sorts of problems.

Late, late show: Jerry Flannery allows the Thomond Park crowd to breathe a sigh of relief after his try against the Newport-Gwent Dragons

With just 10 minutes to go on the clock the Dragons led by a single point and it seemed that Munster's home record was under serious threat. However, Ronan O'Gara landed a penalty to edge the home side in front and in the closing minutes, Jerry Flannery was the last man up from a rolling maul and Thomond Park breathed easily again. Declan Kidney was in defensive mode after the match once more, deciding to praise his side's efforts in difficult circumstances. "How often do golfers go around in 66 or 67?" asked the coach. "Some days, it's 70 or 71. The players are wrecked because of all the effort they've put in. I think there's a danger within the country that we could lose the fun and lose sight of the fact that we always work off small resources. We're looking to compete with the resources the French and English are putting into it. Look at the Sale team now compared with three years ago. They've recruited very well and that obviously had to come from somewhere. We're home-grown, the same as Ulster and Leinster, but I'm not talking negatively because I believe we can win it now as much as any other year."

At lunchtime on New Year's Eve, 14,000 fans packed into the RDS to see Leinster play Munster in the Celtic League. The main attraction was the return of both Brian O'Driscoll and Paul O'Connell to action following spells on the sidelines but after they came through the game virtually unscathed, the main talking points were the

couple of minutes, Marcus Horan, John Hayes and Denis Leamy put in some extraordinary work around the fringes to dampen that particular fire. The donkey work done, Munster started to play. O'Callaghan stole a line-out in Sale territory and with the referee having already signalled a penalty to Munster, they swung the ball wide. O'Gara, Halstead, Murphy and Payne all put the ball through their hands before Ian Dowling dived over at the left-corner flag. O'Gara landed the conversion and the temperature then rose a couple more degrees as Horan and Chris Jones had a conversation with their fists on the floor. Both were sent for a little rest but it worked in Munster's favour, and how.

With Munster in possession inside their own half, O'Gara attempted a dink forward but it was blocked and instead the ball landed in the hands of Barry Murphy. The young centre beat one Sale defender on the run, before turning Daniel Larrachea and Jason Robinson inside out on his way over the try-line. It was magnificent stuff, one of the most memorable tries ever scored in the Heineken Cup at Thomond Park. "I took off initially to chase Ronan's kick and I just got a lucky bounce," Murphy told the press afterwards, as he attempted, without success, to talk down his try. "I was looking to link up with someone initially because I saw two of their lads closing in on me. The lads ran good support lines to take the attention of the defenders away. And I just backed myself to go the whole way."

That gave Munster a barely believable 24-9 lead at the interval and although they struggled to maintain the same pace in the second period, they got the bonus point they so desperately needed when David Wallace squirmed over from close range in the first minute of injury time. It was the first score for either side in the second half but it had come just in the nick of time for Munster. Afterwards, the players attempted to put their emotions into words. "The adrenalin was flowing out there," said Anthony Foley. "Sometimes you're told you can't do certain things and so it's a great feeling when you go and achieve them. They're talking about leaving (Thomond Park) and going somewhere else but, well, I don't know... the atmosphere (here) inspires the players. At the end of the day, it's our families, our friends, the people who live in our towns who come to support us and I don't think any player wants to let them down. It's very close to the heart when we go out there."

Paul O'Connell wondered aloud what it must be like for an opposition player to handle Thomond Park when emotions are high. "It must be very intimidating to run out for your warm-up more than a half hour before a game starts and see the stand full," he said. "You wonder what these people are thinking. When a big hit comes in, all the boys tap each other on the back and then you hear the crowd roaring and getting even more behind you and you want to do it for them as well as yourself."

For Jerry Flannery, a player who'd added so much to the team since taking over from Frankie Sheahan back in October, the real motivation was attempting to beat a team that had been praised to the high heavens by everybody who'd seen them. "We were always aware that Sky Sports build players up in the Premiership so much," explained the hooker. "It's not like we were going, 'these guys are shit', we knew they were really, really good but there was no reason to fear them. If you believe all the hype about players you can go out onto the field and go into your shell. We knew they were good and we respected their strengths, we didn't underestimate them, but we knew what our own scrum and line-out could do. I was just mad keen to get out there. If people build these guys up so much, I just want to have a cut off them and show them what we can do."

Munster had reduced Sale from the most talked about team in Britain to yet another Thomond Park victim and the transformation since that Celtic League game against Leinster was truly remarkable. Munster were a changed side with a new-found confidence and everybody was looking forward to the quarter-finals with an optimism that few would have thought possible before Christmas.

It was ironic, given the way things worked out, that it was left to Leinster to earn Munster their home quarter-final. The day after the province's monumental performance against Sale, their neighbours travelled to the Recreation Ground needing to beat Bath and deny the home side a bonus point in order for Munster to get a home quarter-final and although it was a tough ask, they did exactly that with was only half the story. In between O'Gara's penalties, Bourret had missed two simple kicks from right in the front of the posts, while a break involving Ovidiu Tonita and Julien Laharrague almost saw the busy winger sneak over for a second try. But 19-10 was good enough for Munster and they left the field more relieved than happy at reaching their sixth Heineken Cup semi-final.

"It was always going to be a battle," John Kelly said afterwards, "and much of that was due to Perpignan's approach. They carried the ball very well. All credit to them, they went nine points behind but they never stopped coming at us. This idea of French teams lying down when they go behind is gone. Perpignan are the perfect example of that. They kept at us for 80 minutes and we never felt safe."

Discipline had also played a key part in Munster's success. Over the course of the 80 minutes Perpignan had Nicolas Mas and Nicolas Durand sin-binned for silly infringements, while Munster, for the most part, had kept their bibs clean. "Our discipline held out, that was where it was won," said Marcus Horan after the game. "The penalties were a big thing. We seemed to get ours and put them over. Our discipline was superb. It's important against a team like this that you keep your head and stay focused because it can get frustrating out there. There were a lot of rucks spoiled and moves that broke down because of their indiscipline. The referee did

Flight path: *Paul O'Connell powers over for Munster's only try against Perpignan to set up a mouth-watering semi-final clash with Leinster*

well, he gave us the penalties. We'd prefer to finish them off over the try-line, rather than having to take the kicks, but you've got to take them when you get them."

Their performance wasn't anything like as spectacular as Leinster's had been in France but Munster had still ground out a victory playing somewhere below their best and that was good enough. Even more impressive was the manner with which they dealt with the death of one of their former teammates, Conrad O'Sullivan, who had passed away a couple of weeks before the game. There was a minute's silence in memory of the Cork Constitution out-half before the kick-off and the tears that rolled down a number of the players' cheeks showed the esteem they had held him in. How those players kept their emotions in check during the game is anyone's guess but it's to their great credit that they were able to do so. The victory was a fitting tribute to their former comrade.

The build-up to the all-Irish Heineken Cup semi-final was unique. Rarely has a single game in any code, even an All Ireland football or hurling final, received such media attention. Every old cliché was being dragged out for the occasion but while most were hyperbole of the highest order, there was one that summed the game up nicely. The semi-final was a perfect example of irresistible force meeting immovable object.

Along with the pre-match banter – of which there was plenty – the one activity that united both sets of supporters was the search for tickets. Although the allocation was split evenly between Munster and Leinster, nobody really expected Lansdowne Road to be an equal divide of red and blue on the afternoon of 23 April. Munster fans had become experts at sourcing tickets for big games and that wasn't going to change even if they were going head-to-head with their brothers from Leinster.

Declan Kidney, though, had more pressing matters to deal with. Marcus Horan had pulled a calf muscle in training the week following the Perpignan game and was out of the semi-final. Meanwhile, Ronan O'Gara would have to play despite spending a week in hospital on a drip after a cut he received during the Perpignan match had become infected. Then there was the outside-centre conundrum. Tomás O'Leary had done a half-decent job in the position against Perpignan but John Kelly had played there in the Celtic League games against the Dragons and Edinburgh and the more experienced campaigner was selected in the number 13 shirt.

Munster travelled up on the train the morning before the game, basing themselves at the Radisson SAS on the Stillorgan Road, Ireland's favoured spot before a Lansdowne Road game and a location far enough away from the city centre to cut the players off from the hype. They trained at Lansdowne Road in the afternoon and it was then the worries about Peter Stringer began to surface. The scrum-half was struggling with a pinched nerve in his back but bizarrely Declan Kidney came out and told the media later that day that his number nine might have a bit of bother making the game because of a "bang on the leg". Why the Munster coach felt the need to make up a completely new injury is anyone's guess but it was probably just a start to the mind games that would be played out over the following 24 hours, the kind of cuteness that ensured Munster would inhabit the home dressing room despite the fact Leinster had fully expected to occupy it in the days leading up to the game.

After an early night, the forwards practised their line-outs on the lawns of the hotel and after an 11.30am lunch and a 10-minute team meeting at 1.15pm, Munster boarded the team bus and made their way to Lansdowne Road. Along the route they were greeted by a vista that was reminiscent of that which preceded the semi-final clash with Wasps. Red was the colour of the day, and while there was a fair Leinster representation about the place, the feeling on the team bus was that the support was three to one in their favour. It made an awful lot of difference. Inside the ground, the ratio was something similar and Munster warmed up in front of the East Terrace, or Thomond Park as it appeared to resemble. And lo and behold, Kidney didn't pull Stringer as the scrum-half was declared fit after coming through the warm-up and everything was set for the game half the country had been talking about for three weeks.

There are some rugby observers who believe they can predict the outcome of a game from the very first play and when Malcolm O'Kelly knocked on Ronan O'Gara's drop-off, those mystics felt that the game was Munster's for the taking. How right they were. O'Gara, showing no after-effects of his spell in hospital, kicked Munster in front minutes after O'Kelly's mishap. Before the 10-minute mark, Denis Leamy was credited with a try after Munster had kicked a penalty for the corner and mauled the Leinster pack over the whitewash from the resulting line-out. With Felipe Contepomi struggling to reach anything close to his brilliant best on the day, O'Gara was in complete control of the game and before half-time, the Munster out-half kicked two more penalties to give his side a 16-3 interval lead.

Maul time: *Denis Leamy shunts his way over the Leinster try-line to put Munster in the driving seat*

Rob Henderson had replaced the injured John Kelly at outside centre earlier but within 26 minutes of the second period, Tomás O'Leary was on in his place after the former Lion was forced off with an ankle problem. The number 13 shirt was certainly living up to its unlucky tag. Contepomi kicked Leinster to within 10 points with 11 minutes to go and had Michael Cheika's side scored next, it would have made for an interesting finale. Instead, Munster kept control and O'Gara's brush-off of O'Kelly saw the number 10 saunter to the line for the try that secured the victory. The out-half jumped the hoardings to celebrate with the Munster fans on the south terrace and before the end Trevor Halstead, who'd had a superb game, intercepted a Guy Easterby pass to stroll half the length of the field to apply the icing to the cake. The masses in red on the terraces were in dreamland. They'd felt their side were capable of beating Leinster but not even in their wildest dreams would they have predicted a 24-point victory.

Predictably, there was an awful lot of emotion about the place after the game, particularly from the victorious players. Chief amongst them was Ronan O'Gara, whose leap over the advertising hoarding to greet the Munster fans after his try was one of day's most indelible images. "There was a really intense build-up to the game," he said with his voice wavering slightly. "I definitely felt the pressure, I didn't enjoy the build-up one bit. This morning was horrible. The last 24 hours were horrific, I didn't sleep, just this morning. I didn't eat much and you're just kind of wondering why you do this job. I am kind of saying to myself, 'I should be enjoying this', but I don't enjoy it all. I felt I had a point to prove. I've played Felipe Contepomi plenty of times and I suppose the one time he got on top of me was in the RDS at Christmas and that kind of hurt. So I had a point to prove. I'd heard a lot about him in the build-up so I was keen to show what I was made of. I think it's important that you do your talking on the pitch."

While obviously delighted with the victory, Paul O'Connell, like O'Gara, was a little choked up by it all. His greatest concern after the match – a clear indication of the man's character – was for his Irish colleagues at Leinster and how they would be feeling. "There are guys there on the Leinster team I would have died for a couple of months ago and they would have done the same for us," said the second row. "It's a great win for us and I can understand their predicament. It's going to be a tough couple of weeks for them. It's bragging rights for us but I don't think you saw any of us jumping around the field at the end of the game. We knew we're going to have to play them next year when they're sore. It's like they were in the RDS, gracious. There is a very good, healthy respect between the teams and that showed."

O'Connell's stance was completely understandable but Anthony Foley spoke the words that most Munster fans would have identified with in the immediate aftermath of the victory over their great rivals. "It's great for us country people to come up here and get a result," said the captain, with a grin. "To come up here on such a massive occasion and do what we did does a lot for the game of rugby in Ireland and it does

A game of two halves: while Leinster's Felipe Contepomi wilted in the red-hot atmosphere of Lansdowne Road, Ronan O'Gara excelled. 'I'd heard a lot about him (Contepomi) in the build-up so I was keen to show what I was made of,' the Cork man said after the match. 'I think it's important that you do your talking on the pitch'

Three and easy: *the ratio of Munster fans to Leinster fans on the day of the Heineken Cup semi-final was estimated at three to one.* **Pic courtesy: Liam Kidney**

a lot for Munster people living in Dublin. We're very conscious of the fact that people live their lives through the team and we try to do the best for them as well."

Then, with all the talking nearly done, O'Connell set the tone for his teammates for the weeks before the final. "It's never your season, it's no one's destiny to win it. You need a bit of luck and you need to be the best team in the competition. You need to play for 80 minutes in every game. We're through to the final now, it's a great chance to win it. But it's no one's destiny, it's the best team on the day in the final and producing the goods, with a little bit of luck maybe as well."

And with that they pointed themselves in the direction of home, downing a few pints at O'Neill's Hotel beside Heuston Station before boarding the 9.30pm train to Limerick Junction and then onwards to Cork, Limerick, Kerry or wherever. And just as Paul O'Connell had promised in his post-match TV interview, there were a few more drinks in Jerry Flannery's pub on the corner of Catherine Street in Limerick for those who wanted a truly memorable day to last a little longer.

Kings of the castle:
Rob Henderson and
Marcus Horan show
off Munster's new
arrival as they pass
King John's Castle
in Limerick

CHAPTER 13

MISSION ACCOMPLISHED

20 MAY, 2006

Declan Kidney must have perused his calendar ad infinitum in the days after the Leinster victory. Biarritz had come through their semi-final against Bath in a comfortable fashion and with four weeks to go to the final, the Munster coach needed to draw up a battle plan. His cause was helped in a way by the Celtic League schedulers. After their game against the Borders at Netherdale on 28 April, Munster would play the Ospreys in Wales on 5 May and thanks to the logic of the fixtures men, a postponed game against Llanelli was slotted in for Tuesday, 9 May. That gave Kidney the perfect opportunity to arrange a mini-camp in Wales at a vital time in Munster's preparations, a time that allowed the squad to get some work done away from all the pre-match frenzy that was building back home. Not only that, on completion of the Llanelli fixture Munster would have a full 11 days without a game in the run-up to the final in Cardiff. Things were working out nicely.

But there were a couple of important selection issues to be ironed out in those three Celtic League games. John Kelly's shoulder injury and Rob Henderson's ankle problem, both of which were picked up in the Leinster game, were considered serious enough to put the pair in doubt for the final and just in case they were ruled out, Kidney needed to come up with a back-up plan.

In the first game against the Borders, Mike Mullins started at 13 but he looked slightly off the pace. However, Jeremy Manning made a decent fist of the position when he was introduced during the second half. Munster won the game 41-25, scoring five tries in the process and there was another boost for Kidney with the performance of Christian Cullen at full-back. Now back to something close to full

conservative following their knockout victories over Sale and Bath. With the varied talents of Imanol Harinordoquy, Serge Betsen, Petru Balan, Dimitri Yachvili, Damien Traille, Nicolas Brusque and Sereli Bobo in their ranks, most casual rugby observers would have expected Biarritz to be an all-singing, all-dancing French outfit, one which wouldn't be afraid to take risks on the park. But that wasn't the case.

Against both Sale and Bath in San Sebastian, Biarritz worked themselves into a commanding position early on but then shut up shop and trusted their excellent defence to see them through. Certainly, the trick worked on both occasions but the critics were fuming that such a talented side opted for caution rather than invention. They were a team, to turn the phrase on its head, that somehow appeared to be less than the sum of their parts.

On the back of such criticism, Biarritz captain Thomas Lievremont promised a more positive approach from the Basques in the final. "If we want to beat Munster, there's no way we can play the same way as against Bath and Sale," said the number eight. "We have to offer a lot more, we have to be more ambitious with the ball in hand and if we are limited, uptight and defensive, we won't win. We've proved we're defensively strong, but we failed to show anything in attack. We haven't played a complete game all season long and we really do need one against Munster."

But Lievremont's words had a hollow ring to them. Biarritz had played perfect knockout rugby and in a competition like the Heineken Cup, winning was the only thing that mattered, not tries, not style, not entertainment, just scoring more points than the opposition. The fact of the matter was that the Basques were now in the final and if anything, their approach was going to get even more cautious. There was far too much at stake to start throwing the ball around now.

In the days leading up to the decider, Declan Kidney, as always, kept his cards surgically attached to his chest. The only bit of news coming out of the camp was that Christian Cullen was definitely out for the final, his injury hex striking once more. The team wasn't revealed until 24 hours before kick-off when Kidney appeared at a pre-match press conference at the Millennium Stadium. The good news for the tens of thousands of Munster fans making their way across the Irish Sea was that all the walking wounded had made it. Marcus Horan was back in the front row,

Paul O'Connell had shaken off his ankle problem to take his place in the starting XV, as had Jerry Flannery. Meanwhile, John Kelly had sufficiently recovered from his shoulder injury to be named at outside centre. All four were bound to be a bit rusty but their presence in the team was a huge psychological boost.

The other positive news was that Alan Quinlan had been named on the bench for the final. The flanker had put his head down after suffering the knee ligament injury back in October against Sale and amazingly worked his way back to full fitness by the start of May. Quinlan got some much-needed game time under his belt as a substitute in the Celtic League fixtures against the Ospreys and Llanelli, while the Tipp man also made an impressive cameo in Shannon's All-Ireland League final victory over Clontarf at Lansdowne Road. For a guy who'd been involved with Munster since they first started making the headlines in Europe, it was fitting that he had made it back in time for the province's third Heineken Cup final.

The name of Anthony Horgan in the starting line-up was also welcome. The winger's form had dipped alarmingly around Christmas – after he was chased and tackled from behind by All Black second row Jason Eaton at Lansdowne Road – and he had only really made it into the starting line-up against Leinster because of Munster's problems in the centre. In a revealing interview in the Irish edition of 'The Sunday Times', Horgan explained how difficult it was to watch the quarter-final against Perpignan from the stands, having been on the pitch for so many of the province's big games. "You know those Paddy Power booths out the back of the West Stand, with the television monitors? I watched it there," he explained. "Said I was going to the toilet – went out there and watched it on my own… It just felt wrong to be watching it from the stand, having been out there (on the field) for the last seven or eight years. I never knew it would feel that hard. I don't think I'll do it again til I'm retired. It really hit home, how much it means to be out there."

Back with a bang: Anthony Horgan returned to Munster's starting line-up for the latter stages of the Heineken Cup

It was also nice to see Horgan in the starting line-up because of the manner in which he'd been ruled out of Munster's previous Heineken Cup final in Cardiff. "The Vale of Glamorgan Hotel at 6pm on a Thursday evening – it's crystal clear in my mind. Backs v forwards in a game of tip and we'd managed to win again. What the winners then did was to clap the losers through with a few kicks and smacks as they went. My hand whacked off Claw's and it felt like nothing but I'd soon trouble making a fist. We got it x-rayed and I'd broken two bones across my hand. I wasn't best pleased."

This time around, the only drama in the Munster camp was when Paul O'Connell suffered a slight strain to his neck while practising line-outs on the morning of the game, but he'd be able to take the field. This game was just too important to miss.

———————◗◖———————

As the Munster masses rolled into Cardiff from all sorts of odd places across South Wales and the south-west of England, there was a strange sort of atmosphere in the city. Your average Irish sporting weekend usually involves waking up with a crushing hangover the morning of the game, followed by a desperate search for something greasy to settle the stomach and then a visit to a pub in the environs of the stadium to get the hair of the dog. But while there were those who undoubtedly followed that formula to the letter, an awful lot more were too nervous to stick to their tried and trusted pre-match routine on that fateful day in May. And thus, a visit to the pubs around the Millennium Stadium a couple of hours before kick-off was an unusual experience. Instead of the expected singing, roaring and shouting, there was muted chatter as supporters gathered in groups and assessed Munster's chances.

For most of the chatterers, it had been a bit of a chore both getting a ticket and getting to Cardiff. The city's tiny airport wasn't able to cope with the numbers coming from Ireland and many charter flights had to be directed towards Bristol, Birmingham or London. The search for accommodation anywhere within 60 miles of Cardiff proved an even greater challenge. And then there was the problem of match tickets. Before anybody knew who was even going to be in the final, the ERC had sold somewhere in the region of 50,000 tickets over the internet, and while a good portion of these had been snapped up by Munster fans, it still hadn't sated everybody's appetite. Once the province's clubs, and the Munster Supporters Club, had distributed their allocations, the only place left for those without tickets was the black market or the internet. Online auction company Ebay could have set up a mini-site such was the demand for tickets and although many paid anything between five and ten times' the face value, there was very few moaning about it. The supporters were determined to make the final and they knew that the players appreciated the effort they made to get there.

"We're all fully aware of the sacrifices the fans have made to come watch us over the years," said Donncha O'Callaghan a couple of days before the final. "We know how much people are paying to come on this trip, and I sometimes feel they are being taken advantage of by travel agents and hotels. But they're making a huge effort, they're scrambling for tickets and we know how hard they have to work to come across the type of money they're paying out. From that perspective, we don't want to let these people down. Our supporters are part of the team. I think they know that, they're very special to us."

But if the supporters were part of the team, then they were also every bit as nervous as them. As the clock ticked towards kick-off, the tension was palpable. 'The Fields of Athenry' was given a few pre-match airings but there was little bite or passion in the early anaemic renditions. There were just too many questions to be answered. Would Biarritz be up for the battle? Would Munster freeze on the day? How would John Kelly cope in the centre? Was Paul O'Connell fully fit? Could this team ever bounce back if the worst came to worst and they lost a third Heineken Cup final?

Munster lost the toss and received the kick-off, not something they usually enjoyed doing. "You come out of the dressing room hopping mad and all you've to do is chase and smash in," said Jerry Flannery. "You're on the front foot immediately."

Instead Biarritz were the ones with the early initiative and they turned the screw immediately. The stadium clock was halfway towards the third minute when Philippe Bidabe bounced off John Kelly and released Sereli Bobo down the left for his flirtation with the touchline that, fortunately for Biarritz, touch judge Dave Pearson didn't appear to see. There were boos when the Munster crowd saw that Bobo's left foot, and arguably his right foot as well, had touched the whitewash but Anthony Foley summed up Munster's emotions after that setback on RTE Radio later. "You look at the crowd when they scored their first try and the video screen came up and the boos came out," said the Munster captain. "And the boos came out a second time. Imagine if you were a referee how you would have felt. I said to myself, if there was a 50/50 decision later on in the game we were going to get it… we knew that if push came to shove, we had a decision in our pocket."

But instead of waiting for that decision, Munster took the initiative. Kelly came back to the huddle under the posts and told his teammates that his missed tackle on Bidabe would not be repeated. His word was gospel. Foley's input was simple, when Munster got possession they had to keep it, while Paul O'Connell urged his colleagues to take a quick glance up while they were aligning defensively. You might have imagined there would have been a bit of effing and blinding having conceded a try so early, but no, it was all cool and calm stuff.

Their trusty maul earned them a foothold in the game and after Biarritz had dragged it down illegally, Ronan O'Gara landed a penalty to put Munster on the scoreboard. So far, so good. Then came the ambition, the type that had been lacking earlier in the season, particularly before Christmas. Munster declined an almost certain three

Doing it for kicks: Ronan O'Gara slotted over three penalties and two conversions in the final

Just reward: *Trevor Halstead turns to celebrate his try with players and supporters*

points from a penalty, deciding to kick for the corner instead, and although it took them a couple of phases to earn their reward, they eventually got it. O'Gara chipped a ball over the Biarritz defence from inside his own half and Jerry Flannery and Paul O'Connell were on hand to carry Munster forward. Denis Leamy and David Wallace then had a go as Munster shifted the ball left and with all the French side's forwards buried somewhere on the turf, O'Gara released Halstead on his left and the South African batted aside two defenders on his way over the line.

O'Gara added the convert to put Munster 10-7 in front and although Dimitri Yachvili levelled things up with a penalty, the Irish province's new-found penchant for taking risks was rewarded once more. After O'Gara put another kickable penalty to touch on the right-hand side, O'Connell collected the line-out, O'Callaghan and Leamy had a go around the fringes and with the ball made unplayable, Munster got the put-in to the resultant scrum. Then came Peter Stinger's magic. Criticised for lacking a break in his game since he was probably still in the pram, the scrum-half noticed Sereli Bobo creeping off his wing and in the blink of an eye, he darted right

Pulling a fast one: Peter Stringer outfoxes the Biarritz defence to score his crucial try. **Pic courtesy: Liam Kidney**

around the scrum and dived over the line without a finger being laid on him. "It was just a lack of communication," said Yachvili afterwards. "I don't know what happened. I couldn't believe it when I saw Stringer running around the side. It is something you never see in rugby." Seventy-four thousand spectators in the Millennium Stadium couldn't believe it either and Munster took a seven-point lead into the interval. But would it be enough?

Just seconds into the second period, Shaun Payne turned over Damien Traille in the tackle and Munster were awarded a penalty which O'Gara converted. They were now 10 points up and every red-shirted fan in Cardiff began to believe. And maybe that was the problem in the final 38 minutes. The nervousness in the stands transferred itself to the pitch and Munster started making mistakes, two of which Yachvili punished with successful penalties. The gap was down to four points with 20 minutes left.

Then came a moment that would go down in Munster rugby lore. With 60 minutes and 55 seconds remaining, referee Chris White stopped the clock for a Biarritz injury. A lot of the Munster players, particularly those just back from a spell on the sidelines, were dead on their feet. While they were recovering, an image appeared on the big screen. It took a couple of seconds for people to recognise that it was a shot of thousands of Munster fans watching the game on O'Connell Street in Limerick, but as soon as the image registered with the crowd in the Millennium Stadium, a huge roar worked it's way around the venue.

"I spotted that they were reacting to each other," said Sky Sports' executive director Martin Turner, "that the crowd in the stadium were reacting to the crowd in Limerick. I stayed on it for longer than a usual shot. It seemed like a magnificent moment. I've never seen something like that ever before."

Only those deprived of their senses could have failed to be touched by the moment and the players certainly noticed it. "We saw it and pointed it out to each other," said Paul O'Connell afterwards of the street that many young people in Limerick think is actually named after him. "It inspired us, there's no doubt about that. It was a big moment." Ronan O'Gara agreed. "At that point in the game, it was crucial. These things can be a distraction at times but not this particular shot."

Having been spiritually refuelled, Munster began to cut out the errors that had hampered their game, although Yachvili did narrow the gap to just a single point with a penalty four minutes from the end of normal time. Fortunately, before anybody could ponder Munster's slender advantage, Olivier Olibeau came in the side of ruck inside the Biarritz half and O'Gara kept his cool to knock the resulting penalty between the sticks. The gap was four points again.

As the crowd rose to their feet for the remaining minutes, there was one last scare. Trevor Halstead knocked the ball on in midfield and the Biarritz backline aligned itself menacingly. They went left first to set up a ruck and when the ball was swung back right, Bidabe put Nicolas Brusque through a gap and for the briefest moment it appeared that the French centre was away. But it was a mere trick of the eye, Brusque was wrapped up by John Kelly in the tackle and that was more or less that.

Penalty king: Dimitri Yachvili sets up another Biarritz attack

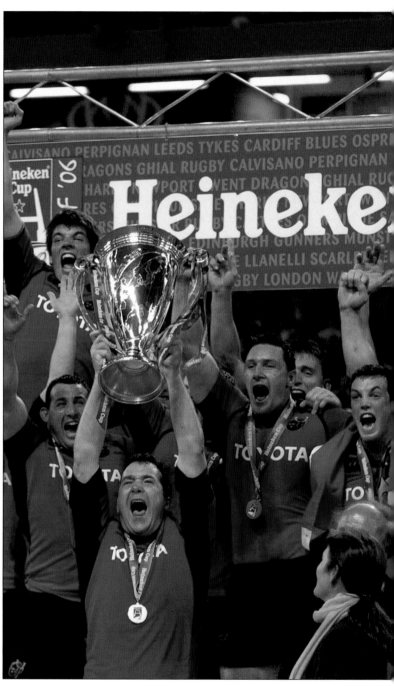

Pic courtesy: Liam Kidney

The one they'd all been waiting for: *after Anthony Foley lifts the Heineken Cup, (clockwise from bottom left) Peter Stringer, Ronan O'Gara, Ian Dowling and Donncha O'Callaghan celebrate their day of days at the Millennium Stadium*

Biarritz ran into each other at the breakdown, Munster were awarded a scrum and Peter Stringer lashed the ball high into the stands. Game over. Munster had won the Heineken Cup. A wave of relief, followed by unbridled elation swept over the Munster hordes in the stands – after so many near-misses, they had finally done it.

Later, the Munster captain attempted to put the enormity of the win into words. It was no mean feat. "When Biarritz were coming back at us, our support kept backing us," said Foley. "They never got on our backs. When you go to an opposition ground, you try and silence the crowd but here, our crowd wouldn't be silenced. People say they're our 16th man and maybe they are. At times out there, it's just awesome to look up and see the amount of red that's around the ground for us. I think they see something in us they can relate to. Because over the years – not alone this year but since 1999 – they've followed us far and wide across Europe. They've put their hands in their pockets and spent their own hard-earned cash just to see us. It's great now that we can finally bring home some silverware. It's for them just as much as it's for us. We all just feel like one, that's the big thing about this team."

But if Munster's search for European glory had finally been realised, Foley was quick to point out that the win was a new beginning rather than an end. "What we achieved here today is magnificent. It's been a journey and that journey isn't over. I think we can kick on from here and we can be competing for this trophy for a number of years to come."

After the official function at the stadium, the Munster party headed to St Andrew's Golf Club near Barry, before departing on their late-night charter flight to Shannon. It was past midnight by the time they sang a few songs with the thousand or so supporters who'd made their way to the airport to welcome them home, and from there the party continued into the early hours of the morning at a function room at the Clarion Hotel in Limerick City. Most were exhausted but as Jerry Flannery put it, "How could you go to bed early on a night like that?"

Over the following few days the celebrations continued. On Sunday, they paraded around Limerick on an open-top bus, while two days later it was Cork's turn to acclaim their European champions on the city's South Mall. In between, and for a few days afterwards, the cup was brought to schools, clubs and pubs around the province. By the end of the week it must have been the most touched relic in Ireland.

Delayed no longer: *Declan Kidney and Anthony Foley arrive at Shannon Airport with the Heineken Cup*

But while most of the celebrations passed in a blur, there were some memories that will remain. The impromptu game of rugby outside the Millennium Stadium about an hour or so after the final whistle will never be forgotten by those who watched or participated in the melee. The scene was wild but good humoured, as was the meeting of touch judge Dave Pearson with a few Munster fans on Westgate Street by the stadium after the game. Pearson was the man who thought the Biarritz winger Sereli Bobo was capable of levitating. "You see that line there," one gent said while pointing at the road markings on the street outside the stadium. "He actually clipped that line on his way over the line, never mind the whitewash on the pitch." Pearson gave his best embarrassed laugh. What else could he do?

Peter Clohessy also got a cameo role in the day's drama. The prop had been called on to do a lap of honour with the team after the game but a guy with a bit of power, an illuminous yellow jacket and probably no rugby knowledge whatsoever was standing in his way. Clohessy's remonstrations weren't working but just as he was

Home are the heroes: *the Munster team bus snakes its way through the thronged Limerick streets*

considering another approach, Sky presenter Dewi Morris slipped him his TV pass and the Young Munster man joined his former comrades on the field.

The craic continued on the rain-soaked stage in Limerick's O'Connell Street the day after the final. Having cruised around town parading the Heineken Cup, the Munster players were in high spirits when they arrived back in the city centre for a live TV broadcast from the celebrations. Marty Morrissey was the first target of their antics, a few of the forwards grabbing hold of the RTE commentator and foisting him high in the air as though he was a trophy himself. They then turned on the unfortunate Peter Stringer. The scrum-half had performed brilliantly the previous day but that didn't save him from a bout of very public slagging. "It was a special move we have called Braveheart," Ronan O'Gara told Limerick 95 FM's Len Dineen of Stringer's vital try. "It's because he's so brave and he has such a big heart," O'Gara added, to the obvious delight of his teammates. The gullible swallowed the yarn but the mischievous glint in O'Gara's eyes told the real story and summed up the spirit within the squad.

It was a typical Munster moment. On more occasions than can be accurately tracked over the past 11 years, successive Munster squads have told the media how much it means to them to be playing rugby, and being successful at it, with their best friends. There's no greater feeling in the world, they've said many times over, and while nobody would ever have doubted the sincerity, here was their comradeship on stage, and on national television, for all to see.

"We've always had a great team spirit within the squad," says Mick Galwey, "and that's stood to us over the years in difficult situations. After the final it was great to see how the lads who were playing on the day treated the fellas who'd hung up their boots. Myself and other former players were made feel involved in the whole celebrations, as though we'd played against Biarritz ourselves. This Munster thing didn't just happen this year, it happened over 11 years and every player will admit that. We had to learn the hard experiences first – how to lose finals, how to finally win away from home, how to come out the right side of tight games. Before this year, I always felt I was part of a great team that never won the Heineken Cup. Now I feel I'm part of a great team that won the Heineken Cup."

Galwey, and each of the 99 players who pulled on that red shirt over the course of Munster's 11-year Heineken Cup odyssey.

Field of dreams:
a revamped
26,000-capacity
Thomond Park is
due for completion
in August 2008

GROUNDS FOR HOPE

Seven days after those magnificent scenes in Cardiff, Munster's week of celebrations finally came to a close at Thomond Park. Aptly enough, Cardiff Blues were the visitors for a Celtic League match that was more about the occasion than the action. The Heineken Cup trophy was on display before the game and it seemed as though half the crowd were intent on having their pictures taken with the cherished piece of silverware. And it was no small crowd. By the time the game kicked off, 13,500 had packed into the ground to set a new home record for a Celtic League fixture. Barely a week after being crowned champions of Europe, the knock-on effects were already plain to see for all associated with rugby in the province.

It is difficult to believe that a little more than a decade earlier, just a handful of journalists and Munster Branch officials ventured to the south of France for the province's first away Heineken Cup fixture against Castres. So much has changed in the interim. The easy-going approach which characterised the opening years of the European Cup is now the stuff of rugby lore. In contrast, the attitude and attention to detail in the modern game is clinical and professional, as is necessary for the provincial side to be competitive. However, to their credit, Munster have maintained a passion and a pride that is all too rare in professional sport. They may be highly-paid sportsmen but they have not strayed too far from their roots and have managed to maintain that common touch. Their secret agent is bond. Not since the heady days of Jack's Army in Italia '90 have a team captured the hearts of Ireland's sporting public to such an extent. It's no exaggeration to state that Kidney's charges have become the sports darlings of the nation. The courage, honesty and modesty of the players, and the relationship that exists between the team and supporters, has created a dynamic around Munster that is special.

It is also a phenomenon that is highly marketable. Indeed, it could reasonably be argued that Munster are now the biggest sports brand in the country. Walk down any street in any town south of a line from Dublin to Galway and somebody attired in the famous red shirt is sure to stroll past. And it's not just in this country. "I couldn't walk down the street in Sydney without somebody in a Munster shirt shouting, 'Hey Alan' at me," says former coach Alan Gaffney. Mick Galwey tells a similar tale. "I've been in America and South Africa since Munster won the Heineken Cup and I've spotted an awful lot of red jerseys in both locations," says the former captain. "It has to be the most famous rugby jersey in the world at this stage." And the most profitable, by all accounts.

Having won the Heineken Cup, Munster are now in a position to reap a rich harvest from their popularity. A genuine 'cash cow' has wandered into the Munster Branch's byre, and while the loot isn't flowing freely yet, the redevelopment of Thomond Park should help things along. Ironically, the evening before that Cardiff Blues match, in a fantastic piece of timing, the Branch unveiled their plans for their new 26,000-capacity stadium at the Clarion Hotel in Limerick. While the existing terracing at the ends of the ground will remain, two banana-shaped stands on either side of the pitch will provide seating for 15,000. Despite the makeover, the stadium is unlikely to lose its famed ferocity as the stands and terraces will still be within touching distance of the pitch. The wrecking ball is due to arrive, planning issues permitting, by early 2007, and the work is scheduled to be finished by August 2008. All going well, the best team in Europe will then have one of the most impressive club rugby venues in Britain or Ireland to call its very own.

The redevelopment is a brave move but it's probably just as well that the Branch are moving ahead with the project given the number of new members that the Munster Supporters Club signed up since Cardiff. At the start of the 2005/06 season, the club had 2,000 full members and 4,000 associate members but having opened the associate membership doors for a single month during the summer of 2006, an additional 5,000 joined. The indications for the future are also good. One of the most striking aspects of the scene around the Millennium Stadium on the day of the Heineken Cup final was the number of young children in attendance. The next generation is already hooked – especially in Tipperary, the fastest-growing rugby county on the island – and it's crucial that that interest is developed.

But if the financials appear sound, then the on-field operations are also in fine fettle. There weren't many additions to the playing staff in the aftermath of the final but that's mainly because Declan Kidney and his backroom team had so much faith in the batch of talented youngsters at their disposal. A couple of years back, particularly after the defeats to Wasps and Biarritz in the knockout stages, there was a worry that the whole Munster bandwagon would grind to a halt because so few new players were coming through. Now, though, there are a string of young hopefuls on the panel who are capable of making the step up to top-grade rugby. Barry Murphy, Ian Dowling, Jeremy Manning and Tomás O'Leary have already challenged successfully for places in the starting XV and there are a host of other youngsters working their way through the province's academy who are more than capable of making the breakthrough.

The likes of Donnacha Ryan, a second row from Shannon who played a lot of rugby at number eight with his club last year, and his teammate Sean Cronin, a hooker who made quite an impression in the All-Ireland League final of 2006, are fine prospects. But it's not just forwards that are coming through. Seasoned observers of the game maintain that Keith Earls, the bustling former St Munchin's College centre, and Denis Hurley, the young full-back from UCC, both have what it takes to make it at the highest level. These lads will have the added bonus of coming into a panel with vast experience and huge ambition, an environment which can only help to develop their talents.

All in all, the foundation stones for success in the short- to medium-term are ready and waiting to be built upon. The next chapter in Munster's history has the potential to be even more exciting and entertaining than those that have gone before.

Young at heart: Jeremy Manning is just one of a string of youngsters vying for a starting role in the Munster XV

HEINEKEN CUP WINNERS

Season	Winner	Result		Venue	Attendance
2005/06	Munster	Munster	23	Millennium Stadium	74,482
		Biarritz Olympique	19		
2004/05	Toulouse	Toulouse	18	Murrayfield	51,326
		Stade Francais	12		
2003/04	London Wasps	Wasps	27	Twickenham	73,057
		Toulouse	20		
2002/03	Toulouse	Toulouse	22	Lansdowne Road	28,600
		Perpignan	17		
2001/02	Leicester	Leicester	15	Millennium Stadium	74,000
		Munster	9		
2000/01	Leicester	Leicester	34	Parc de Princes	44,000
		Stade Francais	30		
1999/2000	Northampton	Northampton	9	Twickenham	68,441
		Munster	8		
1998/99	Ulster	Ulster	21	Lansdowne Road	49,000
		Colomiers	6		
1997/98	Bath	Bath	19	Stade Lescure	36,500
		Brive	18		
1996/97	Brive	Brive	28	Cardiff Arms Park	41,664
		Leicester	9		
1995/96	Toulouse	Toulouse	21	Cardiff Arms Park	21,800
		Cardiff	18		

MUNSTER'S HEINEKEN CUP STATISTICS

Muraro, A Giacon, S Stocco, R Saetti, R Piovan, M Birtig
Subs E Cameran for Giacon (56)
Scorers R Salvan (1 try), K Rolleston (2 pen, 1 cons)

Saturday, 26 September, 1998
MUNSTER 34 – 10 NEATH

MUNSTER B Roche; J Kelly, M Lynch, C Mahoney,
A Horgan; B Everitt, B O'Meara; P Clohessy, M McDermott,
J Hayes, M Galwey (capt), M O'Driscoll, A Foley, A Quinlan,
E Halvey
Subs D Wallace for O'Driscoll (63), I Murray for Hayes (71),
D. Corkery for Foley (72)
Scorers M Galwey (2 tries), M Lynch (1 try), A Quinlan
(1 try), B Everitt (1 con), M Lynch (4 pens)

NEATH G Evans; D Tiueti, J Corderley, T Davies, I Wyn
Jones; M McCarthy, P Horgan (capt); L Gerrard, M Davies,
M Morgan, M Turner, A Jackson, S Martin, B Sinkinson,
R Jones
Subs D Jones for Morgan (50), R Francis for R Jones (67), G
Newman for Jackson (75)
Scorers L Gerrard (1 try); M McCarthy (1 con);
M McCarthy (1 pen)

Saturday, 10 October, 1998
PERPIGNAN 41 – 24 MUNSTER

PERPIGNAN G Bastide; A Joubert, D Plana, N Mathieu, G
Tutard; D Camberabero, J Basset; R Peillard, R Ibanez, S de
Besombes, J Pradal, M James, P Furet, B Goutta, T Lievremont
(capt)
Subs P Meya for Peillard (44), L Salies for Camberabero (48),
G Majoral for Furet (63), S Deroreux for Goutta (65)
Scorers G Tutard (1 try), P Furey (1 try), A Joubert (1 try),
R Peuillard (1 try), R Ibanez (1 try), M Barrau (1 try),
D Camberabero (1 pen, 3 cons), L Salies (1 con)

MUNSTER B Roche; J Kelly, K Keane, C Mahoney,
A Horgan; B Everitt, P Stringer; P Clohessy, M McDermott,
J Hayes, M Galwey (capt), M O'Driscoll, A Foley, A Quinlan,
E Halvey
Subs I Murray for Hayes (29), D O'Callaghan for O'Driscoll
(34), F Sheahan for McDermott (60), D Corkery for
O'Callaghan (60), B. Walsh for Mahony (65)
Scorers B Everitt (1 try), M Galwey (1 try), Penalty try; K
Keane (1 pen, 3 cons)

Saturday, 17 October, 1998
NEATH 18 – 18 MUNSTER

NEATH I Wyn Jones; D Tiueti, G Evans, T Davies,
D Williams; M McCarthy (capt), P Horgan; D Jones,
M Davies, D Penisini, M Turner, A Jackson, S Eggar,
B Sinkinson, S van Rensberg
Subs R Francis for Sinkinson (14), L Gerrard for D Jones (52),
L Richards for McCarthy (73), S Martin for Eggar (73), T
Billups for M Davies (76).
Scorers R. Francis (1 try), P Horgan (1 try), L Richards
(1 con), M McCarthy (2 pens)

MUNSTER B Roche; J Kelly, K Keane, R Ellison,
A Horgan; B Everitt, P Stringer; P Clohessy, M McDermott,
J Hayes, M Galwey (capt), M O'Driscoll, A Foley, A Quinlan,
E Halvey
Subs B Walsh for Horgan (ht), D Wallace for Quinlan (67),

M Lynch for Everitt (71)
Scorers P Stringer (1 try), M Galwey (1 try), K Keane
(2 pens, 1 con)

Saturday, 31 October, 1998
MUNSTER 13 – 5 PERPIGNAN

MUNSTER B Roche; J Kelly, K Keane, R Ellison,
A Horgan; B Everitt, P Stringer; P Clohessy, M McDermott,
J Hayes, M Galwey (capt), M O'Driscoll, A Foley, A Quinlan,
E Halvey
Subs T Tierney for Stringer (50), F Sheahan for McDermott
(62), S Leahy for O'Driscoll (67), D Corkery for Quinlan (70)
Scorers P Clohessy (1 try), K Keane (2 pens, 1 con)

PERPIGNAN G Arandiga; G Bastide, D Plana, N Mathieu,
G Tutard; D Camberabero, J Basset; R Peillard, R Ibanez, S de
Besombes, J Pradal, M James, P Furet, S Deroeux, T
Lievremont (capt)
Subs B Goutta for Furet (50)
Scorers M James (1 try)

Sunday, 8 November, 1998
PADOVA 21 – 35 MUNSTER

PADOVA K Rolleston; V D'Anna, M Piovene, R Salvan,
F Rampazzo; M Berry, F Gomez; P Menapace, A Moretti,
C Cario, A Giacon, S Stocco, R Saetti, R Rampazzo, M Birtig
Scorers K Rolleston (1 try, 3 pens, 1 con), F. Gomez (1 try)
MUNSTER B Roche; J Kelly, K Keane, R Ellison,
A Horgan; B Everitt, P Stringer; D Clohessy, M McDermott,
J Hayes, M Galwey (capt), M O'Driscoll, A Foley, D Corkery,
E Halvey
Subs T Tierney for Stringer (60), M Lynch for Keane (67)
Scorers D Corkery (1 try), B Walsh (1 try), E Halvey (1 try), J.
Kelly (1 try), K Keane (1 try, 2 pens, 2 cons)

Sunday, 13th December, 1998
Quarter-final
COLOMIERS 23 – 9 MUNSTER

COLOMIERS D Skrela; B Lhande, M Carre, S Roque,
M Biboulet; L Labit, S Milhas; S Delpuech, M Dal Maso,
S Graou, JM Lorenzi, G Moro, B de Giusti, P Tabacco,
S Peysson
Subs R Nones for Graue (45), R Tremoulet for Dal Mason
61, R Rysman for Lorenzi (67)
Scorers S Peysson (1 try), B de Giusti (1 try), L Labit (3 pens,
2 cons)

MUNSTER B Roche; J O'Neill, K Keane, R Ellison,
M Lynch; B Everitt, P Stringer; P Clohessy, M McDermott,
J Hayes, M Galwey (capt), M O'Driscoll, A Foley, D Corkery,
E Halvey
Subs D Clohessy for Hayes (40), T Tierney for Stringer (58),
D Wallace for Corkery (65), S Leahy for O'Driscoll (74)
Scorers K Keane (3 pens)

SEASON 1999/2000

Saturday, 20 November, 1999
MUNSTER 32 – 10 PONTYPRIDD
MUNSTER M Mullins; J Kelly, K Keane, C Mahoney,

A Horgan; R O'Gara, P Stringer; P Clohessy, K Wood, J Hayes, M Galwey (capt), J Langford, A Quinlan, D Wallace, A Foley

Subs J Staunton for Mahoney (61), T Tierney for Stringer, M Horan for Clohessy (both 76), E Halvey for Foley, O'Callaghan for Galwey (both 79)

Scorers A Quinlan (1 try), K Keane (1 try), R O'Gara (5 pens, 2 cons, 1 d-g)

PONTYPRIDD B Davey; R Greensdale-Jones, J Bryant, J Corderley, G Wyatt; C Sweeney, P John (capt); M Griffiths, F Vunipola, S Cronk, W James, I Gough, G Lewis, R Parks, D McIntosh

Subs L Jarvis for Sweeney, J Lewis for Corderley, Ntau for Griffith (all 48), M Lloyd for Lewis (70), R Sidoli for Parks, G Williams for Vunipola (both 73)

Scorers G Wyatt (1 try), B Davey (1 pen, 1 con)

Sunday, 28 November, 1999
SARACENS 34 – 35 MUNSTER

SARACENS M Mapletoft; R Constable, J Thomson, K Sorrell, R Thirlby; T Lacroix, N Walshe; R Grau, G Chuter, J White, S Murray, D Grewcock, R Hill, F Pienaar (capt), T Diprose

Subs K Chesney for Murray (55), D Flatman for Grau (60), P Wallace for White (63), P Ogilvie for Hill (65)

Scorers R Grau (1 try), N Walshe (1 try), J Thomson (1 try), M Mapletoft (1 con), T Lacroix (1 con, 5 pens)

MUNSTER J Staunton; J Kelly, K Keane, M Mullins, A Horgan; R O'Gara, P Stringer; P Clohessy, K Wood, J Hayes, M Galwey (capt), J Langford, A Quinlan, D Wallace, A Foley

Scorers K Keane (1 try), M Mullins (1 try), A Foley (1 try), J Staunton (1 try), R O'Gara (3 pens, 3 cons)

Saturday, 11 December, 1999
COLOMIERS 15 – 31 MUNSTER

COLOMIERS JL Sadourny; M Biboulet, S Roque, J Sieurac, D Skerla; M Carre, F Culinat; JP Beyessen, M Dal Maso, P Pages, G Moro, JM Lorenzi, B de Giusti (capt), P Tabacco, S Peysson

Subs B Lhande for Carre, JP Revallier for Lorenzi (both 61), M Marient for Moro (66), C Laurent for Dal Maso (80)

Scorers J Sieurac (1 try), J-L Sadourny (1 try), D Skrela (1 pen, 1 con)

MUNSTER J Staunton; J Kelly, J Holland, M Mullins, A Horgan; R O'Gara, P Stringer; M Horan, K Wood, J Hayes, M Galwey (capt), J Langford, A Quinlan, D Wallace, A Foley

Subs I Murray for Hayes (40), T Tierney for Stringer, D Crotty for Staunton (74), F Sheahan for Murray (77)

Scorers J Holland (2 tries), K Wood (1 try), M. Horan (1 try), R O'Gara (3 pens, 1 con)

Saturday, 18 December, 1999
MUNSTER 23 – 5 COLOMIERS

MUNSTER J Staunton; J Kelly, J Holland, M Mullins, A Horgan; R O'Gara, P Stringer; M Horan, K Wood, J Hayes, M Galwey (capt), J Langford, A Quinlan, D Wallace, A Foley

Subs J O'Neill for Horgan (28), D Crotty for Staunton (53), F Sheahan for Wood, T Tierney for Stringer (76) D O'Callaghan for Langford (79)

Scorers K Wood (2 tries), D Crotty (1 try), R O'Gara (2 pens, 1 con)

COLOMIERS JL Sadourny; P Martinez, S Roque,

J Sieurac, B Lhande; D Skerla, F Culinat; JP Beyessen, M Dal Maso, J Tomuli, JP Revailler, H Manent, B de Giusti (capt), P Tabacco, F Ntamack

Subs W Begane for Tomuli, G Moro for Revaillier (both 40), P Magenide for Ntamack, C Laurent for Dal Maso (both 60), P Pueyo for de Giusti (73)

Scorers P Martinez (1 try)

Saturday, 8 January, 2000
MUNSTER 31 – 30 SARACENS

MUNSTER D Crotty; J Kelly, J Holland, M Mullins, A Horgan; R O'Gara, P Stringer; P Clohessy, K Wood, J Hayes, M Galwey (capt), J Langford, A Quinlan, D Wallace, A Foley

Scorers M Galwey (1 try), J Holland (1 try), K Wood (1 try), R O'Gara (4 pens, 2 cons)

SARACENS M Mapletoft; R Constable, J Thomson, K Sorrell, D O'Mahony; T Lacroix, N Walshe; D Flatman, G Chuter, J White, S Murray, D Grewcock, R Hill, F Pienaar (capt), Tony Diprose

Subs B Johnston for Thomson (21), P Wallace for White (60)

Scorers M Mapletoft (2 tries), D O'Mahony (1 try), T Lacroix (3 pens, 3 cons)

Saturday, 15 January, 2000
PONTYPRIDD 38 – 36 MUNSTER

PONTYPRIDD B Davey; R Greensdale-Jones, J Bryant, S Parker, G Wyatt; L Jarvis, P John (capt); M Griffiths, A Lamerton, S Cronk, G Prosser, I Gough, G Lewis, R Field, D McIntosh

Subs W Jones for Gough (50), J Colderley for Bryant (54), C Loader for Griffiths, M Lloyd for Field (62)

Scorers J Colderly (1 try), R Greensdale-Jones (1 try), B Davey (1 try), R Field (1 try), B Davey (4 pens, 3 cons)

MUNSTER D Crotty; J Kelly, J Holland, M Mullins, A Horgan; R O'Gara, P Stringer; P Clohessy, K Wood, J Hayes, M Galwey (capt), J Langford, A Quinlan, D Wallace, A Foley

Subs E Halvey for Quinlan (50), M Horan for Hayes (69)

Scorers A Quinlan (1 try), A Foley (1 try), D Wallace (1 try), R O'Gara (4 pens, 3 cons, 1 d-g)

Saturday, 15 April, 2000
Quarter-final
MUNSTER 27 – 10 STADE FRANCAIS

MUNSTER D Crotty; J Kelly, J Holland, M Mullins, A Horgan; R O'Gara, P Stringer; P Clohessy, K Wood, J Hayes, M Galwey (capt), J Langford, E Halvey, D Wallace, A Foley

Subs M Horan for Hayes (25), A Quinlan for Halvey (79)

Scorers A Horgan (1 try), D Crotty (1 try), R O'Gara (5 pens, 1 con)

STADE FRANCAIS C Stoltz; C Dominici, F Comba, C Mytton, B Lima; D Dominguez (capt), C Laussacq; S Marconnet, F Landreau, P de Villiers, D Auradou, K Whitley, D George, M Lievremont, R Pool-Jones

Subs R Froment for Goerge (40), L Pedrosa for Landreau (67)

Scorers Penalty try, D Dominguez (1 pen, 1 con)

Saturday, 6 May, 2000
Semi-final
TOULOUSE 25 – 31 MUNSTER

TOULOUSE S Ougier; E Ntamack, C Desbrosse, L Stensness, M Marfaing; A Penaud, J Cazalbou; C Califano, Y Bru, F Tournaire, F Pelous, F Belot (capt), D Lacroix,

MUNSTER'S HEINEKEN CUP STATISTICS

C Labit, S Dispagne
Subs P Bondouy for Desbrosse (70), C Soulette for Califon (72), H Miorin for Dispagne (70), M Lievremont for Lacroix (65)
Scorers J Cazalbou (1 try), M Marfaing (5 pens, 1 con), S Ougier (1 pen)

MUNSTER D Crotty; J Kelly, J Holland, M Mullins, A Horgan; R O'Gara, P Stringer; P Clohessy, K Wood, J Hayes, M Galwey (capt), J Langford, E Halvey, D Wallace, A Foley
Subs F Sheahan for Wood (40), D O'Callaghan for Galwey (78)
Scorers J Hayes (1 try), J Holland (1 try), R O'Gara (1 try, 4 pens, 2 cons)

Saturday, 27 May, 2000
Heineken Cup final
NORTHAMPTON 9 – 8 MUNSTER

NORTHAMPTON P Grayson; C Moir, A Bateman, M Allen, B Cohen; A Hepher, D Malone; G Pagel, F Mendez, M Stewart, T Rodber, D MacKinnon, B Poutney, P Lam (capt)
Subs M Scelza for Stewart (67), J Phillips for Newman (70), J Bramhall for Malone (73)
Scorers P Grayson (3 pens)

MUNSTER D Crotty; J Kelly, J Holland, M Mullins, A Horgan; R O'Gara, P Stringer; P Clohessy, K Wood, J Hayes, M Galwey (capt), J Langford, E Halvey, D Wallace, A Foley
Subs K Keane for Crotty (82)
Scorers D Wallace (1 try), J Holland (1 d-g)

SEASON 2000/01

Saturday, 7 October, 2000
MUNSTER 26 – 18 NEWPORT

MUNSTER D Crotty; J Kelly, J Holland, M Mullins, A Horgan; R O'Gara, P Stringer; P Clohessy, F Sheahan, J Hayes, M Galwey (capt), J Langford, A Quinlan, D Wallace, A Foley
Scorers F Sheahan (1 try), M Galwey (1 try), A Horgan (1 try), R O'Gara (3 pens, 1 con)

NEWPORT M Pini, M Mostyn, J Jones-Hughes, A Marinos, B Breeze; S Howarth, D Edwards; R Snow, J Richards, A Garvey, S Raiwalui, I Gough, P Buxton, J Forster, G Teichmann (capt)
Subs J Prithchard for Jones-Hughes (53)
Scorers B Breeze (2 tries), S Howarth (2 pens, 1 con)

Saturday, 14 October, 2000
CASTRES 29 – 32 MUNSTER

CASTRES F Plisson; U Mola, E Artiguste, G Delmotte, P Garrigues; G Townsend, A Albouy; M Reggiardo, R Vigneaux, L Tsabadze, S Chinarro, J Davidson (capt), A Costes, J Diaz, I Lassissi
Subs A Larkin for Artiguste (33), F Lalague for Chinarro (46), G Bemasat for Tabards (50), C Batut for Vigneaux, D Dima for Reggiardo (both 60)
Scorers P Garrigues (1 try), A Costes (1 try), G. Townsend (5 pens, 2 cons)

MUNSTER D Crotty; J Kelly, J Holland, M Mullins, A Horgan; R O'Gara, P Stringer; P Clohessy, F Sheahan, J Hayes, M Galwey (capt), J Langford, A Quinlan, D Wallace, A Foley
Scorers D Crotty (1 try), A Horgan (1 try), R O'Gara (1 try, 5 pens, 1 con)

Saturday, 21 October, 2000
MUNSTER 31 – 9 BATH

MUNSTER D Crotty; J Kelly, J Holland, M Mullins, A Horgan; R O'Gara, P Stringer; P Clohessy, F Sheahan, J Hayes, M Galwey (capt), J Langford, A Quinlan, D Wallace, A Foley
Subs K Keane for Mullins, J Staunton for Holland (both 77), M Horan for Clohessy, M O'Driscoll, C McMahon for Wallace (all 80)
Scorers A Horgan (2 tries), D Wallace (1 try); R O'Gara (3 pens, 2 cons, 1 d-g)

BATH M Perry; I Balshaw, P de Glanville, M Tindall, K Maggs; J Preston, G Cooper; D Barnes, M Regan, C Horsman, M Haag, S Borthwick, A Gardiner, B Clarke, D Lyle (capt)
Subs A Adebayo for de Glanville (76)
Scorers J Preston (3 pens)

Saturday, 28 October, 2000
BATH 18 – 5 MUNSTER

BATH M Perry; I Balshaw, P de Glanville, M Tindall, K Maggs; M Catt, G Cooper; S Emms, M Regan, C Horsman, M Haag, S Borthwick, A Gardiner, B Clarke (capt), D Lyle
Subs J Preston for Cooper (39), G Thomas for Gardiner (40), J Mallett for Horsman (63)
Scorers J Preston (4 pens), M Perry (2 pens)

MUNSTER D Crotty; J Kelly, J Holland, M Mullins, A Horgan; R O'Gara, P Stringer; P Clohessy, F Sheahan, J Hayes, M Galwey (capt), J Langford, A Quinlan, D Wallace, A Foley
Subs M O'Driscoll for Galwey (27), K Keane for Kelly (73), C McMahon for Wallace (80)
Scorers D Wallace (1 try)

Saturday, 13 January, 2001
NEWPORT 24 – 39 MUNSTER

NEWPORT M Pini, M Mostyn, J Jones-Hughes, A Marinos, B Breeze; S Howarth, D Edwards; R Snow, J Richards, A Garvey, S Raiwalui, I Gough, A Popham, J Forster, G Teichmann (capt)
Scorers M Pini (1 try), M Mostyn (1 try), S Howarth (3 pens, 1 con, 1 d-g)

MUNSTER D Crotty; J O'Neill, J Holland, K Keane, A Horgan; R O'Gara, P Stringer; P Clohessy, F Sheahan, J Hayes, M Galwey (capt), J Langford, A Quinlan, D Wallace, A Foley
Subs M Mullins for Keane (62)
Scorers R O'Gara (1 try, 4 pens, 3 cons, 2 d-gs), M Mullins (1 try), A Horgan (1 try)

Saturday, 20 January, 2001
MUNSTER 21 – 11 CASTRES

MUNSTER D Crotty; J Kelly, K Keane, M Mullins, A Horgan; R O'Gara, P Stringer; P Clohessy, F Sheahan,

J Hayes, M Galwey (capt), J Langford, A Quinlan, D Wallace, A Foley
Subs J Holland for Kelly (40), J Staunton for Crotty (72)
Scorers A Foley (1 try), D Crotty (1 try), R O'Gara (3 pens, 1 con)

CASTRES G Delmotte; D Denechaud, E Artiguste, O Sarramea, P Garrigues; G Townsend, F Seguier; L Toussaint, R Ibanez (capt) M Reggiardo, F Laluque, J Davidson, J Diaz, G Taussac, T Labrusse
Subs A Larkin for Plisson (67), A Albouy for Seguier (57), T Bourdet for Toussaint (55), S Bonorino for Reggiardo (55)
Scorers G Delmonte (1 try), G Townsend (1 pen, 1 d-g)

Sunday, 28 January, 2001
Quarter-final
MUNSTER 38 - 29 BIARRITZ

MUNSTER D Crotty; J Kelly, J Holland, M Mullins, A Horgan; R O'Gara, P Stringer; P Clohessy, F Sheahan, J Hayes, M Galwey (capt), J Langford, A Quinlan, D Wallace, A Foley
Scorers A Foley (3 tries), R O'Gara (7 pens, 1 con).

BIARRITZ S Bonetti; P Bernat-Salles, P Bidabe, N Couttet, S Legg; F Botica, S Bonnet; E Menieu, JM Gonzalez (capt), D Avril, JP Versailles, O Roumat, S Betsen, C Milheres, O Nauroy
Subs T Lievremont for Roumant (48), M Lefevre for Versailles (52), M Irazoqui for Milheres (64), M Lievremont for Betsen, B Daguerre for Couttet (both 70)
Scorers C Milheres (2 tries), S Legg (1 try), S Bonnet (1 try), F Botica (1 pen, 3 cons)

Saturday, 21 April, 2001
STADE FRANCAIS 16 - 15 MUNSTER

STADE FRANCAIS C Dominici, T Lombard, F Comba, C Mytton, R Poulain; D Dominguez, M Williams; S Marconnet, F Landreau, P de Villiers, D Auradou, M James, C Moni, R Pool-Jones, C Juillet (capt)
Subs A Gomes for Juillet (73)
Scorers C. Mytton (1 try); D Dominquez (3 pens, 1 con)

MUNSTER D Crotty; J O'Neill, J Holland, M Mullins, A Horgan; R O'Gara, P Stringer; P Clohessy, F Sheahan, J Hayes, M Galwey (capt), J Langford, D O'Callaghan, D Wallace, A Foley
Subs D O'Cuinneagain for O'Callaghan (70), M Horan for Clohessy (83)
Scorers R O'Gara (5 pens)

SEASON 2001/02

Saturday, 29 September, 2001
MUNSTER 28 - 23 CASTRES

MUNSTER D Crotty; J Kelly, J Holland, M Mullins, A Horgan; R O'Gara, P Stringer; P Clohessy, F Sheahan, M Cahill, M Galwey (capt), M O'Driscoll, J Williams, D Wallace, A Foley
Subs P O'Connell for O Driscoll, M Horan for Cahill (both 53)
Scorers J Holland (1 try), R O'Gara (6 pens, 1 con, 1 d-g)

CASTRES U Mola; F Plisson, G Delmotte, N Berryman,

S Longstaff; G Townsend, R Teulet; L Toussaint, R Ibanez (capt) B Moyle, F Laluque, N Spanghero, A Costes, R Froment, I Lasissi
Subs M Reggiardo for Moyle (57), O Sarramea for Plisson (60), E Artiguste for Mola (71), S Chinaro for Laluque (76)
Scorers U Mola (1 try), R Teulet (6 pens)

Saturday, 6 October, 2001
HARLEQUINS 8 - 24 MUNSTER

HARLEQUINS M Mapletoft; M Moore, W Greenwood, N Greenstock, D Lugar; P Burke, S Bemand; J Leonard, K Wood (capt), A Oliver, G Morgan, S White-Cooper, R Winters, T Tamarua, T Diprose
Subs P. Sanderson for Winters (74), N Burrrows for Greenstock (76)
Scorers D Luger (1 try), P Burke (1 pen)

MUNSTER J Staunton; J Kelly, J Holland, M Mullins, A Horgan; R O'Gara, P Stringer; P Clohessy, F Sheahan, J Hayes, M Galwey (capt), M O'Driscoll, J Williams, D Wallace, A Foley
Subs P O'Connell for O'Driscoll (52), M Horan and D O'Callaghan for Clohessy and Galwey (both 80), C McMahon for Wallace (85)
Scorers R O'Gara (1 try, 2 pens, 1 con, 1 d-g), J. Holland (1 try, 1 d-g)

Friday, 26 October, 2001
BRIDGEND 12 - 16 MUNSTER

BRIDGEND J Taumalolo; G Thomas, J Devereux, J Funnell, D Jones; C Warlow, H Harris (capt); C Loader, G Williams, J Thiel, D Jones, C Stephens, N Budgett, J Ringer, R Bryan
Subs M Molitika for D Jones (69), S Van Rensburg for Bryan (69), C Noon for Thiel (72), A Durston for Funnell (76)
Scorers C Warlow (4 pens)

MUNSTER J Staunton; J Kelly, J Holland, M Mullins, A Horgan; R O'Gara, P Stringer; P Clohessy, F Sheahan, J Hayes, M Galwey (capt), M O'Driscoll, J Williams, D Wallace, A Foley
Subs P O'Connell for O'Driscoll (49), M Horan for Clohessy (57)
Scorers M Mullins (1 try), J Kelly (1 try), R O'Gara (2 pens)

Saturday, 3 November, 2001
MUNSTER 40 - 6 BRIDGEND

MUNSTER J Staunton; J Kelly, J Holland, M Mullins, A Horgan; R O'Gara, P Stringer; M Horan, F Sheahan, J Hayes, M Galwey (capt), P O'Connell, J Williams, A Quinlan, A Foley
Subs P Clohessy for Hayes (51), R Henderson for Kelly (65), K Keane for Staunton (76), C McMahon for Foley (78)
Scorers A Horgan (1 try), J Kelly (1 try), J Staunton (1 try), J Holland (1 try), M Mullins (1 try), R O'Gara (3 pens, 3 cons)

BRIDGEND A Durston; G Jones, J Devereux, G Thomas, D Jones; C Warlow, J Hewlett; C Loader, G Williams, C Noon, D Jones, C Stephens (capt), N Budgett, J Ringer, R Bryan
Subs J Thiel for Noone (60), H Harries for Bryan (72)
Scorers C Warlow (1 pen, 1 d-g)

Saturday, 5 January, 2002
MUNSTER 51 - 17 HARLEQUINS

MUNSTER D Crotty; J Kelly, J Holland, M Mullins, A Horgan; R O'Gara, M Prendergast; P Clohessy, F Sheahan,

MUNSTER'S HEINEKEN CUP STATISTICS

M Horan, M Galwey (capt), M O'Driscoll, J Williams, A Quinlan, A Foley
Subs M Cahill for Clohessy (66), D O'Callaghan for Galwey, Hegarty for Prendergast (both 72), J O'Neill for Mullins, J Staunton for Crotty (both 76), C McMahon for Williams (79), J Blaney for O'Gara (81)
Scorers J Holland (1 try), F Sheahan (1 try), A Foley (1 try), D Crotty (1 try), M Galwey (1 try), A Quinlan (1 try), R O'Gara (5 pens, 3 cons)

HARLEQUINS D Sleman; M Moore, W Greenwood, N Burrows, D Lugar; P Burke, N Duncombe; B Starr, J Roddam, J Dawson, G Morgan (capt), B Davison, S White-Cooper, T Tamarua, T Diprose
Subs R Jewell for Burrows, A Codling for Morgan, M Mapletoft for Burke (57), A Alesbrook for White-Cooper (66), B Douglas for Dawson (72)
Scorers T Diprose (2 tries), P Burke (1 pen, 2 con)

Saturday, 12 January, 2002
CASTRES 21 – 13 MUNSTER

CASTRES R Teulet; U Mola, N Berryman, E Artiguste, S Longstaff; G Townsend (capt), A Albouy; B Moyle, R Vigneaux, M Reggiardo, I Fernandez Lobbe, N Spanghero, A Costes, R Froment, I Lasissi
Subs S Chinarro for Costes (39), G Delmotte for Berryman (68), O Sarramea for Teulet (78)
Scorers R Teulet (1 try, 1 con, 3 pens), O Sarramea (1 try)

MUNSTER D Crotty; J Kelly, J Holland, M Mullins, A Horgan; R O'Gara, M Prendergast; P Clohessy, F Sheahan, M Horan, M Galwey (capt), M O'Driscoll, J Williams, A Quinlan, A Foley
Subs J Hayes for Horan, P O'Connell for O'Driscoll (both 51), R Henderson for Holland (66), D Wallace for Quinlan (68), J Staunton for Crotty (75), D Hegarty for Staunton (78)
Scorers D Wallace (1 try), R O'Gara (2 pens, 1 con)

Saturday, 26 January, 2002
Quarter-final
STADE FRANCAIS 14 – 16 MUNSTER

STADE FRANCAIS S Jonnet; N Williams, F Comba, N Raffault, R Poulain; D Dominguez, F Galthie; S Marconnet, M Blin, P de Villiers, D Auradou, M James, P Rabadan, R Martin, C Juillet (capt)
Subs P Lemoine for Marconnet (67) C Moni for Rabadan (79)
Scorers C Juillet (1 try), D Dominquez (3 pens)

MUNSTER D Crotty; J Kelly, J Holland, R Henderson, A Horgan; R O'Gara, P Stringer; P Clohessy, F Sheahan, J Hayes, M Galwey (capt), P O'Connell, J Williams, D Wallace, A Foley
Subs M Horan for Clohessy (80)
Scorers A Horgan (1 try), R O'Gara (2 pens, 1 con, 1 d-g)

Saturday, 27 April, 2002
Semi-final
CASTRES 17 – 25 MUNSTER

CASTRES R Teulet; U Mola, N Berryman, E Artiguste, S Longstaff; G Townsend (capt), A Albouy; B Moyle, R Ibanez, M Reggiardo, I Fernandez Lobbe, N Spanghero, A Costes, R Froment, I Lasissi
Subs R Vigneaux for Ibanez (40), G Delmotte for Artiguste

(52), D Dima for Reggiardo, S Chinarro for Fernandez Lobbe (both 69), O Sarramea for Teulet (77)
Scorers S Longstaff (1 try), R Teulet (4 pens)

MUNSTER D Crotty; J Kelly, J Holland, R Henderson, A Horgan; R O'Gara, P Stringer; P Clohessy, F Sheahan, J Hayes, M Galwey (capt), P O'Connell, A Quinlan, D Wallace, A Foley
Subs D O'Callaghan for Foley (16), M Horan for Hayes (69), M Mullins for Henderson (82), J Staunton for Crotty (85)
Scorers J Kelly (1 try), R O'Gara (6 pens, 1 con)

Saturday, 25 May, 2002
Heineken Cup final
LEICESTER 15 – 9 MUNSTER

LEICESTER T Stimpson; G Murphy, O Smith, R Kafer, F Tuilagi; A Healey, J Hamilton; G Rowntree, D West, D Garforth, M Johnson (capt), B Kay, L Moody, N Back, M Corry
Subs H Ellis For Hamilton (52), P Freshwater for Rowntree (75), G Gelderbloom for Smith (77)
Scorers A Healey (1 try), G Murphy (1 try), T. Stimpson (1 pen, 1 con)

MUNSTER D Crotty; J Kelly, J Holland, R Henderson, J O'Neill; R O'Gara, P Stringer; P Clohessy, F Sheahan, J Hayes, M Galwey (capt), P O'Connell, A Quinlan, D Wallace, A Foley
Subs J Williams for Foley (52), M Horan for Clohessy, M O'Driscoll for O'Connell (both 62), J Staunton for Crotty (66), M Mullins for Henderson (68)
Scorers R O'Gara (3 pens)

SEASON 2002/03

Saturday, 12 October, 2002
GLOUCESTER 35 – 16 MUNSTER

GLOUCESTER H Paul; M Garvey, T Fanalua, R Todd, T Beim; L Mercier, A Gomarsall; T Woodman, O Azam, P Vickery (capt), A Eustace, M Cornwell, J Boer, P Buxton, J Forrester
Subs E Pearce for Eustace (65), J Simpson-Daniel for Beim (76), C Fortey for Azam (78)
Scorers J Boer (2 tries), M Garvey (1 try), L Mercier (1 try, 3 pens, 3 cons)

MUNSTER J Staunton; J Kelly, M Mullins, R Henderson, M Lawlor; R O'Gara, P Stringer; M Horan, F Sheahan, J Hayes, M Galwey, M O'Driscoll, J Williams (capt), A Quinlan, A Foley
Subs J Holland for Henderson (33), E Halvey for Galwey (59), Blaney for O'Driscoll (72)
Scorers P Stringer (1 try), R O'Gara (3 pens, 1 con)

Saturday, 19 October, 2002
MUNSTER 30 – 21 PERPIGNAN

MUNSTER D Crotty; J Kelly, M Mullins, J Holland, M Lawlor; R O'Gara, P Stringer; M Horan, F Sheahan, J Hayes, M Galwey, M O'Driscoll, J Williams (capt), A Quinlan, A Foley

Subs K Keane for Crotty (79)
Scorers – J Kelly (1 try), A Quinlan (1 try), J Hayes (1 try), R O'Gara (3 pens, 3 cons)

PERPIGNAN M Edmonds; P Bomati, C Manas, F Cermeno, N Couttet; B Bellot, J Basset; R Peillard, A Moreno, N Mas, R Kaireilas, J Daniell, L Maillier, B Goutta (capt), P Murphy
Subs F Sid for Bomati (71), D Marty for Couttet (79), N Laharrague for Bellot (71), S de Bescombes for Mas (76), F Rofes for Mallier (79), S Deroeux for Murphy (65)
Scorers N Couttet (1 try), M Edmonds (1 try, 1 con), N Laharrague (1 try), B Bellot (2 cons)

Friday, 6 December, 2002
MUNSTER 64 – 0 VIADANA

MUNSTER J Staunton; A Horgan, M Mullins, J Holland, M Lawlor; R O'Gara, P Stringer; M Horan, F Sheahan, J Hayes, P O'Connell, D O'Callaghan J Williams (capt), A Quinlan, A Foley
Subs M O'Driscoll for O'Callaghan, S Kerr for Horan (both 60), E Halvey for Foley (64), C McMahon for Lawler (71), J Fogarty for Sheahan (74), M Prendergast for Horgan (77), K Keane for Staunton (79)
Scorers A Foley (2 tries), A Horgan (1 try), P O'Connell (1 try), F Sheahan (1 try), J Holland (1 try), M. Prendergast (1 try), Penalty try, R O'Gara (1 try, 1 pen, 8 cons)

VIADANA C Steyn; M Dolcetto, G Frasca, H Crane, R Pedrazzi; R Pickering, P Roux; M Savi, E de Bellis, L Bocchini, R Denhardt, F Gumiero, M Phillips (capt), A Persico, D Farani
Subs V Jiminez for de Bellis (52), M Avigni for Phillips (55), S Spina for Savi (64), C Bezzi for Gumiero (71), G Vigna for Denhardt (74)

Saturday, 14 December, 2002
VIADANA 22 – 55 MUNSTER

VIADANA C Steyn; M Dolcetto, G Frasca, H Crane, R Pedrazzi; R Pickering, P Roux; M Savi, V Jiminez, L Lidgard, C Bezzi, F Gumiero, M Phillips (capt), A Persico, G Vigna
Subs R Denhardt for Gumiero (45), C Spadaro for Steyn (50), A Buhrmann for Vigna (54), S Aio for Roux (57), E de Belis for Jimenez (64), L Bocchini for Savi (71)
Scorers P Roux (1 try), H Crane (1 try), R Pedrazzi (1 try), C Steyn (1 pen, 1 con), R Pickering (1 con)

MUNSTER J Staunton; J Kelly, M Mullins, J Holland, A Horgan; R O'Gara, P Stringer; M Horan, F Sheahan, J Hayes, P O'Connell, D O'Callaghan J Williams (capt), A Quinlan, A Foley
Subs S Kerr for Horan (59), M Lawlor for Mullins, M O'Driscoll for O'Connell (64), E Halvey for Quinlan (68), J Fogarty for Sheahan, M Prendergast for Stringer, K Keane for Staunton (all 79)
Scorers J Holland (2 tries), A Quinlan (2 tries), F Sheahan (2 tries), M Mullins (1 try), J Kelly (1 try), A Foley (1 try), R O'Gara (5 cons)

Saturday, 11 January, 2003
PERPIGNAN 23 – 8 MUNSTER

PERPIGNAN JM Souverbie; P Bomati, C Manas, F Cermeno, P Giordani; M Edmonds, L Loustau; P Meya, M Konieck, N Mas, R Kaireilas, J Thion, G Le Corvec, B Goutta (capt), P Murphy
Subs C Porcu for Murphy, S de Besombes for Meya (62),

M Dal Maso for Koniek, S Deroeux for Le Corvec (both 78)
Scorers F Cermeno (1 try), P Giordani (1 try), G Le Corvec (1 try), R Kaireilas (1 try), M Edmonds (1 pen)

MUNSTER J Staunton; J Kelly, M Mullins, J Holland, M Lawlor; R O'Gara, P Stringer; M Horan, F Sheahan, J Hayes, M O'Driscoll, D O'Callaghan J Williams (capt), A Quinlan, A Foley
Subs D Leamy for Quinlan (75), M Galwey for O'Driscoll (78)
Scorers A Foley (1 try), R O'Gara (1 pen)

Saturday, 18 January, 2003
MUNSTER 33 – 6 GLOUCESTER

MUNSTER J Staunton; J Kelly, M Mullins, J Holland, M Lawlor; R O'Gara, P Stringer; M Horan, F Sheahan, J Hayes, M O'Driscoll, D O'Callaghan J Williams (capt), A Quinlan, A Foley
Scorers J Kelly (2 tries), M Lawlor (1 try), M O'Driscoll (1 try), R O'Gara (3 pens, 2 cons)

GLOUCESTER H Paul; J Simpson-Daniel, T Fanalua, R Todd, T Delport; L Mercier, A Gomarsall; R Roncero, O Azam, P Vickery (capt), R Fidler, M Cornwell, J Boer, P Buxton, J Paramore
Subs A Hazell for Buxton (51), T Beim for Paul (61), C Collins for Paramore (65), A Eustace for Fidler (75)
Scorers L Mercier (2 pens)

Sunday, 13 April, 2003
Quarter-final
LEICESTER 7 – 20 MUNSTER

LEICESTER T Stimpson; G Murphy, L Llyod, F Tuilagi, S Booth; A Healey, T Tierney; P Freshwater, D West, D Garforth, M Johnson (capt), B Kay, M Corry, N Back, W Johnson
Subs A Balding for W Johnson (47), H Ellis for Tierney (56), J Kronfeld for Kay (67), S Vesty for Healy (67), G Gelderbloom for Tuilagi (75), G Chuter for West (80)
Scorers S Booth (1 try), T Stimpson (1 con)

MUNSTER J Staunton; J Kelly, M Mullins, R Henderson, A Horgan; R O'Gara, P Stringer; M Horan, F Sheahan, J Hayes, P O'Connell, D O'Callaghan J Williams (capt), A Quinlan, A Foley
Subs J Holland for Henderson (67)
Scorers R O'Gara (1 try, 2 pens, 2 cons), P Stringer (1 try)

Saturday, 26 April, 2003
Semi-final
TOULOUSE 13 – 12 MUNSTER

TOULOUSE C Piotrenaud; E Ntamack, X Garbajosa, Y Jauzion, V Clerc; Y Delaigue, F Michalak; P Collazo, Y Bru, JB Poux, D Gerard, F Pelous (capt), T Brennan, J Bouilhou, C Labit
Substitutes J-B Elissalde for Y Delaigue (60), B Lecouls for Collazo (62), W Servat for Bru (71), G Lamboley for Gerard, F Maka for Labit (both 80 mins)
Scorers F Michalak (1 try), J-B. Elissalde (1 pen, 1 con), Y Delaigue (1 pen)

MUNSTER J Staunton; J Kelly, M Mullins, R Henderson, A Horgan; R O'Gara, P Stringer; M Horan, F Sheahan, J Hayes, P O'Connell, D O'Callaghan J Williams (capt), A Quinlan, A Foley
Substitutes J Holland for Henderson (80)
Scorers R O'Gara (2 pens, 2 d-gs)

MUNSTER'S HEINEKEN CUP STATISTICS

Sunday, 3 April, 2005
Quarter-final
BIARRITZ 19 – 10 MUNSTER

BIARRITZ N Brusque; P Bidabe, M Gaitan, D Traille, J Marlu; J Peyrelongue, D Yachvilli; P Balan, B August, D Avril, J Thion, O Olibeau, S Betsen, I Harinordoquy, T Lievremont (capt)
Subs B Lecouls for Balan (58), D Couzinet for Olibeau (63 mins), T Dusautoir for Lievremont (78 mins), J-M Gonzalez for August (80 mins).
Scorers M. Gaitan (1 try), D Yachvili (4 pens, 1 con)

MUNSTER S Payne; J Kelly, M Mullins, R Henderson, A Horgan; P Burke, P Stringer; M Horan, F Sheahan, J Hayes, D O'Callaghan, P O'Connell, A Quinlan, D Wallace, A Foley (capt)
Subs J Holland for Burke (74), J Williams for Quinlan (76 mins), P Devlin for Mullins (84 mins).
Scorers D Wallace (1 try), P Burke (1 pen, 1 con)

SEASON 2005/06

Friday, 21 October, 2005
SALE 27 – 13 MUNSTER

SALE J Robinson (capt); M Cueto, M Taylor, E Seveali', S Hanley; C Hodgson, S Martens; A Sheridan, A Titterell, S Turner, I Fernandez Lobbe, C Jones, J White, M Lund, S Chabal
Subs S Bruno for Titterell (46), B Stewart for Turner (56), D Larrechea for Hanley (64), D Schofield for Fernandez Lobbe (66), V Courrent for Martens, C Day for Jones, R Todd for Seveali' (all 80)
Scorers S Martens (1 try), J Robinson (1 try), C Hodgson (5 pens, 1 con)

MUNSTER S Payne; J Kelly, B Murphy, G Connolly, A Pitout; R O'Gara, T O'Leary, M Horan, F Sheahan, J Hayes, D O'Callaghan, M O'Driscoll, A Quinlan, D Leamy, A Foley (capt)
Subs T Hogan for Quinlan (63), D Wallace for Leamy (72), P Stringer for Pitout, F Pucciariello for Hayes, J Flannery for Sheahan (all 72)
Scorers F Sheahan (1 try), R O'Gara (2 pens, 1 con)

Saturday, 29 October, 2005
MUNSTER 42 – 16 CASTRES

MUNSTER S Payne; J Kelly, T Halstead, G Connolly, A Horgan; R O'Gara, P Stringer, M Horan, J Flannery, J Hayes, D O'Callaghan, M O'Driscoll, D Wallace, D Leamy, A Foley (capt)
Subs B. Murphy for Connolly (80), Manning for O'Gara (80), O'Leary for Stringer (80), Fogarty for Flannery (80), Hogan for O'Driscoll (80), S. Keogh for Foley (80).
Scorers J Kelly (1 try), T Halstead (1 try), A Horgan (1 try), J Flannery (1 try), D O'Callaghan (1 try), R O'Gara (2 pens, 4 cons), J Manning (1 pen)

CASTRES JP Peyrad Loustalet; L Milford, L Marticorena, F Tuilagi, P Christophers; R Teulet, N Mathieu; C Hoeft, R Vigneaux, K Meows (capt), N Spanghero, L Nallet, J Puricelli, P Volley, F Faure
Subs Forestier for Milford (69), Raffault for Tuilagi (32), Albouy for Barrau (62), Capo Ortega for Spanghero (55), Taussac for Faure (67)
Scorers R Teulet (1 try), L Marticorena (3 pens, 1 con)

Saturday, 10 December, 2005
NEWPORT 8 – 24 MUNSTER

NEWPORT A Thomas; G Chapman, S Tuipulotu, C Sweeney, R Fussell; C Warlow, G Cooper; A Black, S Jones, R Thomas, I Gough, P Sidoli, A Hall, J Ringer, M Owen (capt)
Subs G Thomas for R Thomas, L Chateris for Sidoli (both 55), J Bryant for Tuipulotu (67), G Baber for Cooper, R Bryan for Hall (both 72), D Maddocks for Black (76)
Scorers G Chapman (1 try), C Warlow (1 pen)

MUNSTER M Lawlor; J Kelly, T Halstead, G Connolly, A Horgan; R O'Gara, P Stringer, M Horan, J Flannery, J Hayes, D O'Callaghan, M O'Driscoll, D Wallace, D Leamy, A Foley (capt)
Subs B Murphy for Connolly, F Roche for Horan, D Fogarty for Flannery, T Hogan for O'Callaghan, S Keogh for Wallace (all 76), T O'Leary for Foley (80)
Scorers D Leamy (1 try), M Horan (1 try), R O'Gara (1 con, 2 pens, 1 d-g), M Lawlor (1 d-g)

Saturday, 17 December, 2005
MUNSTER 30 – 18 NEWPORT

MUNSTER S Payne; J Kelly, T Halstead, G Connolly, A Horgan; R O'Gara, P Stringer, M Horan, J Flannery, J Hayes, D O'Callaghan, M O'Driscoll, D Wallace, D Leamy, A Foley (capt)
Subs B Murphy for Halstead (71)
Scorers M O'Driscoll (1 try), A Foley (1 try), J Flannery (1 try), R O'Gara (3 pens, 3 cons)

NEWPORT A Thomas; G Chapman, H Luscombe, J Bryant, R Fussell; C Sweeney, G Baber; A Black, S Jones, G Robinson, I Gough, L Chareris, R Oakley, J Ringer, R Bryan (capt)
Subs K Morgan for Thomas, M Owen for Bryan (both 40), R Thomas for Robinson (53), G Cooper for Baber (57), P Sidoli for Gough, D Maddocks for Black (both 63)
Scorers S Jones (1 try), K Morgan (1 try), C Sweeney (2 pens, 1 con)

Friday, 13 January, 2006
CASTRES 9 – 46 MUNSTER

CASTRES P Christophers; Y Fior, N Raffault, F Tuilagi, B Fleming; L Marticorena, N Mathieu; J Castex, D Roumieu, D Attoub, K Ghezal, N Spanghero (capt), R Froment, G Bernad, G Taussac
Subs R Teulet for Marticorena, Purcelli for Froment (both 64), K Hoeft for Attoub (73)
Scorers L Marticorena (3 pens)

MUNSTER S Payne; J Kelly, T Halstead, B Murphy, I Dowling; R O'Gara, P Stringer, M Horan, J Flannery, J Hayes, D O'Callaghan, P O'Connell, D Wallace, D Leamy, A Foley (capt)
Subs T O'Leary for Kelly (58), G Connolly for Halstead (67), F Pucciarello for Horan (70), M O'Driscoll for O'Connell (71), D Fogarty for Flannery (72)
Scorers P O'Connell (2 tries), T O'Leary (2 tries), M Horan (1 try), S Payne (1 try), J Kelly (1 try), R O'Gara (3 cons, 1 pen), J Manning (1 con)

Saturday, 21 January, 2006
MUNSTER 31 – 9 SALE

MUNSTER S Payne; J Kelly, T Halstead, B Murphy, I Dowling; R O'Gara, P Stringer, M Horan, J Flannery, J Hayes, D O'Callaghan, P O'Connell, D Wallace, D Leamy, A Foley (capt)
Subs M Lawlor for Payne, O'Leary for Stringer, F Pucciariello for Horan, D Fogarty for Flannery, M O'Driscoll for O'Connell, S Keogh for Foley (all 83)
Scorers A Foley (1 try), I Dowling (1 try), B Murphy (1 try), D Wallace (1 try), R O'Gara (1 pen, 4 cons)

SALE J Robinson (capt); M Cueto, M Taylor, E Seveali', D Larrechea; C Hodgson, S Martens; A Sheridan, S Bruno, B Stewart, I Fernandez Lobbe, C Jones, J White, M Lund, S Chabal
Subs E Taione for E Seveali' (27), R Wigglesworth for Martens (49), A Titterall for Bruno, C Mayor for Jones (both 69)
Scorers C Hodgson (3 pens)

Saturday, 1 April, 2006
Quarter-final
MUNSTER 19 – 10 PERPIGNAN

MUNSTER S Payne; J Kelly, T Halstead, T O'Leary, I Dowling; R O'Gara, P Stringer, M Horan, J Flannery, J Hayes, D O'Callaghan, P O'Connell, D Wallace, D Leamy, A Foley (capt)
Subs M O'Driscoll for Leamy (37), C Cullen for Payne, Manning for O'Gara (both 80)
Scorers P O'Connell (1 try), R O'Gara (4 pens, 1 con)

PERPIGNAN J Laharrague; C Manas, D Marty, JP Grandclaude, M Bourret; M Edmonds (capt), N Durand; P Freshwater, M Tincu, N Mas, R Kaireilis, N Hiones, G Le Corvec, S Robertson, O Tonita
Subs C Gaston for Kaireilis, V Vaki for S Robertson (both 63)
Scorers M Bourret (1 try, 1 pen, 1 con)

Sunday, 23 April, 2006
Semi-final
LEINSTER 6 – 30 MUNSTER

LEINSTER G Dempsey; S Horgan, B O'Driscoll, G D'Arcy, D Hickie; F Contepomi, G Easterby; R Corrigan, B Blaney, W Green, B Williams, M O'Kelly, C Jowitt, K Gleeson, J Heaslip
Subs E Miller for Jowitt (57), R McCormack for Corrigan (70)
Scorers F Contepomi (2 pens)

MUNSTER S Payne; A Horgan, T Halstead, J Kelly, I Dowling; R O'Gara, P Stringer, F Pucciariello, J Flannery, J Hayes, D O'Callaghan, P O'Connell, D Wallace, D Leamy, A Foley (capt)
Subs R Henderson for Kelly (12), T O'Leary for Henderson (66), F Roche for Foley (76)
Scorers D Leamy (1 try), T Halstead (1 try), R O'Gara (1 try, 3 pens, 3 cons)

Saturday, 20 May, 2006
Heineken Cup final
BIARRITZ 19 – 23 MUNSTER

BIARRITZ N Brusque; JB Gobelet, P Bidabe, D Traille, S Bobo; J Peyrelongue, D Yachvili; P Balan, B August, C Johnson, J Thion, D Couzinet, S Betsen, I Harinordoquy, T Lievremont (capt)
Subs O Olibeau for Couzinet (45), T Dusautoir for Lievremont (52), F Martin Aramburu for Traille (53), B Lecouls for Johnson (63), B Noirot for August (67), C Johnson for Balan (72)
Scorers S Bobo (1 try), D Yachvili (4 pens, 1 con)

MUNSTER S Payne; A Horgan, T Halstead, J Kelly, I Dowling; R O'Gara, P Stringer, M Horan, J Flannery, J Hayes, D O'Callaghan, P O'Connell, D Wallace, D Leamy, A Foley (capt)
Subs F Pucciariello for Horan (63), M O'Driscoll for Foley (71), A Quinlan for O'Connell (76)
Scorers T Halstead (1 try), P Stringer (1 try), R O'Gara (3 pens, 2 cons)

Red mist: *Munster players, including Alan Quinlan, get their hands on the prize at the Millennium Stadium*

BIBLIOGRAPHY

General

English, Alan, 'Stand Up And Fight', Yellow Jersey Press, 2005

Farrelly, Hugh, 'Munster Rugby Giants', O'Brien Press, 2001

Galwey, Mick, 'Galwey: The Autobiography', Irish Rugby Review, 1985

O'Flaherty, Michael, 'The Home of the Spirit – A Celebration of Limerick Rugby', 1999

Van Esbeck, Edmund, 'The Story of Irish Rugby', Stanley Paul, 1986

Newspapers

Sunday Tribune, The Sunday Times, Sunday Independent, The Irish Times,
Irish Examiner, Irish Independent, The Daily Telegraph